A Congreve Gallery

A
Congreve
Gallery

KATHLEEN M. LYNCH

1967

OCTAGON BOOKS, INC.

New York

Reprinted 1967

by special arrangement with Harvard University Press

OCTAGON BOOKS, INC.
175 FIFTH AVENUE
NEW YORK, N. Y. 10010

LIBRARY OF CONGRESS CATALOG CARD NUMBER: 67-18775

Printed in U.S.A. by
NOBLE OFFSET PRINTERS, INC.
NEW YORK 3, N. Y.

To Elizabeth French Lynch

Preface

The following essays throw light from various angles on the personality, background, and times of William Congreve. As Boswell remarked of Johnson, everything relative to a great man is worth observing.

Although he belonged to an age which, on the whole, is very well documented, surprisingly little is known of Congreve's life. He remains a man of mystery, despite the recent excellent biography by Professor John C. Hodges. It is evident that a large number of manuscripts concerning Congreve and those most intimately associated with him must have been destroyed, or lost, or, for reasons that can be surmised, kept in private hands. There is always the possibility, however, that at some future date important Congreve manuscripts will be discovered. Under such circumstances, another biography of Congreve would be required; and all intervening studies from primary sources would contribute something to that work of larger scope.

In this book I have placed emphasis on the friends of Congreve's youth, who played so pleasant a part in his mature life. It has been too often forgotten that Congreve spent his most impressionable years in Ireland, in close contact with younger members of certain Anglo-Irish families. His father's career and the fortunes of these friends led him to take a more than casual interest in Irish affairs.

Congreve's connection, in later life, with the Godolphin circle was the consequence of his friendship with Henrietta, Duchess of Marlborough. I have emphasized this friendship as the most significant personal adventure of Congreve's life. I have included, as pertinent material, an account of Congreve's daughter, Mary, Duchess of Leeds, and of some other members of the Godolphin circle.

The preparation of this book was made possible by a number of grants from the American Council of Learned Societies; a grant from the Research Committee of the Modern Language Association of America; a year's sabbatical leave from Mount Holyoke College; and the kind assistance of President Roswell G. Ham.

I am indebted to the editor of *Publications of the Modern Language Association of America* for permission to reprint portions of two articles published in that journal. My acknowledgments are due to Mr. Bonamy Dobrée and to the Oxford University Press (World's Classics Series) for permission to quote excerpts from Mr. Dobrée's edition of *The Mourning Bride, Poems, & Miscellanies, by William Congreve;* to Mr. R. W. Ketton-Cremer and to Faber & Faber, Ltd., for three excerpts from Mr. Ketton-Cremer's *Norfolk Portraits;* to John Murray for a long quotation from Emily J. Climenson's edition of the letters of Mrs. Elizabeth Montagu and excerpts from Lord Ilchester's edition of the letters of Lord Hervey; and to McGraw-Hill Book Company, Inc., for a brief quotation from *Boswell's London Journal, 1762–1763.*

For the privilege of consulting collections of manuscripts I wish to thank the Duke of Marlborough; the Marquis of Bath; the Earl of Harrowby; the Earl of Ossory; Mr. R. W. Ketton-Cremer; Lieutenant-Colonel F. D. E. Fremantle; the Provost of Trinity College, Dublin; and the Royal College of Surgeons of England. Mr. R. L. Atkinson, Assistant Keeper of the Public Record Office, London, permitted me to examine the Egmont MSS. Professor Robert Halsband generously provided me with transcripts from the Wortley MSS. of manuscript letters and verses by Lady Mary Wortley Montagu. For permission to reproduce photographs of portraits and a manuscript letter I owe

PREFACE

thanks to the Duke of Leeds; Ruth, Dowager Countess of Chichester; the National Portrait Gallery; the Royal College of Physicians; and the New York Public Library.

Many persons have advised and assisted me in a variety of ways. I am grateful to the staffs of the British Museum and the Public Record Office, London. From Professor John C. Hodges I have received substantial aid. I am indebted, also, to Mr. Thomas Ulick Sadleir; Captain C. G. T. Dean; Mr. R. R. James; Mr. G. H. Holley; Mr. Humphrey Whitbread; Mrs. Walter Burns; Mr. C. K. Adams; Mr. Derek Rogers; Mr. H. A. C. Sturgess; Mr. E. A. P. Hart; Mrs. Standish Henry Harrison; Miss Hilda U. Walsh; Miss P. Beryl Eustace; Professor Emmett L. Avery; Professor Emeritus Dorothy Foster; Professor Charlotte D'Evelyn; Miss Flora Belle Ludington; Miss Barbara Hubbard; the Reverend W. S. Evans; the Reverend R. J. Higgitt; the Reverend J. H. McCubbin; Mr. G. Lloyd Lewis; Miss Kate Collyer; Mrs. George Collyer; and Miss Pearl R. Felice.

KATHLEEN M. LYNCH

South Hadley, Massachusetts
April 1951

Contents

xi

Illustrations

WILLIAM CONGREVE

16

Reproduced from the painting in the Kit-Cat Club series of portraits by Sir God-frey Kneller, by permission of the National Portrait Gallery.

LETTER FROM CONGREVE TO KEALLY, SEPTEMBER 28, 1697

32, 33

The first of Congreve's letters to be reproduced, from the manuscript in the Berg Collection, New York Public Library, by permission of the Library.

HENRIETTA, DUCHESS OF MARLBOROUGH

64

Reproduced for the first time from a painting, probably by Sir Godfrey Kneller, in the Stanmer Collection, on loan in the Brighton Art Gallery, by permission of Ruth, Dowager Countess of Chichester. (This is probably the portrait which Congreve bequeathed in his will to Henrietta, Duchess of Newcastle.)

FRANCIS GODOLPHIN, SECOND EARL OF GODOLPHIN

80

Reproduced from the painting by Jonathan Richardson, by permission of the National Portrait Gallery.

ILLUSTRATIONS

A Congreve Gallery

William Congreve

*T*he majority of Congreve's critics, since his own time, appear to agree that little can be said of his personality and character and that what can be said is not very pleasant. It is true, of course, that biographical data concerning Congreve are disappointingly scanty and are likely to remain so. On the other hand, such evidence as is available has often been misinterpreted and as often ignored. Nor have certain regrettable misinterpretations and omissions been exposed. It has been asserted that Congreve has been "singularly fortunate" in his critics and biographers, despite "some unimportant exceptions." [1]

The fact of the matter is that posterity has refused to accept Congreve as the delightful person in whom his friends rejoiced. His contemporaries found him above criticism. They considered his scholarship unimpeachable, his wit unsurpassed, his taste flawless. He was the best of companions, the most loyal and understanding friend. His private life impressed them as neither uneventful nor unseemly.

The most remarkable of Congreve's literary friendships was his friendship with Dryden. In the last decade of his life, Dryden was exhilarated by the meteoric career of the young dramatist whom he welcomed as his spiritual son. It was Congreve's scholarship which first commended him to Dryden. This "excellent young man" translated the eleventh satire in Dryden's Juvenal and corrected the manuscript of Dryden's *Aeneid*. Congreve's translation of two passages from Homer made Dryden wish that his youthful friend had the leisure to translate all of Homer "and the World the good Nature and Justice, to encourage him in that Noble Design, of which he is more capable than any Man I know." [2]

The discovery of Congreve's dramatic genius was a rich satisfaction. On reading *The Old Bachelor,* Dryden observed that "he never saw such a first play in his life." He revised it for the stage, lest it "miscarry for want of a little Assistance." [3] In the summer of 1693 he confided to Jacob Tonson: "I am Mr. Congreve's true Lover, & desire you to tell him, how kindly I take his often Remembrances of me: I wish him all prosperity, & hope I shall never loose his affection." As a common friend, though "much more mine," [4] Dryden insisted, Congreve was able to ease the tension between Dryden and his exacting publisher.

On December 12, 1693, Dryden undertook to introduce Congreve to Walsh by sending the latter a copy of *The Double-Dealer.* Dryden admitted:

[The play] is much censured by the greater part of the Town; and is defended only by the best Judges, who, you know, are commonly the fewest. Yet it gains ground daily, and has already been acted Eight times. . . My verses, which you will find before it, were written before the play was acted. but I neither alterd them nor do I alter my opinion of the play. [5]

Regarding Dryden's verses to Congreve, no one is likely to quarrel with Edmund Gosse's statement: "Perhaps since the beginning of literary history there is no other example of such fine and generous praise of a young colleague by a great old poet." [6] The amazing achievement of Congreve's "blooming Youth," said Dryden, could not offend his "foil'd" contemporaries:

> So much the sweetness of your manners move,
> We cannot envy you because we Love.

He counseled affectionately:

> Maintain Your Post: That's all the Fame You need;
> For 'tis impossible you shou'd proceed.
> Already I am worn with Cares and Age;
> And just abandoning th' Ungrateful Stage:

Unprofitably kept at Heav'ns expence,
I live a Rent-charge on his Providence:
But You, whom ev'ry Muse and Grace adorn,
Whom I foresee to better Fortune born,
Be kind to my Remains; and oh defend,
Against Your Judgment, Your departed Friend!
Let not the Insulting Foe my Fame pursue;
But shade those Laurels which descend to You:
And take for Tribute what these Lines express:
You merit more; nor cou'd my Love do less.[7]

Dryden lived to see the first cool reception of *The Way of the World*. On March 12, 1700, he wrote to Mrs. Elizabeth Steward: "Congreve's New Play has had but moderate success; though it deserves much better." [8] The elderly dramatist's death in the same year deprived Congreve of the friend whose opinion of his work must have gratified him more than any other homage which he ever received.

"I loved Mr. Dryden," wrote Congreve in his dedication to the Duke of Newcastle of Dryden's *Dramatic Works*. He praised Dryden's "exceedingly humane and compassionate" nature and reflected: "To the best of my knowledge and observation, he was, of all the men that ever I knew, one of the most modest." Of Dryden's literary work, commented Congreve, "I may venture to say, in general terms, that no man hath written in our language so much, and so various matter, and in so various manners so well." [9]

The friendship of Congreve and Swift was not a literary friendship at all. Swift was, indeed, struck by Congreve's youthful precocity. But after *The Double-Dealer* had been unfavorably received, he preferred not to send to Congreve the verses in which he had announced: "Godlike the force of my young Congreve's bays." [10] Some years later on a rainy evening Swift dipped into a volume of Congreve's plays left by a servant in his room and "read in it till twelve, like an owl and a fool." [11] The remark has been interpreted as a compliment and as the reverse. Congreve's private opinion of *A Tale of a Tub* was, at any rate, not flattering.[12] And a profound difference in temperament separated the genial dramatist and the indignant satirist whose chief aim was "to vex the world rather than divert it." [13]

Nevertheless, there was a cordial relationship between the two men which ended only with Congreve's death. During Swift's residence in London they saw much of each other. When Congreve was well, Swift found it pleasant to laugh with him for hours, even over "a bowl of bad punch" or sipping "nasty white wine." When Congreve was ill, Swift sat in his lodgings with him, also for hours, impressed by the fact that, although almost blind and never free from gout, "poor Congreve" was "as chearful as ever." Swift took some pains to persuade the Earl of Oxford to prevent Congreve from losing his government post under a Tory ministry; and "so I have made a worthy man easy, and that is a good day's work." [14] After his return to Ireland, Swift depended upon Pope and Gay to keep him informed as to Congreve's health. Gay assured Swift that Congreve "always mentions you with the strongest expressions of esteem and friendship." [15] Writing of Swift to Pope, Congreve confessed: "it is a great pleasure to me, and not a little vanity, to think that he misses me." [16]

When Congreve died, Swift shared with Pope his "grief for the death of our friend Mr. Congreve, whom I loved from my youth, and who surely, besides his other talents, was a very agreeable companion." He did not attempt to conceal his sense of bereavement: "Years have not yet hardened me, and I have an addition of weight on my spirits since we lost him, though I saw him so seldom, and possibly if he had lived on, should have seen him no more." [17]

Congreve's early fame enabled him to assist Pope, who was eighteen years his junior. In 1706 he read Pope's *Pastorals* in manuscript and apparently recommended them. Pope was always grateful because Congreve "loved . . . my lays," which Swift only "endured." In 1715 Pope acknowledged Congreve's continued, although futile, "endeavours to enrich me." In the last year of Congreve's life, Gay wrote to Pope: "Mr. Congreve admires, with me, your fortitude, and loves, not envies, your performances, for we are not dunces." [18] After her quarrel with Pope,

Lady Mary Wortley Montagu declared that Pope's poetry and conversation had been "perpetual jokes" to Congreve and that he had been "particularly pleasant on that subject." [19] Under the circumstances, the value of such evidence may be questioned. However, the few letters of Congreve to Pope which have survived are formally written, and the greater warmth of friendship appears to have been on Pope's side.

Pope turned to Congreve for "your condolence" when he and Gay were "suffering under a criticism." He was distressed by Congreve's ill health. "The calamity of your gout," he deplored, "is what all your friends, that is to say, all that know you, must share in." When the Duchess of Marlborough engrossed Congreve's time and attention, Pope made no derogatory comment on Congreve but merely noted that the ladies are "the destroyers of their best friends the men." After Congreve's death, he observed: "Mr. Congreve's death touches me nearly. It is twenty years and more that I have known him." [20] His moving dedication to Congreve of his translation of Homer's *Iliad* indicates a very genuine regard for "one of the most valuable men, as well as finest writers of my age and country" and a very real satisfaction in "placing together . . . the names of Mr. CONGREVE, and of A. POPE." [21] As Macaulay remarked, "There was not a duke in the kingdom who would not have been proud of such a compliment." [22]

Pope, Congreve, and Lady Mary Wortley Montagu for some years made up a notable trio. How ardent was Congreve's friendship with Lady Mary it is impossible to tell. The letters which he sent to her when she was in Turkey, sometimes enclosed in Pope's letters, have been destroyed. The impression remains that she pursued him, and with increasing tenacity in proportion as his interest in her declined. She would perhaps have liked him as a lover. She found him a charming companion, and affirmed: "I never knew any body that had so much wit as Congreve." [23]

In 1716 Pope wrote to Lady Mary that he had given Congreve a letter of hers, and added:

His health and my own are now so good, that we wish with all our souls you were a witness of it. We never meet but we lament over

5

you: we pay a kind of weekly rites to your memory, where we strow flowers of rhetoric, and offer such libations to your name as it were a profaneness to call toasting.[24]

In another letter Pope assured her: "Mr. Congreve is entirely yours, and has writ twice to you." In a third he declared that Congreve "no way deserves to be thought forgetful of you." [25]

In replying to Pope, Lady Mary spoke of "my few friendships" and told him: "I am still warmly sensible of yours and Mr. Congreve's, and desire to live in your remembrances, though dead to all the world beside." She expressed her pleasure in returning home, for "I long much to tread upon English ground, that I may see you and Mr. Congreve, who render that ground classic ground." [26] By 1719 Congreve may have been perceptibly aloof, for Lady Mary reproached him, as he informed Pope, for not letting her know that he was at Ashley; having "the goodnesse for me to believe" [27] that he had been there all summer without writing to her. His friendship with Henrietta, Duchess of Marlborough, removed Lady Mary from his circle. There seems never to have been any open quarrel, as there was between Lady Mary and Pope. In 1735 she wrote to Dr. Arbuthnot concerning "Mr. Congreve, who was my friend." [28]

Among Lady Mary's unpublished manuscripts is a rough draft in her handwriting of some unfinished verses, which she probably composed soon after Congreve's death.

To the Memory of Mr Congreve

Fare well ye best & loveliest of Mankind
where Nature wth a happy hand had joyn'd
ye softest temper with ye strongest mind
In pain could counsel & could charm w^n blind

In this Lewd Age when Honor is a Jest
he found a refuge in his Congreves breast
superior there, unsully'd, & entire
& only could wth ye last sigh expire

his wit was never by his Malice stain'd
No rival writer of his Verse complain'd

for neither party drew a venal pen
to praise bad measures or to blast good men

. . . .

If in a distant State blest spirits know
ye scenes of sorrow of a World below
This little Tribute to thy Fame approve
a Trifling Instance of a boundless Love [29]

In his delightful poem, "Mr. Pope's Welcome from Greece,"
Gay praised "friendly Congreve, unreproachful man!" [30] Like
Swift, Gay admired Congreve's "cheerful temper," despite ill
health. In February 1723, Gay wrote to Swift: "I passed all the
last season with Congreve at the Bath, and I have great reason
to value myself upon his friendship; for I am sure he sincerely
wishes me well." [31] These two most amiable men were naturally
attracted to each other. It is not known to what extent Gay succeeded Congreve in the affections of the younger Duchess of
Marlborough. She may have perceived in Gay something of the
gentleness and sweetness which had endeared Congreve to her.

More surprising is Congreve's friendship with the irascible
Dennis, who attacked in venomous fashion most of the men of
letters of the day, but expressed only unbounded admiration for
Congreve. Dennis admitted that he had received many favors
from Congreve and professed himself "perfectly yours." [32] No
doubt, Congreve handled him tactfully. He is credited with the
statement that "it was of the two Evils better to have Dennis's
Flattery than his Gall." [33] He is said to have persuaded Pope and
Addison to "silence" Dennis by subscribing for some of his books.
And he addressed to Dennis his essay, "Humour in Comedy."

The most felicitous of Congreve's letters was written to
Dennis from Tunbridge Wells on August 11, 1695. It was a letter
which he obviously enjoyed writing, for he ran "into length
like a Poet in a Dedication, when he forgets his Patron to talk
of himself." He began with a graceful compliment:

Before I came to Tunbridge, I proposed to my self the Satisfaction of Communicating the Pleasures of the Place to you: But if I
keep my Resolution, I must transcribe, and return you your own

7

Letters; since I have met with nothing else so truly Delightful. When you suppose the Country agreeable to me, you suppose such Reasons why it should be so, that while I read your Letter I am of your Mind; but when I look off, I find I am only Charm'd with the Landskip which you have drawn. So that if I would see a fine Prospect of the Country, I must desire you to send it me from the Town; as if I would eat good Fruit here, Perhaps the best way were, to beg a Basket from my Friends in Covent-Garden. After all this, I must tell you, there is a great deal of Company at Tunbridge, and some very agreeable . . . But were the Company better, or worse, I would have you expect no Characters from me; for I profess myself an Enemy to Detraction; and who is there, that can justly merit Commendation? I have a mind to write to you, without the pretence of any manner of News, as I might drink to you without naming a Health; for I intend only my Service to you. I wish for you very often, that I might recommend you to some new Acquaintance that I have made here, and think very well worth the keeping; I mean Idleness and a good Stomach. You would not think how People Eat here; every Body has the Appetite of an Oastrich, and as they Drink Steel in the Morning, so I believe at Noon they could digest Iron. But sure you will laugh at me for calling Idleness a New Acquaintance, when, to your Knowledge, the greatest part of my Business, is little better. Ay, But here's the Comfort of the Change; I am Idle now, without taking pains to be so, or to make other People so; for Poetry is neither in my Head, nor in my Heart. I know not whether these Waters may have any Communication with Lethe, but sure I am, they have none with the Streams of Helicon. . .

Turning to the subject of the theater, Congreve continued:

. . . now I talk of the Stage, pray if any thing New should appear there, let me have an Account of it: for tho' Plays are a kind of Winter-Fruit, yet I know there are now and then some Windfalls at this time of Year, which must be presently served up, lest they should not keep till the proper Season of Entertainment. 'Tis now the time, when the Sun breeds Insects; and you must expect to have the Hum and Buz about your Ears, of Summer Flies and small Poets. . .[34]

It is no wonder that Dennis rejoiced in such a correspondent. He wrote to Congreve: "the gaiety of your Letters relieves me considerably. Then what must your Conversation do? Come up and make the Experiment; and impart that Vigour to me which Tunbridge has restor'd to you." [35]

In "An Account of the Greatest English Poets," Addison ranked "harmonious Congreve" [36] as Dryden's successor. According to Steele, it was to Congreve that Addison owed his introduction to Charles Montagu. Between 1699 and 1702, in the course of his European tour, Addison wrote three letters to Congreve which have been preserved. They are Baedeker letters, as Addison himself realized, for he apologized for almost carrying Congreve "from room to room" [37] in the gallery of Versailles. After his first years in London, Congreve saw less of Addison than of Pope or Gay. In 1708 he wrote to Joseph Keally: "I have made your compliments to Mr. Addison, having seen him once by accident. It is not so familiar a thing to see him as it was ten years ago." [38]

Steele seems to have had a stronger personal affection for Congreve. He believed that Congreve excelled in "ev'ry way of Writing" [39] but admired most of all his friend's character. In his dedication to Congreve of his *Poetical Miscellanies*, he wrote:

As much as I esteem you for your excellent writings, by which you are an honour to our nation, I chuse rather, as one that has passed many happy hours with you, to celibrate that easy condescension of mind, and command of a pleasant imagination, which give you the uncommon praise of a man of wit, always to please, and never to offend. No one, after a joyful evening, can reflect upon an expression of Mr. Congreve's that dwells upon him with pain.

In a man capable of exerting himself any way, this (whatever the vain and ill-natured may think of the matter) is an excellence above the brightest sallies of imagination. [40]

Eight years later, in dedicating to Congreve the second edition of Addison's *The Drummer*, Steele commended Congreve's "equanimity, candour and benevolence" and spoke of him as "one whom every wise and good man looks upon with the greatest affection and veneration." [41]

Congreve was "a particular favourite with the ladies . . . He indulged none of those reveries, and affected absences so peculiar to men of wit." [42] There was some contemporary gossip about his *tendre* for Anne Bracegirdle, who played the successive roles of his heroines and to whom both Congreve and Rowe, "when they gave her a Lover in a play seem'd palpably to plead their own Passions." [43] It was known that Mrs. Bracegirdle was Congreve's neighbor, assumed that she was his mistress, and hinted that she might have been his wife by a private marriage.[44] It was also known that the Earl of Scarsdale [45] succeeded Congreve as her admirer and left her a legacy of one thousand pounds. In the main, the distaste for publicity of both Congreve and Mrs. Bracegirdle was respected. One of Congreve's detractors in the Collier controversy could find nothing worse to say of this affair than that it was Congreve's custom to "Ogle his Dear Bracilla, with sneaking looks under his Hat, in the little side Box" [46] over the stage. In *Memoirs of the Life, Writings, and Amours of William Congreve* (1730) there is no account of this or any other of Congreve's amours. It was generally recognized, no doubt, that Anne Bracegirdle's reputation was "in good hands." [47] Even after Congreve fell in love with Henrietta, Duchess of Marlborough, he remained on terms of friendship, but not of intimacy, with Mrs. Bracegirdle and left her two hundred pounds in his will. She had "the highest veneration" for him "and joined with her Grace [the Duchess of Marlborough] in a boundless profusion of sorrow upon his death." [48]

The friendship of Congreve and the younger Duchess of Marlborough attracted the attention of many of his contemporaries. The extravagance of the Duchess's grief at his death and her manner of showing it could not escape comment and, in some quarters, ridicule.[49] Her elaborate monument to Congreve in the south aisle of Westminster Abbey records

> how dearly
> She remembers the happiness and Honour She enjoyed in
> the Sincere Friendship of so worthy and Honest a Man,
> Whose Virtue Candour and Witt gained him the love and
> Esteem of the present Age and whose Writings will be the
> Admiration of the Future.

It is probable that Henrietta sponsored James Thomson's elegiac verses on Congreve and rewarded him generously for praising those varied talents which "Hallifax approv'd and Marlbro' mourns." [50]

Among Congreve's titled friends, Sir Richard Temple, Viscount Cobham,[51] was the most congenial. A contemporary writer conjectured: "Thus Horace lov'd Augustus, thus was lov'd." [52] This was one of the longest of Congreve's friendships, dating back to his earlier years in London, when he was able to drink with Temple and Delaval "six nights in seven." [53] Congreve admired Cobham's unpretentious goodness:

> Affecting none, all Virtues you possess,
> And really are what others but profess.

He considered him his "sincerest Critick." It was for Cobham that, shortly before his death, he sketched a finer portrait of himself than any of his critics has ever painted:

> Come, see thy Friend, retir'd without Regret,
> Forgetting Care, or striving to forget:
> In easy Contemplation soothing Time
> With Morals much, and now and then with Rhime,
> Not so robust in Body, as in Mind,
> And always undejected, tho' declin'd.[54]

At his country seat at Stowe, where Congreve had been so welcome a guest, Cobham erected in 1736 a monument to his friend's memory, as "a poor Consolation for . . . his loss." He paid tribute in his Latin inscription to Congreve's "piercing, elegant, polished Wit and civilized, candid, most unaffected Manners." [55]

It was the consensus of opinion of Congreve's many friends: "Beyond the Poet, we the Person Love." [56] This does not imply that the poet was in the least undervalued. Among his contemporaries, perhaps only his Puritan critics and Congreve himself [57] took exception to Dryden's claim that Heaven had endowed Shakespeare and Congreve equally. Addison considered *Love for Love* "one of the finest Comedies that ever appeared upon the English Stage." [58] To Steele Congreve was a sacred name. He devoted a whole *Spectator* paper [59] to condemning the corrupt morals of Etherege in *The Man of Mode,* but seems

never to have thought of his friend Congreve as belonging to
Etherege's school. None of his contemporaries presumed to up-
braid Congreve for retiring from the stage; it was merely regretted
that he had done so. Young reflected:

> Congreve. . . crown'd with lawrels fairly won,
> Sits smiling at the Goal while Others run,
> He will not write; and (more provoking still!)
> Ye Gods! he will not write, and Maevius will.[60]

Dennis observed aptly, "most Persons" thought, that Congreve
"left the Stage early, and Comedy has quitted it with him." [61]

Congreve's literary reputation remained secure. There is no
occasion to review here the just tributes which he has received
from many able pens. But as a man, posterity has treated him
shabbily. The chorus of praise with which his friends acclaimed
his personal qualities had died out by the middle of the eighteenth
century. The brilliant achievement of his ten years of playwrit-
ing, while recognized by Johnson, was lost sight of by others,
who preferred to stress the much longer period of inactivity
which followed. Macaulay explained:

Two kinds of ambition early took possession of his mind and often
pulled it in opposite directions. . . He longed to be a great writer.
He longed to be a man of fashion. Either object was within his reach.
But could he secure both? . . . The history of his life is the history
of a conflict between these two impulses. In his youth the desire of
literary fame had the mastery; but soon the meaner ambition over-
powered the higher, and obtained supreme dominion over his mind.[62]

The life of a complex human being was reduced to its simplest
terms; and its low points (there appeared to be no high ones)
were faithfully repeated by each successive critic.

It was assumed that laziness was a basic trait of Congreve's
character. It was noted that he made a fortune from a number
of absurd government sinecures, to which he clung by flattering
rival ministers. His later life was viewed as a dismal tale of
increasing infirmities: and it was objected that he led a padded
existence, coddled by "the great and splendid." [63]

Congreve has been damned for the very amiability which charmed his contemporaries. The worst has been made of what could not be put out of the picture. It has been inferred that a man who was everyone's friend, with "an ear at everybody's service," [64] could have been no very hearty friend to any one. Macaulay declared that Congreve was "not a man of warm affections." [65] Leigh Hunt doubted if he "ever risked any thing, or encountered any kind of martyrdom or privation, to benefit anybody." He found "the conclusion . . . unavoidable, that [Congreve] was negatively rather than positively amiable, and must be ranked among the agreeably selfish. (What a blessing if all the selfish were equally agreeable!)" [66]

To negative amiability has been added the charge of frivolity and insincerity. From Johnson to Thackeray there was a growing conviction that Congreve's reading of life was frivolous, if not perverse; and this notion was extended to include his character. Lamb considered (without objecting) that Congreve "spread a privation of moral light" [67] over his fairy-tale world. It was assumed that Congreve's own life lacked such moral light—in fact, any light at all.

Voltaire's account of his visit to Congreve had a mischievous effect on the latter's reputation, as it seemed to offer indisputable evidence that Congreve was a snob. Voltaire reported:

Il était infirme & presque mourant quand je l'ai connu. Il avait un defaut, c'étoit de ne pas assez estimer son premier metier d'autheur, qui avoit fait sa reputation & sa fortune. Il me parloit de ses ouvrages comme de bagatelles au dessous de lui; & me dit à la premiere conversation, de ne le voir que sur le pied de gentilhomme qui vivoit trés uniment. Je luis repondis, que s'il avoit eu le malheur de n'être qu'un gentilhomme comme un autre, je ne le serois jamais venu voir, & je fus trè choqué de cette vanité si mal placée.[68]

Johnson censured Congreve for the "despicable foppery" [69] of his reply to Voltaire. Lamb, however, protested with some spirit: "I think the impertinent Frenchman was properly answered." [70] The episode has been placed in its true light, at last, by Dobrée, who assails the common assumptions that it is "intolerable vanity to pretend to that ease of mind for which everybody strives, and that nobody has any business to be successful in the art of possessing his soul in peace." [71]

Congreve's relations with women have been regarded as further proofs of his worldly heart. On this subject Thackeray expended his eloquence:

What an irresistible Mr. Congreve it is! . . . with such a grace, with such a fashion, with such a splendid embroidered suit—you see him with red-heeled shoes deliciously turned out, passing a fair jewelled hand through his dishevelled periwig and delivering a killing ogle along with a scented billet.

A touch of Steele's tenderness is worth all his finery—a flash of Swift's lightning—a beam of Addison's pure sunshine, and his tawdry play-house taper is invisible. But the ladies loved him and he was undoubtedly a pretty fellow.[72]

Congreve has been severely criticized because he "jilted" Mrs. Bracegirdle, drawn from her by the rank, wealth, and beauty of Henrietta, Duchess of Marlborough, at whose table he became "as regular . . . as the wine." [73] It has been the fashion to denounce the "absurd and capricious" [74] will in which he neglected his needy relatives, gave a niggardly two hundred pounds to Mrs. Bracegirdle, and left ten thousand pounds to the Duchess of Marlborough, a sum "to her superfluous and useless." [75] The story of Henrietta's devotion to Congreve's image has been repeated with variations and with some reflections on her "insanity."

Until recently, there has been no probing into the history of either one of these ladies, and they have been left, where they were found, in dusky niches. Congreve was undeniably discreet in his amours. His well-bred gallantry has perhaps rankled with critics who would have preferred to find more flame than smoke.

There have been three full-length biographies of Congreve. Edmund Gosse wrote the first of these, printed in 1888. Always readable, in this instance Gosse seems not to have relished his task. He was irked by a paucity of materials and acknowledged that Congreve's personality eluded him. One reads with astonishment his tribute to Thackeray's "few marvellous pages" [76] on Congreve. With considerable severity Thorn-Drury [77] has pointed out numerous errors in Gosse's book. The omissions are equally unfortunate. Like most of Congreve's critics, Gosse has been more of a snob than Congreve and has overlooked Congreve's connections with ordinary humdrum mortals. His preoccupation with notable figures led Gosse to believe that the "dear Charles" (Charles Mein) with whom Congreve and Jacob Tonson traveled to the Low Countries was "Charles Gildon the critic." [78] Shocked by such a conjecture, Thorn-Drury observed: "I can hardly imagine a wilder guess among all Congreve's contemporaries." The same critic comments with perfect justice: "It doesn't seem to occur to Gosse that the large majority of any man's friends and acquaintances must be more or less undistinguished people." [79]

Gosse evaluates Congreve in these words:

There were no salient points about Congreve's character. Though an old bachelor, he was not eccentric; though a man of pleasure, he was discreet. No vagaries, no escapades place him in a ludicrous or in a human light. He passes through the literary life of his time as if in felt slippers, noiseless, unupbraiding, without personal adventures." [80]

This is a fine bit of writing which effectively takes all of the color out of Congreve's life.

Discouraged, perhaps, by such a verdict and by the lack of fresh documents, scholars made no attempt to improve upon Gosse's biography for over forty years. In 1931 D. Crane Taylor published a "critical biography," in which he claimed to present "much new information." [81] Taylor follows, but in pedestrian fashion, the broad outlines of Gosse's book, repeats some of his errors, adds others of his own, and contributes little of consequence that is new. He dismisses Congreve's good friends, Luther, Fitzgerald, Amory, and "Charles" (whom, like Gosse, he assumes to be Charles Gildon) with the casual statement: "Who these people are we have no idea." He assigns to the second Earl of

Godolphin his father's office of Lord High Treasurer and concludes, without investigation, that the second Earl was "a
dullard." At times he gives a false impression of Congreve. Although he quotes frequently from Congreve's letters to Keally,
he discounts their revelation of the writer's personality, merely
because Congreve excluded from them "the privacies of his life."
A grave misreading of Congreve's character may be inferred
from Taylor's comment that the dramatist retired from the theater an "embittered man." [82]

Ten years after Taylor's attempt, John C. Hodges published
a scholarly biography of Congreve.[83] Hodges settles disputed
points regarding Congreve's family. He visited the scenes associated with Congreve's youth, examined carefully all available
school and college records, and paints the first illuminating picture of the dramatist's life in Ireland. He notes a number of Congreve's later contacts with Irish friends, including members of
the Boyle family, and especially Richard Boyle, third Viscount
Shannon. He also throws light on Congreve's friendship with
Jacob Tonson. Of Congreve's official life, hitherto so sketchily
treated, and of his financial circumstances he gives the first detailed and coherent account. Hodges does much towards break-
ing down the Congreve myth. So scrupulously has he performed
his task that there appears to be no occasion for a fourth biography, until accident discloses sources of information which
patient scholarship could not detect.

Some of the gaps in our knowledge of Congreve may have
to be permanent. Others can be filled. There is a good deal which
has not been recorded about Congreve's friendships. His wide
circle of friends must be recognized as wider than has commonly
been supposed. With a number of his Irish friends, now shrouded
in oblivion, he was on terms of intimacy; and to one of them,
at any rate, he was more warmly attached than to Swift or Pope.

All of his Irish associations meant much to Congreve.[84] The
present writer first reviewed the life of his most intimate Irish
friend, Joseph Keally.[85] In his letters to Keally it was his custom
to send his regards to "Robin and the rest." [86] One of the following essays concerns Robin Fitzgerald and his family. The other

WILLIAM CONGREVE

Irish correspondents whom Congreve mentions most often are Thomas Amory and Henry Luther, to whom only passing reference has been made by his biographers.

Both Amory and Luther were Trinity College men. Amory received his B.A. degree in 1681; Luther in 1688.[87] Amory was among the Irish Protestants, including Keally and Fitzgerald, who fled to England in 1688. He settled in Bunratty, county Clare, and when he died in 1728 left a considerable estate. Luther was the son of John Luther, a merchant of Youghal and several times mayor of that town. He was admitted to the Middle Temple in 1688; was town clerk of Youghal in 1700; was called to the Irish Bar; and represented Youghal in the Irish Parliament for some years. He lived in Dublin and later in Balliboy, King's County, and was the owner of large properties in county Cork.[88]

Once Keally's long silence made Congreve feel charitable towards "that brute Luther" and disposed to forgive the omissions of Tom Amory, "if I could ever have been angry with [him]." Amory saw something of Congreve during at least two visits to London. In "term-time" Congreve wrote to Luther in Dublin. By 1710 his bad eyesight obliged him to write less often to both Keally and Luther.[89]

Charles Mein [90] was an Irishman who settled in London and was the frequent companion of Congreve's leisure hours. He held several posts in succession at the Custom House and at the time of his death in 1735 was Examiner of the Duties on Wine and Currants.[91] Under the date of October 8, 1710, in his *Journal to Stella,* Swift describes him in humorous fashion:

Yesterday I was going with Dr. Garth to dine with Charles Main, near the Tower, who has an employment there: he is of Ireland; the Bishop of Clogher knows him well: an honest, goodnatured fellow, a thorough hearty laugher, mightily beloved by the men of wit: his mistress is never above a cook-maid.[92]

In "Mr. Pope's Welcome from Greece," Gay includes, among boon companions, "wond'ring Maine, so fat with laughing eyes." [93]

Mein appears to have enjoyed life in an easygoing, pleasant

manner. Congreve mentions one occasion when Mein "very narrowly escaped being arrested, and that near the custom-house" and was "forced to go out of town." At times Congreve felt impelled to curb the dissipations of this jovial friend. He told Keally: "I have preached as I ought to Mein, and he has edified as he ought." [94] Congreve toured Holland with Mein in 1700 and was much entertained by the whimsicality of his fellow-traveler:

Whenever we have seen any thing extremely surprising, chiefly in painting, though the picture has been the most solemn, the most devout, the most moving, both in the subject and the expressions of the passion; as soon as our Charles began to be touched with it, he always burst out a laughing, which I like mightily; and so he did the first time he heard Abell sing.[95]

Mein indulged in violent alternations of high and low spirits. When Keally was suffering from a broken leg, Congreve wrote: "I have not seen Mein since I received your letter; but I expect that he should hang or stab himself when I tell him. I think he ought to do no less who affected to fast upon the news of Lord Donegal's death, and got drunk the night following." Congreve found such fluctuations of mood a safeguard against boredom. He assured Keally: "Mein is, as you hope, fat, rich, and melancholy; very variable when awake, and nothing but his sleepiness makes him tolerable." Betwixt gaiety and gloom, "our Charles" throve "prodigiously," growing steadily fatter, until, said Congreve, "we can't sit on the same side of a coach, though I am no fatter than I use to be." Like all jesters, Mein had his soberer side. He had scholarly tastes and was "of all men the hardest to be pleased with any modern essays." [96]

Congreve's relations with Edward Porter and his wife, Frances, have been largely disregarded, despite the familiar tone of his letters to them. Probably as a Middle Templar Congreve made the acquaintance of Edward Porter, in the days when the latter was "of the Inner Temple." [97] For some years they were neighbors in Arundel Street, where Porter lived "against" the Blue Ball. In or before June 1706 the Porters moved to Surrey

Street, and Congreve soon afterwards moved to lodgings in their house.

It has been taken for granted that Mrs. Porter was the "talented actress."[98] But it was Mary Porter, an unmarried woman, who was Mrs. Barry's successor in tragic roles. In the will that he drafted on February 26, 1725,[99] Congreve left to Frances Porter a bequest of fifty pounds. Her death (1727) preceded Congreve's (1729) and her husband's (1731).[100] Edward Porter's will reveals the interesting fact that his wife was Anne Bracegirdle's sister. Dying without heirs and in comfortable circumstances, he left bequests in "good British money" to "our Sister," Anne Bracegirdle; to "our brother," Hamlet Bracegirdle, and to each of his children; and to Justinian, the son of John Bracegirdle. He made "my dear and only Sister Joyce," the wife of John Green, his residuary legatee and provided adequately for her children. His will was signed "att Arundell Street."[101]

Five letters which Congreve wrote to Edward Porter give an agreeable impression of their friendship. During his tour of Holland and Belgium, Congreve never failed to drink the healths of his neighbors in Arundel Street. He spent a summer holiday at Ilam in Staffordshire, and described to Porter its romantic solitudes:

this place . . . is so much out of the world that nothing but the last great news could have reacht it. I have a little tried, what solitude and retirement can afford, which are here in perfection I am now writing to you from a black mountain nodding over me and a whole river in cascade falling so near me that even I can distinctly see it.

From Stowe in Buckinghamshire, he sent New Year's greetings:

I am by a great fire yet my ink freezes so fast I cannot write. the Hautboys who playd to us last night had their breath froze in their instruments till it dropt of the ends of em in icicles by god this is true.[102]

To Mrs. Porter Congreve wrote a gay, bantering letter from Rotterdam on September 27, 1700:

I Leave you to Judge whither Holland can be said to be wanting
in Gallantry, when it is Customary there to enclose a Billet doux to
a Lady, in a letter to her husband I have not so much as made mention of this, to yours: & if you tell first, let the sin fall upon your
head instead of his. for my part I keep the Commandments, I love
my neighbour as my selfe, & to avoid Coveting my neighbour's wife
I desire to be coveted by her; which you know is quite another thing.
about 5 weeks since, I wrote a very passionate letter to you from Ant-
werp which I believe you never receivd, for just now it is found,
carefully put up by my Man, who has been drunk ever since. I understand you have not been in the Country, I am glad of it; for I
should very much have apprehended the effects which solitude might
have produced, joynd with the regrett which I know you feel for
my absence. take it for granted that I sigh extreamly . . . I would
have written to y^r Mother but that I have changed my religion twice
since I left england, & am at present so unsettled, that I think it fit
to fix before I endeavour to convert her to my opinion which I design
to do as soon as I know what it is. I have discoursd with friers &
monks of all orders, with zealots enthusiasts & all sectaries of the re-
formd churches. & I had the benefit to travel 12 leagues together in
Guelderland with a mad Phanatick in a waggon, who preachd to me
all the way things not to be written. pray take care that Mr Ebbub
has good wine for I have much to say to you over a bottle under-
ground: & I hope within 3 weeks to satisfie you that no man upon
the face of the earth nor in the Cellar is more dear neighbour y^r
ffaithful

> & affectionate humble
> servant than
> W: C: [103]

Anne Bracegirdle, Frances Porter's sister, was Congreve's near
neighbor in Howard Street. In his letters to Keally he often
included her in greetings from "all the neighbourhood." To his
letter to Porter from Calais on August 11, 1700, he adds a postscript to the effect that Charles (Mein) "is just writing to M^{rs}
Anne" and exerting himself "to send something besides the
Ballad, to please her much." [104] When Anne Bracegirdle died
(1748), she left a large legacy to her nephew, Justinian Bracegirdle, bequeathing the residue of her estate to her niece, Martha
Bracegirdle.[105] It may be hoped that any further discoveries con-

cerning the Porters will increase our limited knowledge of "charming Bracegirdle." [106]

Perhaps the most significant of Congreve's attachments was for Henrietta, Duchess of Marlborough. The nature of this friendship, well known in his lifetime but afterwards little noted, was discussed by the present writer some years ago. [107] It was the opinion of some of his contemporaries that Congreve was not only Henrietta's lover but also the father of her youngest daughter, Lady Mary Godolphin. If this was the case, the mystery of his will, so baffling to most of his critics, is explained. If Congreve left his fortune to the mother of his child, with the intention of providing for that child, he stands acquitted of the charge, repeatedly made against him, that he unkindly neglected those to whom he was most indebted. It would be gratifying if we knew more about this love story; in any case, it lends interest to Congreve's "placid" later years.

Congreve's life was not dull. He had as many interesting and stimulating friends as a man could have; and he was well qualified to appreciate them fully, whatever their station in life. To one of them he gave his heart. His love poetry, although not to the taste of the present age, reveals that he was more "romantic" than Gosse would concede.

He was loved by and loved two very beautiful women, one of whom was highly gifted. To Henrietta, Duchess of Marlborough, the prematurely aging dramatist owed an Indian summer adventure in love which contributes something towards placing him in the "human light" in which Gosse could never find him. Having written his comedy, Congreve had the experience of living it. The familiar trio of the Restoration stage appeared in real life: the bored wife, the indulgent husband, the discreet and graceful lover. But the husband was a man of character, whose "honesty and justice" [108] Congreve himself recognized; and the lover was kinder and wiser than any Restoration gallant.

Congreve found life good. As an artist, however, he was always capable of a certain detachment from it. Hazlitt hinted at his poetic fastidiousness; [109] and Dobrée, always discriminating, has noted his "poet's longing for beauty." [109] In his brief but fruitful career as a dramatist, Congreve aimed at perfection and did not fall far short of it. In retirement he lived "without regret." Had he not been an acute and delighted observer of the graces and follies of men, he could not have written *The Way of the World*. His last verses [111] reflect his unfailing enjoyment of this world's ever curious, unchanging pageant.

Joseph Keally

O ver sixty years ago Edmund Gosse observed: "We should know little or nothing of what happened to Congreve between 1700 and 1710 if it were not for the Keally letters."[1] The further statement must be made that in over two hundred years little or nothing has been discovered concerning the friend to whom those letters were addressed. Gosse knew only that Joseph Keally was of Kellymount, Kilkenny, and that he was a relative of Bishop Berkeley. One of Congreve's recent biographers, D. Crane Taylor, unaware of Keally's early death, deplores the "most regrettable" loss of letters later in date than those of George Monck Berkeley's *Literary Relics* but concludes that Congreve and Keally "unquestionably remained close friends."[2]

There are many obstacles in the way of an adequate knowledge of Joseph Keally's life. The worst that fate could do to obliterate a family happened promptly in his case. On May 21, 1713,[3] he died at the age of forty, on the threshold of a promising career. Three days before his death, he made his will, of which only an abstract remains, the original document having perished when the Public Record Office of Dublin was destroyed in 1922. Elizabeth Keally, his widow, survived him thirty years. His son, Joseph, a successful young counsellor at law, died "after a long illness" on May 8, 1749,[4] at the age of thirty-eight. The following year, on July 10, Kellymount House, which travelers had been in the habit of stopping to admire and had pronounced "a very handsome Seat," [5] was "entirely consumed, by an accidental fire." [6] Keally's son, Joseph, by his marriage to Dorothea, daughter of Sir Thomas Molyneux, had an only daughter, Elizabeth, who died in Bath in June 1761, in her eighteenth year.[7] The last surviving member of Keally's family was his daughter, Elizabeth, who died unmarried on January 8, 1783, in her seventy-eighth year.[8] In her will there is no mention of nephews or nieces. Keally's brother, John, with whom he had constantly corresponded, had died in Portugal. John Baptist Keally, John's son by his marriage to Hannah Stepney, left no children. In May 1754 the Prerogative Court granted him administration of the estate of his maternal grandfather, Lancelot Stepney of Cork.[9]

The scarcity of available Keally documents must be attributed, in part, to the fact that Joseph Keally's line was short-lived. At the death of his daughter, Elizabeth, forty-three letters written to Keally by Congreve, five by Addison, four by Steele, and three by the second Duke of Ormonde [10] came into the possession of John Monck Mason, grandson of her maternal uncle, George Monck, and one of the executors of her estate. They were published with other letters in 1789 in a volume of *Literary Relics,* edited by George Monck Berkeley, great-grandson of Rebecca Monck Forster, a sister of Keally's wife.

It has been impossible to discover what disposal was made of these manuscripts at Berkeley's death; but some of them, at any rate, were not destroyed. Two of the letters and the address leaf of a third are now in the New York Public Library.[11] One is in the Morgan Library in New York; [12] one in the library of the Historical Society of Pennsylvania.[13] Three are in private hands.[14] The British Museum has one of Congreve's letters to Keally which is not in Berkeley's volume,[15] besides one of Keally's letters to John Ellis [16] and two of Charles Mein's letters to Keally.[17] Four of Keally's letters to the second Duke of Ormonde are in Kilkenny Castle. It may be inferred that other "lost" manuscripts are still in existence and may eventually be brought to light.

Joseph Keally was the great-great-grandson of Maurice O'Kelly, who fled from King's County after the massacre of the

Irish at Mullaghmast in the reign of Queen Elizabeth and settled in Gowran, county Kilkenny, where he changed his name to Keally. His son, Maurice, had a son, Patrick, the father of John Keally of Kellymount, county Kilkenny. John Keally married Elizabeth, eldest daughter of Captain Joseph Cuffe of Castle Inch, county Kilkenny. Joseph Cuffe had commanded a troop of horse under Cromwell in 1649, had assisted in the capture of Cork, and had received considerable grants of land under the acts of settlement.[18]

Death overtook John Keally *in medias res*. He was High Sheriff of county Kilkenny in the year of his death, 1678. A young man of thirty-six, he left three small children, Joseph, aged five, John, aged four, and Elizabeth. A second daughter, Ellen, was born after his death. At the time of his death, he was building a new house, probably Kellymount House. In his will, drawn up on April 8, 1678, he made ample provision for his wife and children and assigned numerous bequests to relatives, his children's nurses, and other servants. Twenty pounds were to be distributed among the poor of Gowran. When his new house was finished, the workmen were to have an additional thirty shillings. His brother-in-law, Agmondisham Cuffe, was to have "my best horse & furniture & my best sword & belt & my best Mare & Colt." [19]

On the 5th of May, 1685, Joseph and his brother, John, became pupils at Kilkenny College. Here, for nearly a year, Congreve, three years older than Joseph, must have been a fellow student, until he entered Trinity College, Dublin, in April 1686. Other schoolmates, during the next three years, were George, Charles, and Thomas Monck, and Joseph Cuffe.[20]

Kilkenny College, which was under the patronage of the Duke of Ormonde, was in a flourishing condition. In July 1686 it was visited by the Earl of Clarendon, who had come to Kilkenny to witness, against his will, the disbanding of Protestant soldiers out of "two very gallant regiments of horse" [21] by the Earl of Tyrconnel, acting as the agent of King James. One might hear the complaints of the soldiers "as one went along the streets." [22] At his Grace's school, all was well, "considering the great discouragement all things are under here, in which the very schoolboys have their share, who would be more humorous if the times were more serene. The master is certainly a very industrious man. There are in the school fifty-one." [23] Two years later, in a letter written to the Duke of Ormonde on September 24, 1688, the Bishop of Kildare commended "the care and industry of Dr. Hinton, the Master of the School at Kilkenny." [24] Yet within a few months, Dr. Hinton was driven out by Tyrconnel's soldiers, who converted the schoolhouse into a hospital for their men. [25] These were cheerless days for Irish schoolboys. When King James visited Kilkenny on March 22, 1689, he was informed: "Our barns are changed into armouries, our shops are metamorphosed into magazines . . . our very children are better skilled in the book of exercise than in the horn-book." [26]

Joseph Keally must have left Kilkenny when Edward Hinton fled to England, if not before. He had probably had time to complete his grammar-school studies. Between December 1688 and March of the next year, Irish Protestants came over to England in great numbers. [27] Among them were Elizabeth Keally [28] and her widowed mother, Martha Cuffe, both of whom are listed in the Act of Attainder passed by King James's Irish Parliament in the summer of 1689 as persons who "are and for some time past have been absent out of this Kingdom" [29] and whose properties were to be vested in King James for his use, unless by a certain date their claims to those properties should be allowed. The same Parliament attainted Martha Cuffe's eldest son, Agmondisham Cuffe, who had been removed by James's government as mayor of Kilkenny in December 1687. [30] The first Duke of Ormonde, an old man in exile in England, a year before his death remarked sadly that "it is so far come to pass that I had rather live and die in Carolina than in Ireland." [31] By November 1689 the Protestants who had remained in Ireland were in a miserable condition, excluded from holding office and deprived of their estates; many were in prison. King James had entrenched Dublin, planting cannon at the ends of the streets. [32]

Elizabeth Keally placed her son, Joseph, in Pembroke College, Oxford, where he matriculated on May 30, 1689. According to the

buttery books of the college, he was in residence fairly con-
tinuously until June 13, 1690, when his name was dropped from
the books. It was probably an auspicious moment for his return
to Kilkenny. On June 14 King William landed in Ireland; and
on July 6, after the Battle of the Boyne, he was welcomed in
Dublin "with great acclamations and demonstrations of joy." [33]
One of the Irish Protestants reinstated by William was Agmondisham Cuffe, the chief person on whom the King relied to convey
ammunition and provisions for his camp.[34]

On the 6th of February, 1693, Joseph Keally was admitted to
the Middle Temple,[35] where his friend Congreve had been in
residence for two years. Although there is no evidence that
Keally had chambers here, it may be assumed that he spent the
next three or four years of his life pursuing his legal studies in
London and seeing much of William Congreve.

In the autumn of 1697, Keally went back to Ireland, and thereafter was only an occasional visitor in London. During the next
fifteen years, he corresponded more or less regularly with Congreve, whose letters supply most of our information concerning
him.

Berkeley edited Congreve's letters to Keally in such a fashion
that their full value does not become apparent until they are rearranged. Seven dated letters [36] are misplaced by a year, because
of Berkeley's treatment of Congreve's Old Style as New Style
dates, a practice followed also by Dobrée and Taylor. The dates
of two letters [37] are misread, and two undated letters [38] are misplaced. Dobrée altered the position of four letters,[39] but otherwise
followed Berkeley's arrangement.

The rearranged letters include: one for 1697; two for 1700;
three for 1701; two for 1702; one for 1703; six for 1704; three for
1705; four for 1706; one for 1707; nine for 1708; one for 1709;
five for 1710; three for 1711; [40] two for 1712. It is reasonable to
think that a certain number of letters are missing. One is tempted
to suppose that Congreve may have written to Keally at least
half a dozen letters a year.

At the time of Keally's return to Ireland in 1697, the Irish
coasts were infested with privateers.[41] Congreve had felt con-

cerned for his friend's safety, and wrote to him on September 28, 1697, after receiving word of his arrival: "I thought you were either drowned or a prisoner at St Maloes; which would have been a worse thing, if not for you, at least for your acquaintance; for I would not willingly hear any more of St Maloes." He continued:

You must not wonder if the peace which affects all Europe should in some measure influence me. It has indeed put a stop to my intended pilgrimage for St Patrick's. I am sorry you are like to have no better an effect of your own. . . My Lord D. of Ormond, whom I waited on yesterday, talks of going for Ireland on Monday next.[42] I would not miss such an opportunity if it were not thought absolutely necessary for me to stay here. I believe my Lady Duchess and the good Bishop [43] will have their books at that time. . . Tell the good Bishop I must have very good fortune before I am reconciled to the necessity of my staying in England at a time when I promised myself the happiness of seeing him at Kilkenny. I would say something very devout to the Duchess; but you are a prophane dog and would spoil it. If the Bishop would sanctify my duty to her, I would requite him in my way. . .[44]

The letter implies that Keally was returning home with the hope of obtaining advancement through the assistance of his patron, the second Duke of Ormonde. He could depend on the good will of the Bishop of Ossory and of the Duchess of Ormonde, the novelty of whose welcome in Kilkenny was beginning to wear off.[45]

In Trinity Term, 1700, Keally was called to the Irish Bar.[46] In the same year he and his mother made an order in the Court of Claims in Dublin by which they might be legally entitled to the interest on eight hundred acres of land in the townland of Duningy, on which they held a mortgage by a deed dated May 14, 1677. The claim was "allowed and enforced." [47]

On May 28, 1702, Keally wrote to John Ellis, Under Secretary of State, enclosing a letter which he begged to have forwarded to his brother, John, in Portugal. He apologized for having been "so troublesome" with similar requests, "but I hope ye necessity I ly under will in some measure plead my excuse, for what ever Letters I have sent any other way have miscarried." [48] The letter is signed: "Jos. Kelly"; and it is probable that from 1702 on Keally used this spelling.[49]

On October 10, 1704, Charles Mein wrote to Keally that, as instructed, he had opened Keally's letter to Congreve, in the latter's absence, and had delivered the enclosure to the Duke of Ormonde, "whose answer was y^t he shou'd see you soon, & wou'd be very glad to serve you." The letters to John Keally had been forwarded by a trustworthy person, as Congreve had reported. Mein commented that he considered himself a slightly better correspondent than Keally, who never writes "but upon business, tho in six months time." [50]

Political honors came to Joseph Keally at the age of thirty-two. In March 1705 [51] he became M.P. for the borough of Doneraile, which he continued to represent for the following six years. At the death of Standish Hartstonge on May 31, 1705,[52] the post of Recorder of Kilkenny became vacant. On the same date Richard Nutley applied to the Duke of Ormonde, but in vain, for this post and that of Second Judge of the Palatinate of Tipperary.[53] The office of Recorder was given to Joseph Keally on June 2,[54] and on June 22 Robert Blennerhassett received the other appointment.[55] It was perhaps in response to a letter to the Duke of Ormonde, written on December 27, 1705, apropos of further vacancies,[56] that Keally was made Attorney-General of the Palatinate of Tipperary.[57] Looking on at these events, Congreve ventured a plausible prediction: "I am, dear Recorder and Judge *in futuro,* already in wisdom, gravity, and understanding, yours, and so is all the neighbourhood." [58]

Meanwhile, Congreve's letters to Keally dealt chiefly with personal details. He forwarded John Keally's letters from Portugal; purchased a lady's necklace, according to instructions; reported the death of a favorite dog; described in some detail the ravages of a November hurricane; and gave an account of Mr. Howard's progress on the portrait which Keally had requested. Keally's visit to London in the autumn of 1705 made it possible for him to act as Congreve's proxy with a difficult landlord,[59] when Congreve was out of town. By December [60]

Keally was back in Ireland, and the chronicle of domestic affairs was resumed.

In the summer of 1706 Keally suffered an accident. He informed the Duke of Ormonde that his broken leg was "well sett and cured" by "an excellent French Surgeon whom y^r Graces Grandfather planted in Kilkenny." His illness delayed him in the preparation of an address to the Queen from the city of Kilkenny which the Duke of Ormonde was to convey to her Majesty.[61] Congreve's anxiety was in due course dispelled, and he reflected: "I hope your leg is so well that it makes not any unnecessary addition to the gravity of your walk." [62]

On the 5th of June, 1707, Joseph Keally "of the parish of St. Mary in the City of Kilkenny, Esq." married "Elizabeth Monke, of the parish of St. Peter in the City of Dublin, Spinster." Elizabeth Monck was the granddaughter of Charles Monck, Surveyor-General of the customs of Ireland, and of Sir John Blennerhassett, Baron of the Exchequer. She was the youngest daughter of Henry Monck of St. Stephen's Green, Dublin. Both Congreve and Steele congratulated Keally on his marriage; and the latter commented that being a husband "is at least a snug, if not a rapturous condition." [63] There are also references in Congreve's letters to the births of Keally's daughter, Elizabeth, in 1708 and his son, Joseph, in 1711.[64]

Like other Irishmen of his period, Keally was willing, when conditions seemed favorable, to practice the art of "dancing attendance" on ministers.[65] When Lord Wharton [66] was Lord Lieutenant of Ireland, such an errand brought Keally to London in the early spring of 1710. "I went and made your compliment to Lady Wharton," explained Congreve in a brief letter, "and she will be glad to see you when you please." [67] On April 13, after Keally's return to Ireland, Addison noted the success of his mission: "Lady Wharton was speaking to me two mornings ago with great esteem of you, and tells me that my Lord is fully determined to put you into the appeals when in Ireland, which I did not think fit to make the least doubt of." [68] On June 23, 1710, Keally was appointed Commissioner of Appeals.[69] In the same month he waited upon Lord Wharton with a report from a committee of the Irish House of Commons which had been appointed to consider the navigability of the river Barrow.[70]

To this year belongs the most delightful of the letters to Keally which have survived. On December 29, 1710, Charles Mein wrote as follows:

I have seen a letter of y^{rs} to Mr Congreve wherein there is some honourable mention made of me, & when you say (pleasantly enough) y^t you fancy these latter times make me look as if I had seen a Serjeant, you little think how much you have exceeded y^r own conceit; for I have been kept in close durance for these six weeks, of & on, by an ugly hurt in my leg, wch is not yet cured, & wch makes me sympathize with poor Robin in his gout, his temperance, & his impatience; & I am litter'd about, as he us'd, with a multitude of unread Books. I find you expect to be let into ye mysterys of ye Times, Intrigues of Partys &c. Know this for once, that you on ye other side of ye Water are all in ye dark, & so are like to be for us here, who live in so pure a light. . . & hurts ye aking sight. You say you read [hist]ory, by w^{ch}, no doubt, you mean that you are Wise; but I say, Travel. . . is it to behold in History, as it were in a mirrour, ye Face of antient [tim]es; to be able by a quick, piercing & delicate Wit so to fit ye Past wth ye Present y^t it may serve on all occasions as a most prudent & faithful—Counsellor, neither to be awed by fear, nor corrupted & led aside by Interest; if at ye same time you are unaquainted with ye humours & manners of ye age you live in.—Travel I say. But I beseech you, my dear, old, & bosome friend, be not inquisitive. Have ye gout with F^{z}Gerald, drink wth Luther, & go powder'd among ye Beau Monde like y^r Servant, but I entreat you, nay I conjure you (for ye States sake) not to be inquisitive. Travel, I say again.[71]

Congenial advice this might have been; but for a man in Keally's position extensive travels were out of the question. The difficult little journeys to Kilkenny, to Dublin, and to London sufficed and may even have shortened the life of Congreve's dear Judge *in futuro*.

Congreve found politics wearisome, although, as Keally desired, he gave him the news of the town. He was glad to have Howard's portrait of his friend, "which is like you, but too warmly painted, as you hinted." He sent Keally books and prints and sponsored the making of his Holland shirts by Mrs. Porter;

and he welcomed the visits of John Keally. From Congreve's letter dated October 29, 1712, it appears that Keally was intending another London visit. "Mrs. Porter went to the Bath almost on purpose to meet you and bring you up with her . . . If you design to come this winter, pray go on board the packet-boat, that you may not be liable to any uncertainty but that of the wind." [72]

In May of the following year Keally died. His "most sorrowful mother" placed a tablet to his memory and his father's in the church of Gowran, where he was buried. Her inscription commends her son's "Parts and Integrity," which "rendered him a Useful Man to his Country, and an Ornament and Credit to his Family."

From these few sources emerge the dominant traits of Joseph Keally's character. Ambition was the keynote, as Congreve recognized. "I find you are resolved to be a man of this world, which I am sorry for, because it will deprive me of you." With affectionate pride Congreve followed Keally's career. But his own aims were of another sort. "Ease and quiet," he admitted, "is what I hunt after. If I have not ambition, I have other passions more easily gratified. Believe me I find none more pleasing to me than my friendship for you." [73]

Keally's letters to the Duke of Ormonde are obsequious, in the manner of the day. His Grace was properly flattered and graciously proposed: "I desire to hear from you often. I intend to trouble you sometimes with my thoughts." Among Keally's friends, Addison was best qualified to appreciate his worldliness. To a man who could well understand such diplomacy Addison confided: "I have had incredible losses since I saw you last; but this I only communicate to yourself: for I know the most likely way to keep a place is to appear not to want it." [74]

Keally's career meant much to him; yet his interests were by no means narrow. He enjoyed plays and music and had an excellent literary taste. Congreve sent him an elaborate account of the production at Dorset Garden of *The Judgment of Paris,* with musical settings by Eccles, when "our friend Venus [Mrs. Bracegirdle] performed to a miracle." [75] The letters include discerning comments on plays by Rowe and Cibber and notes on

London 7br 28: 97:

Dear Jo:

I thought you were either drown'd or a prisoner at
St Malloes, which would have been a worse thing
if not for you at least for yr acquaintance for I
would not willingly hear any more of St. Malloes.
You must not wonder if the Peace which affects all
Europe should in some measure influence me. it has indeed
put a stop to my intended pilgrimage for St Patrick;
I am sorry you are like to have no letter an offect
of yr own. may be I may stay in England to as little
purpose as you left it; but I am advised to try. My
D: D: of Ormond whom I wait on yesterday talks of
going for Ireland on monday next. I would not
miss such an opportunity if it were not thought
absolutely necessary for me to stay here. I believe
my Lady Duchess & the Good Bishop will have their

LETTER FROM CONGREVE TO KEALLY (RECTO)

books at that time. I have no news of any kind to send you. I have not been bottom since I receiv'd yr. Letter but Amory I just now parted with who is yours. Jonny Marsh is here. as for Luther I find him told by yr. account & his own proceeding unalterable. and I hope Champs & you will come over together. pray give my hearty service to my Cosen Congreve. tell the Good Bishop I must have very good fortune before I am reconcil'd to the necessity of my staying in England at a time when I promis'd my Self the Happiness of seeing him at Kilkenny. I wou'd say something very devout to the Dutchesse but you are a prophane dog & wou'd spoil it. if the Bishop wou'd sanctifie my Duty to her I wou'd require him in my way. prithee Keally distribute my service in a most particular manner & make me popular amongst those acquaintance whom I have forgott let me hear when I may expect you & make haste to your

W. Congreve

the changing fortunes of the playhouses. It was gratifying to Congreve that Keally was unfavorably impressed by *A Tale of a Tub*.

I am not alone in the opinion, as you are there; but I am pretty near it, having but very few on my side: but those few are worth a million. . . Bottom admires it, and cannot bear my saying, I confess I was diverted with several passages when I read it, but I should not care to read it again. That he thinks not commendation enough.[76]

On receiving from Keally a Latin ballad,[77] Congreve observed: "I think it is as well as the thing will bear, and so does Mein, who continues of all men the hardest to be pleased with any modern essays." [78]

Another bond between Keally and Congreve was their mutual sense of life's little ironies. In the midst of the formalities which his correspondence with the Duke of Ormonde naturally imposed, Keally noticed that the annoying stubbornness of his fellow members in the Irish House of Commons had amusing aspects:

The buisnesse of the supply has given greater difficulty to your Graces opposers than any thing else, for they that had given such violent reasons against voting for two years when requested by your Grace found themselves greatly embarrassd in changing their resolution now with any tolerable grace, therefore they found out the Expedient of giving ye former duty's but for one year & three quarters (instead of two years,) which was unanimously carried, which finesse coud not but make us merry & putt every one in mind of the spanish Fryar whose conscience was so squeamish att taking the fifty, yet coud easily digest ye nine & forty peices.[79]

In a letter to Congreve Keally made laughing mention of Mein, fancying that "these latter times" made him look as if he had "seen a Serjeant"; and Mein, himself a humorist, found the apt rejoinder quoted above and enlarged on the "conceit." Steele felt impelled to write to Keally "very freely." With the charm that marks many a *Tatler* paper, he rattled on:

You shall from henceforth have every post from me my circular of what passes with the gazette. Mr. Congreve is at Newmarket. Mr. Addison is your servant. The taste for plays is expired. We are all

for operas, performed by eunuchs every way impotent to please. . .
My way of life should make me capable of entertaining with much
politics; but I am not a bit wiser than you knew me.[80]

In spite of his gravity on occasion, Keally provoked levity
on the part of his friends. Congreve jested with him about
Robin's weakness for taverns and widows and the idiosyncrasies
of Charles Mein. Even in Congreve's most serious moods a tone
of gentle banter intruded. Having expressed his regret that Keally
was likely to become preoccupied with professional cares, he
hastened to add: "However, think of me, as I am nothing
extenuate. My service to Robin, who would laugh to see me
puzzled to buckle my shoe; but I'll fetch it down again." The
most solicitous of his letters, on the subject of Keally's accident,
Congreve concluded with a humorous reference to the caprices
of Mein.[81]

The letters furnish eloquent evidence of Keally's gift for
friendship. He had the grace to inspire its generous enthusiasms,
regardless of long absences and "frail paper and packet-boats."
Congreve reminded him: "My neighbours are very much yours;
and if you drink not their healths daily, are before hand with you
in a kind remembrance." [82] Addison considered "one of the
greatest benefits of my place in Ireland to have been the opportunity it gave me of making so valuable a man my friend." [83]
The warmth of Mein's attachment to Keally may be guessed from
the phrase: "my dear, old, & bosome friend." [84]

Congreve's friendship had deeper roots. Quietly, unostenta-
tiously, with the mind's full approbation, he gave to one what
the multitude would not have understood. He was "not apt to
care for many acquaintance" and never intended "to make many
friendships." The most reasonable of men, he found separation
"the greatest trial" of "my philosophy." Only once again did he
refer to a matter so deeply felt, repeating: "I make use of my
philosophy, and love you as ever." It was a friendship of complete understanding and consequently without reserves. Congreve
could be "plain" with Keally concerning the frailties of "honest
Robin" whom they both loved. Keally's "friendly sense" of a
personal loss could be relied on: "I know you are no stranger to

sentiments of tender and natural affection, which will make my concern very intelligible to you, though it may seem unaccountable to the generality, who are of another make." When Keally was ill, Congreve showed a similar concern: "I am sure you know me enough to know I feel very sensibly and silently for those whom I love." [85]

This was the most enlightened sort of friendship, for it was unexacting. When one of Keally's rare visits to London was constantly postponed, Congreve felt "tantalized." He remarked however: "I have no great faith in your promises; yet I am willing to expect your performance, and hope you will celebrate the ensuing festival in Arundel-street." Untouched by the pettiness of personal pique, he could write twice to Keally's once, having found it "a tedious while since I heard from you." When the news of Keally's marriage came "by report," Congreve assured him: "though I long to hear from you, yet I hope you will be so much taken up with joy, that you will not very soon find time to excuse your neglecting to inform me of an adventure so important to you." It was also by report that he was informed of the birth of Keally's daughter and the marriage of Robin Fitzgerald to Keally's sister, Ellen. "You are close husbands of your pleasures in Ireland," wrote Congreve; "and we old friends must always have the first news of you from common fame." There was much in Keally's life that Congreve never expected to share. With no jealous regrets he could play the part of onlooker; and "all who love you" could claim his affectionate regard.[86]

Perhaps few friendships have been so complete, so secure from the hazards of alteration. Congreve closed his letters with such phrases as: "I am entirely yours;" "I am just as I used to be, and as I always shall be, yours." The town might be dull and Congreve "not much otherwise"; but "in dullness or mirth, dear Keally," he professed himself "yours." It was of no importance that there should be "any news or business in your letters." And when Congreve was living entirely at home and seeing no one, the logic of friendship required that "I write to you because I will write to you, and always must desire to hear from you." His eyesight failed, so that it was difficult for Congreve to write letters. His gout increased, and the friend of his youth must know that he could no longer "jump one-and-twenty feet at one jump upon Northhall Common."[87] But so sturdy a friendship was proof against all vicissitudes due to ill health, weariness, or disillusion.

Congreve wrote the last of his published letters to Keally on October 29, 1712. With unabated solicitude, he observed: "I this instant received yours of the 22d, and the first thing I do is to answer it."[88] He had been expecting to see Keally "every day this summer, or at least this autumn," and still hoped for a winter visit. Mrs. Porter and Mein are mentioned. Although worried over politics,[89] Congreve jested about his fears: "News! No, Sir, no news, I thank you; nor no glimpse. But one thing I'll tell you, whenever it comes, it will be no longer a glimpse, but a glare: and so my service to Robin and all friends."[90]

Perhaps Keally made the winter journey and saw his friend once more; perhaps business or illness kept him in Ireland. Six and a half months later, he was dead. For seventy years, his family carefully preserved this correspondence; and it remains both a memorial to Keally and the only intimate record of Congreve's unpretentious life.

The Fitzgeralds of Castle Dod

*I*t is a matter for conjecture whether William Congreve and Robert Fitzgerald were childhood friends. Their fathers may have met in Youghal, perhaps through their mutual acquaintance with Richard Boyle, second Earl of Cork, during the period (1674–78) when Lieutenant Congreve was stationed in the garrison there. During those years, William Fitzgerald was Clerk of the Crown and Peace for the County and City of Cork. At any rate, young William and "Robin" had an opportunity to see much of each other as fellow students at Trinity College, Dublin, which they entered in the same year (1686), both as pensioners, at the respective ages of sixteen and fifteen.[1]

Robert Fitzgerald was descended from ancient Irish and English families. His remote paternal ancestors were the Gherardini Dukes of Tuscany, who migrated from Florence to Normandy, and whose descendants established themselves in England, and then in Ireland. In 1170 Maurice Fitzgerald came to Ireland, assisted Richard Strongbow, the second Earl of Pembroke, in reducing the country, and received grants of Irish lands.

Robert's grandfather, Richard Fitzgerald, son of Richard Fitzgerald,[2] was descended from John FitzThomas of Callan, whose great-grandson was Maurice FitzThomas, first Earl of Desmond. When Gerald FitzJames, fourteenth Earl of Desmond, was slain in rebellion in 1583, his lands, covering over a million acres, were forfeited to the Crown. He had devastated "the fair plains of Munster" and left the town of Youghal an uninhabitable ruin. Queen Elizabeth paid out half a million pounds to suppress her richest and most formidable subject.

It may be assumed that in this great feud Richard Fitzgerald's closest relatives [3] were on the Queen's side. His grandfather may have been a ward of the Queen and may have borne arms in support of his sovereign against the rebel Roman Catholic chieftains. Richard Fitzgerald was a devout, almost fanatical Protestant.

On the maternal side, Robert Fitzgerald was connected with the Anglo-Norman Percivall family, which had long been established in Somerset. His grandfather, Richard, married Alice, youngest daughter of Richard Percivall of Sydenham (1550–1620), by his second wife, Alice, daughter of John Sherman of Ottery St. Mary.

As a young man, Richard Percivall won the favor of the Queen by deciphering and translating some Spanish letters, thrown overboard by a Spanish commander and salvaged by an English captain, giving the first certain information regarding the Spanish Armada. The Queen took Percivall "under her own peculiar care," and he was made Commissioner and Remembrancer for the Court of Wards. In 1616 he settled in Dublin, where he served as Clerk of the Commission for Wards in Ireland.[4] Before his death, he sold most of his English property and made large purchases in county Cork.

Sir Philip Percivall,[5] his son, was a distinguished figure in Irish political life. His marriage to Katherine, daughter of Arthur Usher, allied him with many prominent Anglo-Irish families. Through purchases, leases, and transfers of forfeited lands, he became owner of over sixty-two thousand Irish acres.

When Sir Philip's first child, Judith, was baptized on January 1, 1627, his sister, Alice, stood as godmother.[6] By 1631 Alice had married Richard Fitzgerald; and on August 18 of that year, the latter stood as godfather to Sir Philip's son, Richard, who was christened on that date.[7] By 1632 brother Richard was acting as Sir Philip's agent in various business transactions.[8]

Fitzgerald was living in Dublin when, on January 26, 1634, he began his active career in the Irish House of Commons, representing Strabane, county Tyrone. He was soon serving on various parliamentary committees[9] and was found useful in the drafting of petitions. On May 2, 1636, Sir Philip made him his deputy in the offices of Clerk of the Crown in the Court of Chief Pleas, Clerk of the Common Pleas, and Custos Brevium.[10] On February 6, 1637, he was appointed Clerk of the Crown and Peace for the County and City of Cork.[11]

In 1636 Sir Philip procured for his brother-in-law a lease of part of Castle Dod, in the parish of Ballyhay, in the barony of Orrery and Kilmore, county Cork. This "little broken castle" and eighty English acres, which were among the forfeited lands of Gerald, fourteenth Earl of Desmond,[12] had been included in a seignory of twelve thousand acres assigned in 1587 to the English undertaker, Hugh Cuffe.[13] In 1592 Cuffe was required to yield half of his seignory to William Power; but in 1594 he received other lands to make up a full seignory. Cuffe forsook his Irish lands in 1598, when the Irish in Munster revolted and all but three or four of the English undertakers fled to England.[14]

His rents at Castle Dod helped Richard Fitzgerald to pay his debts. In a letter which he wrote to Sir Philip Percivall in May 1637 he complained that "this terme proves badd, & answeares not my expectation by the one halfe."[15] He had loaned money too liberally, and "good Kinde Cosens have abused my Softenes." One of the cousins, William Fitzgerald,[16] was grateful enough to describe "cossen Richard" as "a tried honest man if there bee on[e] in the world."[17] Whether advisedly or not, Richard Fitzgerald continued to make loans to his relatives and others. In November 1641 his debtors included his widowed sister, Mary Dixon, of Clondurre, county Meath; his brother, William, of Sellunyin and Ardmaye; and the young Earl of Kildare,[18] who owed him one hundred pounds.[19]

In 1640 Sir Philip undertook to purchase for himself from Maurice FitzGibbon the half plowland of Coolcam, "which is the only parcell between me & my Brother FitzGerralds lands."[20] In the same year John Hodder, Sir Philip's steward, leased Castle Dod from Fitzgerald, with the understanding that "if ever he or his Wife come to live there to put me out I am to hold it again at the same Rent when they leave dwelling there themselves." [21]

If Richard Fitzgerald had entertained any thought of leading a country gentleman's life, he was obliged to renounce such a frivolous notion. On November 11, 1640, the Irish House of Commons appointed him one of a committee of thirteen carefully chosen members to "repair to England" and present to the King "the Grievances of this Kingdom." [22] Various letters were exchanged, in the months that followed, between the House and its committee. The committee interviewed the King on December 11 and reported progress, although it hinted that nothing could be gained unless the subsidies which had been ordered were levied without delay. King Charles sent two letters of vague promises, and the committee was urged not to relax its efforts. On July 2, 1641, Richard Fitzgerald received permission to return to Ireland, since his personal affairs required his presence at home. Although the work of the committee was not finished, the House was "desirous to comply with him in his Desires, in Regard of the great Testimony he hath given of his Integrity and good Endeavours in the public Services, committed to his Charge." [23]

Storm clouds were gathering. The Earl of Strafford had been beheaded in May; his Irish army had been unwisely disbanded but not paid off; and two ineffectual Lords Justices [24] governed in Dublin, while across the Irish Channel the relations of King and Parliament became increasingly strained. In October the Irish Rebellion broke out in the north of Ireland; and the south had a few weeks' respite to prepare for inevitable invasion. It was a dark hour for Munster, whose Lord President, Sir William St. Leger, had only a handful of men to defend the province and neither money nor supplies.

The old Earl of Cork,[25] who had recently returned to Ireland, took prompt action. At his own expense, he fortified Youghal to withstand a siege and to serve as a much-needed port of entry for English aid. He supplied St. Leger with funds; put his second son, Lord Dungarvan,[26] into the field with five hundred men; and financed the defense of Castle Lyons by his son-in-law, Lord Barrymore, of Lismore by his fourth son, Lord Broghill,[27] and of the town of Bandon by his third son, Lord Kinalmeaky. Sir Philip Percivall took similar action on a smaller scale, committing the defense of four castles to John Hodder. The latter assembled a company of eighty English tenants of Sir Philip and Richard Fitzgerald, armed half of them, and arranged to have Fitzgerald's men "fly to Castle Dod, which I have made very strong." [28] Hodder himself withdrew to Liscarrol, convinced that Sir Philip must hold that fort at whatever cost.

In the midst of these distractions, the Lords Justices dispatched Richard Fitzgerald to England, as their special agent, to attend the King and his Council and solicit aid to suppress the Rebellion. The Earl of Leicester, absentee Lord Lieutenant of Ireland, was especially requested to listen to Fitzgerald's account of Irish affairs, "he having had long experience here and being able to inform you in many particulars very needful for your Lordship's knowledge in these times." [29] Fitzgerald left Ireland on November 29, although November 5 was the date originally set for his departure. He must have found it difficult, on short notice, to wind up his affairs in Munster. Sir Philip Percivall also hastened to England on a mission to the King.

In January the two brothers-in-law were in Chester, where arms for Ireland were awaiting shipment. It had been Alice Fitzgerald's intention to join her husband. But having crossed to Beaumaris, she was detained there by "extreme foule wether" [30] for at least a month. Her eldest son, William, and Sir Philip's eldest son, John,[31] were with her, and probably her daughters, Elizabeth [32] and "Nanny"; [33] but another son, John,[34] remained in Ireland with his nurse.

Of Alice Fitzgerald's correspondence, only two short letters, which she wrote to Sir Philip from Beaumaris, have survived. She was a most affectionate sister, disposed to rely on her brother and eager for his advice. In her letter of December 28, 1641, she informs him: "heere is a very good free scoule and the boyes ware at scoule before crismas and we live resnable cheape yet I wolde fane live nere you." [35] Both families were soon established in London. In April 1642 Sir Philip returned to Ireland as Commissary General of Victuals for the army.

For a time the rebel forces in Munster contented themselves with skirmishes, cattle raids, and farm burning. The Protestant gentry shut themselves up in their castles, or took the greater precaution of removing to the fortified towns. The Earl of Cork spent "a heavy and sorrowful Christmas" in College House in Youghal. Defended by only two hundred of his tenants, the town was "very weak and ruinous"; and the Earl was obliged to admit: "We are now at the last gasp." Lord Broghill, "full of hot blood and courage," resented being confined at Lismore, which he swore should not be surrendered while he remained alive.[36]

Meanwhile, Richard Fitzgerald proceeded with his difficult liaison duties in England as the agent of the Lords Justices. It was his misfortune to have to address his petitions to a Lord Lieutenant whose hands were tied by the contradictory orders of King and Parliament. He scrupulously performed his task and at first gave "both the Lords Justices good satisfaction in his solicitation, and my Lord Lieutenant also." [37] Yet it soon became apparent that only a trickle of men, money, arms, and food could be expected from England. Instead of ten thousand foot, fourteen hundred arrived. Instead of two hundred thousand pounds, sixteen thousand, five hundred, then eleven thousand, five hundred were sent. Richard Fitzgerald was instructed to use "all possible importunity" [38] to secure for the army "twenty thousand pair of shoes at the least"; but soldiers continued to march (if at all) barefooted and often with bleeding feet.

The Lords Justices were thoroughly disheartened. In the first two years of the war, only the raising of the siege of Drogheda and the victory at Liscarrol gave them the slightest encouragement. There were intolerable delays in the arrival of promised supplies; the disaffected soldiers threatened to disband; and the harassed agent was regularly reminded that the arms from Holland or the drugs for the surgeons had not come, and he was "never to give over, but to be incessantly solicitous," or "all will be lost." [39] Looking back on this trying experience, Richard Fitzgerald complained to Sir Philip: "my greate Masters in Ireland . . . requited me unworthily for my extraordinarie fidelitie and diligence, but it may be theire expectations not being answeared they may likewise complaine: there is a Judge above." [40]

In the winter of 1642, Lord Inchiquin [41] was in England, raising and arming a regiment by his own efforts. He wrote from London to Sir Philip Percivall: "I shall nott neede to send you any news of this place, for dick fitzGerrald says he will doe it for mee, but this I will say that neyther he nor I may safely write what wee beleeve." [42] In the early spring, Sir Charles Vavasour, Inchiquin, and William Jephson brought reënforcements to Youghal. Their assistance was much needed, for Lord Mountgarret had already invaded Munster with a large army. In February, as Lord Broghill's chaplain reported, Castle Dod had yielded to the invaders "uppon quarter for which the Lord President [St. Leger] was highly offended with the Counstable of the said Castle, but his Lordship is mercifull to all Protestants though he much hates a coward." [43] The first great battle of the war, in which Lord Kinalmeaky was killed, was fought on September 3 of this year in a plain near Liscarrol. Although the rebels had captured Percivall's strongest castle the day before, they were now completely routed. In the words of an English participant in the battle: "advantages they had of us every way, only we were Virtute pares, and necessitate superiores." [44]

In the eight years which followed, Castle Dod shared the fate of other Munster castles and changed hands a number of times. Sometimes John Hodder was able to collect the semiannual rents, but more often not. English tenants lost all of their cattle. Many farms were abandoned; and when corn was planted, little of it was harvested. After two years of such vexations and the negative miseries of inconclusive engagements and uneasy truces, vigorous fighting broke out in the spring of 1645, when Lord Castlehaven quickly reduced nearly all of Munster. One by one, Sir Philip's castles surrendered; the province was ravaged to the walls of Cork, which was crowded with refugees; and Youghal was besieged and seemed likely to fall. In the autumn, the tables were turned. Youghal was relieved, and Castlehaven's depleted forces went into winter quarters.

In the spring of 1644 Sir Philip Percivall returned to England. On June 7, 1645, Richard Fitzgerald wrote to him from London, expressing in guarded terms his concern over both English and Irish affairs. He feared that "this somers warre" would disturb the universities. There was much talk of the Earl of Leicester being lost.[45] Colonel Jephson had hopes of raising men for Munster; but before he succeeded, "the rascall enemy" might do much mischief. At this critical moment,[46] "I conceave it better for you to be absent then present, for the businis concerning yo^u will be laid aside at this time." [47]

In the spring of 1646 there was a disagreement between Richard Fitzgerald and Sir Philip, the cause of which it is impossible to determine. Both felt aggrieved. In a letter of May 4 Fitzgerald conceded:

one hower every day I would gladly spend wth yo^u to make up this unhappie breach betwene us, wch hath wrought more perturbation of minde in mee then all the crosses and losses I ever had, and many visitts I have made to take some opportunities to renew our former amitie but had not power to begin discourse to that end since yo^u once expressed yor selfe that I dissembled wth yo^u, be not reserved henceforth neither be tarte in reprooving nor lett us looke strange one upon another when wee meete its not well that so much notice is taken of our difference. God mend whats amisse, and preserve us to see better daies.[48]

Sir Philip replied that he had endured "frivolous and unjust calumniations." A few days later, his brother-in-law made another plea to "lay aside all that is paste and . . . be more intimate for the future." And peace was made, although Sir Philip endorsed this second letter: "Bro. fzGerald. In his old strayne of causeless Jealousies, haveing indeed iniured me." [49]

On July 11, 1646, the Committee of Both Houses for Irish Affairs approved an order to the effect that Richard Fitzgerald be appointed agent for soliciting the bringing in of assessments for Ireland in the counties and cities of Worcester, Hereford, Monmouth, Radnor, Glamorgan, Pembroke, Brecknock, and

Montgomery.[50] The task was certainly an exacting one, but it had
its compensations. Sir Paul Davis, Sir Philip's brother-in-law, was
a more generous master than the Lords Justices. Nor was Fitzgerald a man to shy away from difficulties, especially when the
fate of Ireland was at stake.

He discussed his new duties in a series of fairly long letters,
which he wrote to Sir Philip between December 1646 and August
1647. Losing no time, he applied himself with his usual energy
to an undertaking in which "in truth many a one might have bin
baffled." Most of the Welsh counties were refractory; Welshmen
were "not forward" to part with their money; and the collector
sweated for every shilling. Once Fitzgerald sat up all night "in
frostie cold weather," issuing warrants for a local committee
which found excuses for not signing them. Coöperation was as
welcome as it was rare. He begged Sir Philip to commend to
Lord Broghill Mr. Rotherick Gwyn of Llanellwell in Radnor-
shire, a kinsman of the Earl of Cork, and praised Major General
Mitton as "a verie reall & plaine dealing gentleman," by whose
order the committee for Montgomeryshire subscribed. Welsh
journeys were "scattered and wilde" and must be made on horse-
back, or even on foot. With a touch of melancholy humor, Fitzgerald describes a night journey which he made with a cowardly
servant from Usk to Chepstow: "at 12 of the Clock at Night [I]
loaded my mony upon a packe horse wth my fearefull Janizarrie,
and a stoute fellowe on foote wth a Long Staffe and a pistoll, and
a young man to drive the packe horse and soe came to Cheape-
stowe by three of ye clocke." [51]

It was a lonely life, and Richard Fitzgerald felt very keenly
his separation from all members of his family. He was vexed not
to be with Sir Philip at Easter, predicted difficulties for him
in the House of Commons, worried over Lady Percivall's health,
and rejoiced that his nephew, Jack, was at Cambridge. He sent
loving messages to his "deare wife and children" and was most
heartily grateful for Sir Philip's goodness to them, since they
"could not have subsisted wth out yo[u]." The last of these letters
ends with an earnest petition: "I have bin of Late troubled w[th]
some thoughts of my wife and children, I feare Nanny is ill

because of a dreame I had of her I beseech yo[u] continue yo[r] love to them, and my praiers shall be for yo[u] and yo[rs]." [52]

Fears for Ireland, as well as domestic anxieties, distressed Richard Fitzgerald. He longed for news of Dublin, alarming though it was, and listened apprehensively to the reports of travelers. He resented the neglect of Inchiquin by Lord Lisle, who, on his arrival in Munster, excluded the General from his councils, treating him so rudely that Inchiquin resumed fighting, which he preferred to starving, and managed to win several victories, but remained under suspicion. Fitzgerald regarded his friend as one of "the verie champions of the allmightie" and asserted that the objection of "the brotherhood" (the Independent party) that Inchiquin was Irish was enough to make a man disdain the reformation of these days. Inchiquin's wants, said Fitzgerald, were "discouragements to my hearte." [53]

Sir Philip Percivall died on November 10, 1647, heartbroken because he foresaw the King's tragic doom.[54] On November 13 Inchiquin won a great victory at Knocknanoss, near Kanturk. Nothing is known of the rest of Richard Fitzgerald's life. It can only be surmised that, like Sir Philip, he was a Royalist at heart and that he sympathized (if secretly) with Inchiquin, when the latter declared for the King and thereafter coöperated with Ormonde [55] in the King's service. King Charles was beheaded on January 30, 1649. It may not have been long afterwards that Fitzgerald died, while collecting assessments in Wales.[56] His widow received in Bristol the Castle Dod rents for Easter of that year.[57]

It is apparent from his letters that Richard Fitzgerald was an able man, who felt that his talents were not appreciated. He took pride in his work, whether congenial or not, and put up a stiff resistance to whatever obstacles it presented. He had strong political and religious convictions, which he defended with ardor. He valued learning and relished Latin phrases. His temper was variable, perhaps irritable, and he was quick to take offense. He was, however, a devoted husband and thoughtful father; and he was warmly attached to his brother-in-law, whose "uprightness" he proved "by the touchstone of time." [58]

Aided by Lord Broghill, whose support he demanded and won, Oliver Cromwell quickly conquered most of Munster in 1649–50, although the Rebellion did not end in that province until the fall of Limerick in October 1651. John Percivall, who had been a college friend of Henry Cromwell, regained most of the estates which his father had lost and was knighted in 1658. Alice Fitzgerald recovered Castle Dod, after Colonel Moyler Power had collected the Michaelmas rent for 1649. She arrived in Cork in May 1650; and in August John Hodder turned over to her a larger sum than he had received from her untilled lands, "or else she might have perished." In March 1651 William Fitzgerald joined his mother in Cork.[59]

It was fortunate that there were persons of influence who took an interest in "Mr. Fitzgerald's son." By 1653 young Fitzgerald had become the secretary of Lord Broghill. In a letter of February 23 of that year, he informed his cousin, John Percivall, of his arrival in Youghal with his Lordship. He wrote letters for Broghill, conducted estate business, and was sent on various errands to London and back to Youghal. On one of these journeys, in August 1654, he escorted Lady Broghill to London. In the autumn of 1654 his mother, accompanied by Nanny, visited her goddaughter, Judith Clayton, in Mallow.[60]

In 1657 Fitzgerald witnessed in London an impressive piece of pageantry, of which, on May 27, he gave John Percivall the following account:

I much doubt my long silence has layd me und^r yor censure. . . The chief cause of my Long forbearance was ye desire I had to balast so light a thing as a sheet of paper from me wth ye event of ye grand deliberation, wch has kept ye whole Christian world in suspense untill Munday, ten aclock [May 24, 1657], when the Parlim^t mett his Highn^{es} in ye Painted Chamber & made good their first offer to him wth name of King under ye stile of Protector, wch he accepted.[61]

Lord Broghill had recently made an eloquent speech, which his young secretary may have copied out, in which he urged Cromwell to take the title of King.

Because of ill health, Fitzgerald gave up his post with Lord

Broghill at the end of 1657 and went to London "to putt my self into yᵉ handes of able physitians." He wrote to Percivall:

in order to yᵉ supporting of yᵉ great expense of entertaining Doctors & following a course of Physick my Lord has promised to gett me a place among yᵉ Clerkes of yᵉ Counsele at London if any be vacant, wᶜʰ I pitch upon rather than any under Thurloe, because yᵉ duety is easier by much, wᶜʰ as my condition is is a thing I must principally look after and yᵉ salary is 100ˡˢ p year wᶜʰ would be sufficient for a single man; and from thence I suppose yᵉ step may be easier when I shall have recovered health enough [for] yᵉ irregular hours of a Secretary of State.[62]

In his absence, John Percivall managed his cousin's financial affairs and agreed also to advise Mrs. Fitzgerald "how to carry her self to Coll. Hodder." As his father had taken counsel with Sir Philip, so did William Fitzgerald with Sir Philip's son, "knowing wᵗ has past yᵉ teste of your judgemᵗ needes noe other tryalle." [63]

Fitzgerald's correspondence furnishes no hint of what London physicians were able to do for him during what proved to be a brief London visit. He seems to have found love the best doctor, for he married in London rather suddenly in May 1658. His cousins, William Dobbins and Sam Percivall, flattered themselves that they had made the match, and the former assured John Percivall: "She is a good wife to him everye waie." Of this elusive young woman we know only that her Christian name was Charity. In November 1658 the young couple were living in Mallow.[64] The next May Fitzgerald wrote to Percivall from Newtown. He was still in search of employment and hoped that Lord Broghill and Sir John would recommend him to the Lord Lieutenant.[65] An office of his father's for which he had been angling became available, and on March 1, 1660, he became Clerk of the Crown and Peace for the County and City of Cork.[66]

The Restoration brought Fitzgerald several honors and real prosperity. In the spring of 1660, his patron, Lord Broghill, was created Earl of Orrery and appointed one of the Lords Justices and Lord President of Munster. In 1661, at the new Earl's request, Fitzgerald was granted a free pardon.[67] In April 1662 he was made Sole Examinator to the Commissioners appointed by the King to execute the Act of Settlement.[68] When the Commissioners were changed, he was confirmed in his post at the insistence of Orrery, who requested the favor for "an old servant of mine." [69] Orrery had the town of Rathcogan, near Castle Dod, rechristened Charleville, in honor of Charles II, and closed it to all persons except "good Protestants." He established in Charleville manufactures of linen and woolen goods, held his presidency court there, and built for himself a fine mansion, where he resided until 1668.

Through Orrery's influence, Fitzgerald obtained a seat in the House of Commons, as member for Lismore, which he held from 1661 to 1666. Under different conditions, his career in Parliament was less outstanding than his father's had been. But on one occasion, at any rate, he impressed the House, when, in November 1665, he ably defended the loyalty, during the late rebellion, of John Fitzgerald of Inismore, county Kerry.[70]

Sir John Percivall died in 1665, leaving Lady Percivall with young children, who were placed under the guardianship of her father, Robert Southwell.[71] In 1668 the Earl of Orrery resigned as Lord President of Munster and was impeached in the House of Commons. As these circumstances altered his prospects in Ireland, William Fitzgerald went to England and entered the Middle Temple on May 19, 1669.[72] On September 2, 1671, the King directed letters patent to be passed, admitting Fitzgerald to the society of the King's Inns in Dublin and constituting him Counsellor at Law in all the courts of Ireland.[73] In 1673 he was appointed deputy subcommissioner of prizes in the province of Munster to Robert Fitzgerald of Kinsale. He proved himself "very diligent" in the Prize Office in Cork and was granted a suitable salary.[74]

While the Percivall children were growing up, Fitzgerald's name seldom appeared in the correspondence of that family. His only son, Robert, was born about 1671; and he was also the father of four daughters: Elizabeth,[75] Mary,[76] Catherine, and Charity.

After completing his education and travels, Sir Philip Percivall,[77] Sir John's eldest son, settled in Ireland in 1679 as master
of Burton, county Cork. The one letter in which he refers to
William Fitzgerald, written to Sir Robert Southwell[78] in August
1680, expresses his satisfaction that

To morrow the man who impeached my cosen Fitzgerald of so many
heighnous things, will come into ye custome house, and there declare
whoo twas [Sir Richard Kyrle?] that sett him on to doe him that mis-
cheif. . . tis said he will cleare him selfe very handsomely, w^h I am
very glad of.[79]

Sir Philip died in 1680, at the age of twenty-four, and his title
and estates passed to his brother, Sir John.[80]

The second Sir John Percivall was very fond of cousin William. His cousin advised him about his brother's monument; and
the best sort of lands to purchase; and shipments from Lisbon
and Brazil; and the marriage of Helena Percivall. A stern judgment on one of Helena's suitors was regarded by her brother
with some amusement and "a Grain of Allowance."[81] But Sir
John respected his cousin and made every effort to be of service
to him.

William Fitzgerald made some dangerous enemies, who, in
Sir John's opinion, treated him shabbily. In November 1683 he
went to England to present his case, bearing with him a most
cordial letter which Sir John had written to Sir Robert Southwell
in his behalf:

My Cousen Fitzgerald being bound for England I can not lett
him goe without giving him some proofs of my willingness to serve
him there att least as farr as my Interest reacheth. I have written to
Sr Edward Dering concerning him & make ye same request to You.
His Misfortune is to be left out of ye Commission of ye Peace the last
Assizes when divers others of suspected Loyalty were putt out:
And this Company reflects upon him as alike culpable. This lights
heavy on ye Innocent, not only because 'tis unexpected but because
it toucheth them in the tenderest part they have. I doe unfeignedly assure you that I have not heard of any one step made by him that
might subject him to ye least severity of this kind; Butt on ye contrary
he appears to me & to all others with whom I converse very well af-

fected both to ye State and ye Church, & of great Moderation towards all Parties. Soe y^t it is very probable the blow came from some private hand, by wch he was unhappily misrepresented in y^t Conjuncture. If he needs either your Counsel or good word to sett him right again I beseech You afford him both; & your favor shall not be accounted for onely by him but allsoe by [me].[82]

Sir Robert seems to have been unable to offer assistance, although he wished the commission for Fitzgerald "before any man in Ireland." Fitzgerald's consolation, which he valued "above all my former hopes," was that Sir John had "soe fully owned me not only as y^r relation (wch is my greatest honor,) but as y^r friend (wch is a tye stronger than that of blood)." [83]

The friendship was broken by Sir John's early death in April 1686, on the eve of another Irish rebellion. For the third time, William Fitzgerald assisted with a heavy heart at the funeral of the head of the house of Percivall. When Lady Percivall and her children went to England to live with Sir Robert Southwell, Fitzgerald parted sadly with "all the remains of Sir John Percivall." He wrote to Sir Robert:

it is some content to us that they [Sir John's family] are goeing from these dangers & mischeifs wch are generally apprehended must in a short time inevitably fall upon us here but principally that they are goeing under your care who can best supply the losse of soe good a father. I pray god continue you to them till you have fully and like yor self discharged that trust. I am infinitely obliged by your great kindenesse when I had the honor to wayte on you at yor house & for ye assurance of your favor in yor Lett^r by Mr French. I finde my self in my owne Country wthout friendes, & wholy without employm^t & with a family of five children growne up to yeares that make y^t very chargeable soe that if any thing falls in your way by wch you might putt any buisnesse in my hands, you may doe an act wch tho I am not of ye Religion y^t teaches men may meritt of God, I am sure you would infinitely of me, and also meet wth a recompence in Heaven. I wish you all happinesse & delight in yor retirement & ingenious diversion wth ye Odyssey & every thing else.[84]

Fitzgerald was in ailing health. The following March, when Lady Percivall needed the services of the kind cousin whom she had been able to command "absolutely," she had to be told of "Mr. Fitzgeralds weakness and inability for buisness"[85] and of the fact that no one was available to assist her. On September 4, 1687, the Dowager Countess of Orrery was informed by her son, Captain Henry Boyle,[86] that "Mr. [William] Fitzgerald of Castledod died last week."[87]

He died a disappointed man. In the closing years of Charles's reign, retirement seemed the only course for the capricious King's friends and those whom they befriended. And the accession of James dashed all Protestant hopes. William Fitzgerald had his father's qualities, but a less aggressive nature; and when fortune frowned, he was more disposed to droop. In spite of his reverses, he had considerably increased his estates;[88] and he enjoyed at intervals, as his father had not, the country diversions which Castle Dod afforded.

In June 1686 William Fitzgerald's son, Robert, entered Trinity College, Dublin, having completed his preparatory studies under Lewis Prythergh of Charleville. Margery Conron, wife of Richard Conron, reported to Lady Percivall that she had sent her servant "with Robin to the Colledge."[89]

There is no indication that Robin distinguished himself as a student. According to the college buttery book, he attended regularly the mathematics and logic lectures, but missed eighteen Greek and Latin lectures. His absences from chapel averaged four a week, his record being only a little better than Swift's.[90] Socially, he profited by his brief college days, judging by the lasting friendships which he made with William Congreve and Henry Luther.

The calm routine of the university was soon broken. Already in the summer of 1685, King James was favoring the Irish Catholics, the army was passing into Catholic hands, and the emigration of Irish Protestants had begun. In 1686, in county Cork, the rebels were strong enough "to come in numbers with a piper playing before them, and carry off the stock and cattle of protestants in the middle of the day."[91] When Tyrconnel returned to Dublin as Lord Lieutenant in January 1687, the disarmed Protestants were at the mercy of his recently recruited soldiers; and in the months which followed, all who could manage to do so fled to England.

Robert Fitzgerald remained at Trinity College for only sixteen months. His name does not appear in the buttery book after the week beginning October 8, 1687. In that year or the following year, he left Ireland, perhaps with his widowed aunt, Elizabeth Lloyd of Dublin, and two of her children.[92] He was in England until the autumn of 1690, a member of that dejected coterie of "gentlemen of Ireland," attainted by King James's Parliament, who lingered in London, waiting for brighter prospects to dawn in their native country.

These Protestant refugees were a large group, drawn together by common hopes and fears. Among the more notable figures were the second Earl of Cork, the Earl of Orrery,[93] Lord Clifford,[94] and Captain Henry Boyle. There were many gentlemen from Cork, including Dr. Rowland Davies, Dean of Ross, who kept a meticulous journal of his English exile. Robert Fitzgerald is mentioned twice in the pages of this journal. On March 21, 1690, Davies "spent the evening with Robert Fitzgerald and Mr. Brooks at the King's Head near Temple Bar, where Mr. Brooks treated." On April 3 of the same year, Davies dined near the Swan in Exchange Alley with Samuel Morris, Robert Fitzgerald, and Mr. Windham.[95]

The Irish exiles assembled in small groups in their favorite coffeehouses and taverns. If the Earl of Orrery was of the company, they chose the expensive French eating-house, Pontack's, where a dinner cost five shillings a head. At the Roebuck, King's Head, Dolphin, and Royal Oak, supper prices were from sixpence up. In the coffeehouses one might read the disquieting news of King James's campaign in Ireland. Hawes Cross, who was later to marry Robert Fitzgerald's sister, Mary, spent a gloomy evening at the Gun making his will.[96] One might wait upon a possible patron;[97] or haunt the Court of Requests; or try to borrow money at fifty per cent on the reduction of Ireland. It may be assumed that Robert Fitzgerald frequented the Theatre Royal in Drury Lane, where he may have seen Shadwell's masterpiece, *Bury Fair* (*c*. April 1689), Crowne's *Sir*

Courtly Nice (May 31, 1689), revived at the Queen's command, and (perhaps with Congreve) Lee's *Massacre of Paris* (October 1689) and Dryden's *Don Sebastian* (December 4, 1689).

King William's victory at the Boyne on the first of July, 1690, marked the defeat of the Irish Roman Catholic party and served as a signal for home-coming Protestant refugees. On October 7 a pass was issued for William Congreve, Robert Fitzgerald, and others to travel from Bristol to Ireland.[98] Congreve was to pay a visit of only a few months, Robin to remain in Ireland for over two years. It was a dismal scene which the young master of Castle Dod revisited. Orrery's house in Charleville and Burton House had been burned, and Castlemartyr, the seat of Captain Henry Boyle, plundered. A great part of Cork had just been destroyed, when the city surrendered to the Earl of Marlborough. The rebellion ended with the reduction of Limerick in October 1691; but the Percivall lands, and presumably Robert Fitzgerald's, lay waste until the spring of 1692.

On February 22, 1693, Fitzgerald was admitted to the Inner Temple.[99] He may have crossed to England with Joseph Keally, who entered the Middle Temple in the same month.[100] Congreve's letters of a later date hint that Robin was better acquainted with coffeehouses than with the law and was a thoroughly amiable and light-hearted companion. During the next two or three years, Robin probably saw many plays with Congreve, including Congreve's own comedies, *The Old Bachelor* (Drury Lane, March 1693), *The Double-Dealer* (Drury Lane, *c.* December 1693), and *Love for Love* (Lincoln's Inn Fields, April 1695). He must have been interested in the dedication of *The Old Bachelor* to Lord Clifford, nephew of his father's patron, and of *Love for Love* to the sixth Earl of Dorset, brother of Mary, Dowager Countess of Orrery.

If Congreve spent a part of 1696 in Ireland,[101] Fitzgerald may have again made the journey with him and may have settled in Ireland at that time. The young Irishman completed his legal studies in Dublin and was called to the Irish Bar in 1700.

There are cordial references to Robin in thirty-one of Congreve's forty-four letters to Joseph Keally. The first reference is in a letter of December 10, 1700, in which Congreve sends a message to Amory and Robin, comments on the delightful fact that both Mein and Robin do not change, and declares: "I am Robin's." In a letter of January 28, 1701, Congreve seems to indicate that Robin had recently returned home from a London visit and had neglected to send Mein a sum of money which he had borrowed from him, to the embarrassment of Mein, who had barely escaped an arrest. It is evident that "inhuman Robin" was an irregular correspondent. Congreve "always punctually answered" his letters and considered a "kind" reply an event worth recording.[102]

Although he had confidence in Keally's future, Congreve had some doubts about that of "poor Robin" and begged Keally to lend a hand to the latter, whose "guts were not naturally made for mounting."[103] Yet there are signs that Robin was at last beginning to take life seriously. For eight years, from 1703 to 1711, he represented Charleville in the Irish House of Commons, where he must have exerted himself in the interests of his county, for in 1705 he was made a freeman of the city of Cork.[104]

Robin was often in Congreve's thoughts. In describing to Keally the big storm of November 1703, Congreve added the detail: "The King's-Bench walk buildings[105] are just as before their roofs were covered. Tell that to Robin." As he grew fat, Congreve was amused to reflect that fat Robin "would laugh to see me puzzled to buckle my shoe." Congreve's duties as one of the managers of the new Haymarket Theatre prompted a merry device for getting Robin to London, and he wrote to Keally in February 1705: "My service to Robin. Tell him I shall want a fat box-keeper." Robin came to England, perhaps with Keally, in the autumn of 1705, remaining until past the middle of December, when he parted reluctantly from his old friend. In a letter to Keally, written on December 15, 1705, Congreve remarked: "Robin talks of going every day. I would have him stay till the weather is a little settled; for if he should be cast away you know your water swells a man; and what a thing were he if he were swelled? I know he sends you all the news from the Smyrna . . ."[106]

Recurring attacks of gout were the price Robin paid for too much London gaiety. On June 8, 1706, Congreve wrote to Keally: "I am sorry Robin Fitzgerald continues in so ill a state of health. I must be plain with you on his account: He did not live at a rate in this town to hope otherwise. Nothing but an absolute and continued regularity, and that with very good prescriptions, can recover so ill a habit of body. I wish he would take care of himself, or rather that he could." [107] His malady may have been aggravated by formidable Irish feasts, at which "Nonsense and wine . . . flowed in plenty" and "gigantic Saddles of Mutton and Brobdingnagian Rumps of Beef" weighed down the table.[108]

Gout and convivial spirits alternately depressed and exhilarated Robin. In March 1708, Congreve wrote: "I am very much concerned Robin has not better health. Our fat friends have suffered. King of the Royal Oak died last week, and poor Cornigh the taylor this week; so there is once more a widow and a well customed house for Robin, if he be in condition to venture." Nor was Robin too ill to "venture," although he made his own choice of a wife. On July 10 he married Joseph Keally's younger sister, Ellen. Congreve congratulated Keally on "the engrafting of Robin, to whom I wish much happiness with your sister." [109]

No doubt, Congreve took an affectionate interest in Fitzgerald's career. He told Keally that he would have been glad to see Robin "strut about the hall as great as the prince of Conde." [110] Robin's professional advancement, however, occurred after Keally's death and the close of the Keally correspondence. He became Second Sergeant at Law on December 18, 1714, and Prime Sergeant at Law on June 23, 1717.[111] His domestic happiness was increased by the birth of a daughter, Elinor, in 1715.[112]

It may be inferred from his business transactions that he became a successful man of affairs. It was his custom to spend the Christmas holidays at Castle Dod, on which occasions John Bowerman, to whom he had leased the lands of Ardnageehy and Ballydrydeen, presented his landlord with "a fat Wether and a Couple of Fatt Capons," as the terms of his lease required.[113] Perhaps Fitzgerald was in Cork in May 1722 when Lord Shannon,[114] one of the Lords Justices, was given the freedom of the city.[115] It is a temptation to fancy that a bond between Congreve and Lord Shannon may have been their mutual friendship with "honest Robin."

Fitzgerald's death, caused by a fall from his horse, occurred on January 21, 1725. An anonymous author wrote some very bad but sincere verses in his memory, paying tribute to his talents and integrity:

> . . . Fitz-Gerald God's resolved that We!
> Should loose *Apollo* and a *Lawyer* in thee . . .
> Curs'd be that Horse, that ended the sweet Days
> Of him, that was both Just and Good always. . .
> He ne'er was Brib'd, nor against Conscience would
> Do ought was wrong, for Silver or for Gold.[116]

In his will, of which only an abstract exists, Fitzgerald made provision for his wife and only child and left bequests to his sisters,[117] nephews, and nieces.[118]

His daughter, Elinor, a child of ten when he died, was the last of the Fitzgeralds of Castle Dod. At the age of twelve, she lost her mother, also. Ellen Fitzgerald had appointed her cousin, John Cuffe, guardian of the estate of her "dearly beloved Daughter," and the Honorable Mrs. Downes (widow of Dive Downes?) the child's personal guardian. Among Mrs. Fitzgerald's bequests, were four hundred pounds to her niece, "Jeane Kely," daughter of her brother, John; fifty pounds to her brother, John; and one hundred and ten pounds to two of her servants, "in Consideration of their faithful Behaviour in my Sarvis." [119]

On January 12, 1734, Elinor Fitzgerald married William Stewart, third Viscount Mountjoy, afterwards first Earl of Blesington,[120] the nephew of her cousin, Lady Blesington.[121] In 1736, in accordance with the terms of her marriage contract, Castle Dod was sold to Henry Harrison [122] for twelve thousand pounds, to pay the debts of Elinor's young husband.[123] Her son, William, was born in Dublin on March 14, 1735.[124] She survived both her son [125] and her husband, and died in London on October 1, 1774.

Her will suggests that Robin Fitzgerald's daughter had an affectionate and generous nature. She desired to be buried in Silchester (Hants), between the remains of "my ever beloved and honoured Lord and our Dear Son Lord Mountjoy." To her husband's cousin, Admiral John Forbes,[126] she bequeathed her husband's plate and her portrait, and to his younger daughter, Maria Elinor, her goddaughter, her diamond cross and other jewels. She left the sum of five hundred pounds to "John Kelly Esquire my Relation [127] to whom my dear Lord was very good." [128]

Henrietta
Duchess of Marlborough

*A*mong the shadowy figures that make up the circle of Congreve's most intimate friends, Henrietta, Duchess of Marlborough, seems to have suffered most from the gossip of her own age and from the more detached but still biased estimates of later critics. Not one of her contemporaries spoke a really decisive word in her favor; and the earlier biographers of Congreve preferred to dismiss her as an amusing eccentric. Leigh Hunt, however, chose to linger over this minor portrait, commenting on "the slow yet sensitive mind" of the Duchess and concluding that she loved Congreve "with all the heart she had, and a great deal of obstinacy." [1]

Henrietta Churchill was born on July 19, 1681, the eldest of the four daughters of John Churchill, afterwards first Duke of Marlborough, by his wife, Sarah, second daughter of Richard Jennings. On April 23, 1698, at the age of seventeen, she married Francis Godolphin, the only child of Sidney Godolphin, afterwards first Earl of Godolphin, by Margaret Blagge. Henrietta was a Lady of the Bedchamber (1702–12) to Queen Anne, who had contributed generously to her marriage portion and who acted as godmother to her eldest son. At the Duke of Marlborough's death in 1722, she became Duchess of Marlborough. She died on October 24, 1733.

Francis Godolphin, her husband, was born on September 3,

1678. He was educated at Eton and at King's College, Cambridge, where he received his M.A. degree in 1705. He was styled Viscount Rialton from 1706 to 1712, becoming Earl of Godolphin on his father's death in the latter year, and was created Baron Godolphin of Helston in 1735. Among the numerous offices which he held in the course of a long life, were those of Cofferer of the Household (1704-11, 1714-23); Lord of the Bedchamber (1716-23); Groom of the Stole (1723-27, 1727-35); Privy Councillor (1723); Governor of the Scilly Islands (1733-66); and Lord Privy Seal (1735-40). He died on January 17, 1766.

Of Henrietta's five children, two, Margaret and Henry, died in infancy. Her eldest son, William Godolphin, Marquis of Blandford (c.1700-1731), died in the lifetime of his parents. Henrietta was survived by two daughters, Henrietta, Duchess of Newcastle (1701-1776), and Lady Mary Godolphin, afterwards Duchess of Leeds (1723-1764).

The junior Duchess of Marlborough has been remembered only because of her friendship with Congreve. Unfortunately, none of Congreve's letters to her have been preserved, nor any references which he made to her, except those in his will. She has a place, although a small one, in the correspondence of a number of his famous friends, on whom she made an impression, chiefly unfavorable.

Swift could not forgive her for having snubbed him. On March 1, 1713 he noted in his *Journal to Stella:*

I . . . went to sitt with Lady Clarges,[2] I found 4 of them at whist, Lady Godolphin was one. I sat by her, & talked of her Cards &c, but she would not give one Look, nor say a word to me. She refused some time ago to be acquainted with me. You know, she is Ld Marlboroughs eldest Daughter. She is a fool for her Pains, & I'll pull her down.[3]

To Pope Henrietta was an intruder, whose presence he resented, since she deprived him of a witty and amiable companion, who renounced his society for hers. In 1722 Pope wrote to Gay, with a touch of asperity: "Pray put Mr. Congreve in mind that he has one on this side of the world who loves him; and that there are more men and women in the universe than Mr. Gay and my Lady Duchess of M[arlborough]."[4] Four years later, in a letter to Swift, Pope lamented: "I cannot help thinking, when I consider the whole short list of our friends, that none of them except you and I are qualified for the mountains of Wales . . . Mr. Congreve is too sick to bear a thin air; and she that leads him too rich to enjoy anything."[5]

Lady Mary Wortley Montagu was still more unsympathetic. She seized the occasion, when Henrietta's youngest daughter was born in 1723, to declare that her "poor friend" had exposed herself "to a most violent ridicule."[6] Subsequently, Lady Mary remarked that Henrietta did not often invite her to Bononcini's concerts at her house; and she referred to the Duchess and herself as "two people who are resolved to hate with civility."[7] Three politely ironic notes which Henrietta wrote to Lady Mary indicate that the two ladies were well matched in the delicate art of pretended friendship. In one note Henrietta observes: "I am sure you wont dislike to have Mr Congreve tomorrow if you can get him for he is like all good things hard to come at. and 'tho I shant add to ye company I have witt enough not to spoyle it, which you must allow is being tolarable. what hour woud you have me come."[8]

Although it cannot be determined at what date Henrietta became acquainted with Congreve, it may have been about 1706 and cannot have been later than 1714. She had no doubt felt flattered by his poetical tributes to her brother[9] and to her father-in-law.[10] Her mother names "Congreve & several Poets"[11] last in a list of the bad company which Henrietta kept after she went to live at Godolphin House, the residence of her father-in-law. On November 27, 1711, Lady Strafford wrote to her husband: "The world says Lady Har. Rialton has latly been in Pickell for her sins, and Lady Jersey[12] in the same way; if they are as bad as the town says they are, I wonder they are ever out of it."[13] But whether or not Congreve was then involved in Henrietta's sins, we do not know. It appears to have been in 1714 that her mother found Henrietta one day "at Ombre with Mr Congreve" and detected their mutual embarrassment.[14]

A romantic account of Congreve's courtship of Henrietta was published shortly after her death, under the title, "The Secret History of Henrada Maria Teresa." Henrada (Henrietta) is described as the eldest daughter of a great general, who "cut out his Fortune with his Sword," and Jenina (Sarah Jennings), "a woman of deep penetration" and "aspiring Nature." Among her many suitors, Henrada selected as her husband Count Adolphus (Lord Godolphin), "a complete Gentleman . . . Chaste; Charitable, Even-temper'd, Good-natur'd, and a most kind and indulgent Husband," with whom she lived happily for many years.

As she was a Lady of Wit and Spirit, she took a secret Pleasure in reading Poetry, of which she was a good Judge; but the Works of Congravino [Congreve], gave her the greatest Satisfaction. To give him what is due to his Character, he was one of the best of the Age, and [showed] a peculiar Talent in writing Comedies, wherein he never failed of some double Entendre's, to raise a becoming Blush in the Fair Sex: And when he made Love his Subject, he writ such Softness, that he made a deep Impression in their Hearts. This was the Fate of Henrada, who was captivated with his Poems. If, says she, the bare Reading of the Works of this Gentleman, can have such an Effect upon our Minds, what Wonders must he needs be capable of performing when we hear the Words from his own Mouth? From that day she studied how there might be an Interview between them; and as Secrecy was a material Point in this Case, it was some time before she could accomplish her Design: At last she determined to write to him, which she did to the following Effect

Signior Congravino,

If you have the Spirit of an English-man, you will not refuse a Woman's Challenge; meet me therefore this Evening in the Inamorate's Grove at the Back of the Palace.

A trusty servant delivered this letter, and the meeting took place. Henrada went to the assignation in disguise, attended by a female servant, who acted as sentinel. Seated with her on a green bank, Congravino read, at Henrada's request, "a particular Page, which treated of Love," from a volume of his poems which she had brought in her pocket. She squeezed his hand, and he read on with much grace. The reading was interrupted by word from the servant that Count Adolphus was walking through the grove. Henrada hastily gave Congravino a diamond ring which she took from her finger, unveiled, was embraced by him, and retreated, unseen. The next afternoon she went to his house "in cog," and remained there two hours.

Some time afterwards, having discovered that she was with child, she contrived to spend a whole season with Congravino in lodgings at Aix la Chapelle (Bath), where they carried on their intrigue so discreetly that no one was aware of it. On her return to town, she refused to tell Count Adolphus the name of her lover, and "they were seperated by Consent from Bed, and in that State they continued for twelve Years."

At length Henrada was delivered of a Daughter, of whom all the Care imaginable was taken; and she was brought up in the House with her Mother. Much about this Time the Countess's Father died, whereby his Titles descended to her, and with them a large Estate to support the Dignity. Little Miss, encreasing in Years, had the Happiness of pleasing her Mother, who perceived in her the Wit and Sprightliness of the Father, who dying a few Years after, placed such an entire Confidence in Henrada, that he made her his sole Heiress and Executrix, not in the least doubting but she would take care of his Daughter. 'Tis true, he did not recommend the Child to her, which he imagined would be fruitless, being persuaded that Henrada would always look upon her with an Eye of Tenderness and Affection. She took as much Care of her Education, as if she had been her Legitimate-Daughter, and no Pains or Cost were spared to make her an accomplished young Woman. She would not permit her to be called by any other Name than her Father's, for whom she retained a grateful Remembrance, and, as it is said, shed many Tears, when she looked earnestly upon Miss. . .

Whether Henrada laid too much to Heart the Death of Congravino, I cannot take upon me to determine; she did not survive him above five Years; at last being seized with a lingring Distemper, she was advised to take the Country Air, but relapsing several times, and her Constitution being greatly impaired by her Sickness, she was at last constrained to pay the last Debt to Nature.

When she was sensible of the Approach of Death, she called for Miss, gave her her Blessing, and having made her Will, left her all her Father's Estate, by whom she was impowered to leave it to whom she pleased, and made a very large Addition to it. She died a Penitent, and was sorry she had wronged so good a husband as Adolphus.[15]

Over against this picturesque narrative, which is correct in certain details, we can merely set the following facts. Congreve, Henrietta, and Gay spent the season of 1722 in Bath;[16] and in September of that year Pope deplored Congreve's apparent infatuation for the Duchess.[17] On November 23, 1723, Lady Mary Godolphin was born. In September 1726 Congreve was seriously ill of "a fever, and the gout in his stomach" at Henrietta's house, Windsor Lodge, where Dr. Arbuthnot, probably at her insistence, visited him "for near three weeks together every day."[18] On the 3rd of May, 1728, Lady Mary Godolphin was sent to Bath. The next day Congreve and the Duchess made the same journey together.[19] They spent a long season in Bath and were still there in October.[20] When Congreve died, Henrietta paid the most extravagant homage to his memory. In her later years, according to her son,[21] she was sometimes on terms with her husband, and sometimes not. Lord Godolphin showed solicitude for her in her last illness and grief at her death.[22]

In the will[23] which he drew up on February 26, 1725, after assigning various small legacies, Congreve left the bulk of his fortune, amounting to over ten thousand pounds,[24] to the Duchess of Marlborough, for her "Sole and Separate use & wherewith her said Husband or any after taken Husband of her . . . shall not intermeddle or have any controuling power over." He appointed Lord Godolphin sole executor "in Confidence of his honesty and justice." To Henrietta, Duchess of Newcastle, he bequeathed "the Dutchess of Marlboroughs picture by Kneller," and to Lady Mary Godolphin, still an infant, "her Mothers picture Enamelld in Miniature together with my white brilliant Diamond Ring." In a codicil dated January 29, 1728, he annulled more than half of his legacies, and left it "absolutely in the power and determination" of Henrietta to pay or not to pay these, to take from or add to them.

Following Congreve's death, there was a good deal of com-

HENRIETTA, DUCHESS OF MARLBOROUGH

ment and speculation concerning his liaison with the Duchess of Marlborough. In February 1729 Anne, Viscountess Irvine, wrote to her father, Lord Carlisle:

The young Duchess has made herself very particular upon Mr. Congreve's death: he left her executrix, by which she gets 7,000 pounds in wrong, I think one may say, to a great many poor relations he had, and some say a son by Mrs. Bracegirdle. The Duchess buried him handsomely, and showed so great an affection for his dead body that she quitted her house and sat by his corpse till he was interred.[25]

For the enlightenment of posterity, Horace Walpole recorded:

When the younger Duchess exposed herself by placing a monument & silly epitaph of her own composition & bad spelling to Congreve in Westminster abbey, her Mother, quoting the words, said, "I know not what pleasure She might have had in his company, but I am sure it was no honour." [26]

The legend that Henrietta made a fantastic use of Congreve's fortune may be traced back to Edward Young, who declared:

The duchess showed me a diamond necklace (which Lady Di used afterwards to wear), that cost seven thousand pounds, and was purchased with the money Congreve left her. How much better would it have been to have given it to poor Mrs. Bracegirdle.[27]

It has been assumed that Pope had Henrietta in mind in his description of Philomede in "Of the Characters of Women." These lines were first published in 1751, having been excluded, like the portrait of Atossa (Sarah, Duchess of Marlborough), from the 1735 edition of the poem. The proud peeress who "sins with Poets thro' pure love of wit" [28] resembles Henrietta, although at least one detail of the portrait does not suit her. It seems rather clearer that Pope aimed at her the deadly last line of his suppressed portrait of the Duke of Marlborough: "Madness and Lust (said God) be you his heirs." [29]

The reputation of Congreve's patroness was rudely attacked by anonymous writers in two verse satires: *The Female Faction* (1729) and *The Amorous D[uc]h[e]ss* (1733). The author of the former poem offers sarcastic advice to Gay, who had been encouraged in the publication of *Polly* by Henrietta's generous subscription of one hundred pounds.[30] Gay is urged to repay the favors of "great Almeria" (Henrietta), who, imagining that Alphonso (Congreve) survives in him and charmed by his homage, will treat her husband's "vast merits with *polite Neglect*." [31] Almeria will be most obliged if her admirer will provoke the anger of her foe, Clodia (Sarah, Duchess of Marlborough).

The author of *The Amorous D[uc]h[e]ss* relates how "Great Hotonta" (Henrietta) employed an artist "of best known Skill" to make a wax statue of "Comick Con" (Congreve).[32] For years she visits at frequent intervals the case where this curio is kept. Then one day Tom, moving the statue to another room, drops and breaks it. Hotonta, frenzied with grief, summons Connelia (Lady Mary Godolphin) to help her collect the precious fragments.

Congreve's successive biographers have never failed to do justice to Henrietta's curious way of remembering her famous friend by a lifelike effigy. Theophilus Cibber in *The Lives of the Poets* notes that the Duchess placed every day at her toilet table an image of Congreve, "to which she would talk as to the living Mr. Congreve, with all the freedom of the most polite and unreserved conversation." [33] Thomas Davies in his *Dramatic Miscellanies* describes the image as "an automaton, or small statue of ivory . . . which was every day brought to table. A glass of water was put in the hand of the statue, which was supposed to bow to her Grace and to nod in approbation of what she spoke to it.[34] In the *Biographia Britannica* Andrew Kippis, quoting "a respectable correspondent," adds:

This Lady, commonly known by the name of the young Duchess of Marlborough, had a veneration for the memory of Mr. Congreve which seemed nearly to approach to madness. Common fame reports, that she had his figure made in wax after his death, talked to it as if it had been alive, placed it at table with her, took great care to help it with different sorts of food, had an imaginary sore on its leg regularly dressed; and to compleat all, consulted Physicians with relation to its health.[35]

More recent critics have not been averse to repeating such statements, omitting the word of caution which Kippis appends that, since the story "is grounded only on common report, there is the highest probability of its being greatly exaggerated."

Unfortunately, Henrietta never spoke out. The few letters which she wrote that have survived disclose only what she was to other people and not her essential self. She is most communicative in her letters to her mother, Sarah, Duchess of Marlborough; but these have been so deliberately edited and footnoted with Sarah's comments that they frequently seem to bear more strongly the impress of the mother's than of the daughter's personality.

All of Henrietta's letters to acquaintances and friends exhibit the "slip-slop" [36] style that Leigh Hunt claimed for one of them. They are carelessly written in a large, sprawling hand and indicate that their author was too much occupied with the business of living to be seriously concerned with epistolary art.

Three letters referring to Congreve have been published. On January 22, 1729, Henrietta wrote to George Berkeley, requesting him to be one of the pallbearers at Congreve's funeral.[37] A second letter to Berkeley, written six days later, evidently accompanied some gift, for the Duchess observes:

The last letter I writ to you was upon allways having thought that you had a respect and a kind one, for Mr Congreve. I dare Say you believe I coud sooner think off doing the most monstrous thing in the world, then Sending any thing that was his, where I was not perswaded it would be valued. The number off them I think So off, are a mighty few indeed.[38]

On November 29, 1729, Henrietta wrote to Jacob Tonson's nephew, Jacob Tonson, begging him to persuade his uncle to let her have the Kit-Cat Club portrait of Congreve "yt I would give the world for," [39] in exchange for another portrait of Congreve by Kneller.

Several manuscript letters by Henrietta are in the British Museum. In a letter to Mrs. Howard, on January 30 (1723), Henrietta objects that Mrs. Bellenden "has in all Companys Said things off me that I am not Capable off" and has been the first person, "however ungrateful People have been," to ridicule one who has been kind to her out of charity.[40] Henrietta wrote a letter to Mrs. Clayton (undated) in the hope that the latter would interest the Queen in the case of Lady Dillon, "a mighty good woman, and a very agreeable one and very misarable now, to have her Child she doates of, in these unfortunate Circumstances."[41]

The most personal of these letters (October 26, 1720) is addressed to Lady Evelyn.[42] Henrietta explains: "I had thanked you last night for the favour of your letter but had the headach and you know how I bear pain. I have not yet been pleased one minute Since I left you." A few comments are made concerning mutual acquaintances and some portraits which Henrietta had given and received. Although the letter is not long, the writer concludes: "I think for me I have Said So much in this letter and in the way of telling too, that it Shall Serve my most dear friend for Some time." A postscript follows: "Sr John will tell you about the Stocks Plague and King. I wish I was kissing Sid: hearing miss Ann read who I realy thought was Sorry when I came away, and Seeing miss Mary Cry."[43] Sir John and Lady Evelyn were friends for many years of both Henrietta[44] and her husband, Lord Godolphin. Another evidence of Henrietta's interest in Lady Evelyn's children is supplied by one of the letters (May 14, 1718) of Sir John Evelyn to his wife, in the remark: "I saw Lady Godolphin before dinner in a roome litterd with things for Wotton, she says she cant gett a Japan trunk to her mind, & therefore will send Miss Anne a Japan Cabinet—instead of it."[45]

Forty letters written by Henrietta to her mother, Sarah, Duchess of Marlborough, have been preserved in Blenheim Palace. Most of these are undated, and some of them are unsigned. It is probable that the most revealing of the daughter's letters[46] were destroyed by Sarah in a mood similar to the one in which, after a brief reconciliation with her daughter, Mary, Duchess of Montagu, she burned "all former letters that I might never more see how she had used me."[47] The kindest letters were kept.

Judging by these, Henrietta's girlhood was the happiest period of her life. She was warmhearted, impulsive, and rather romantic and was proud of sharing her mother's confidence, as her younger sisters could not. Even then, her effusive protestations of affection were not always all that her mother required. The weighing and measuring of affection grew wearisome; and there were times when too much perseverance was needed to please and to be pleased. Letter writing in itself was not exhilarating. Once Henrietta asks forgiveness for "this horrid Scraull," and another time she admits, at the close of a passage which she has copied: "I am in pain for fear my Dear mama Shoud be angrey y^t this is ill writ, and Spellt, but if y^u will beleeve me, I am in Such hast, I hardly know w^t I do, and therefore hope y^t y^u will forgive all faults." [48]

The letters represent three phases in Henrietta's relations with her mother. It is possible to date seven roughly as belonging to the period from about 1692 to 1701. [49] They were written when she was a girl and in the years following her marriage. The first letter was sent to Sarah when she was in St. Albans because of her mother's illness. Henrietta declares that a letter from "my dear mama" would make her the "over joyest creature in the world." She wishes to be remembered to friends in St. Albans and adds: "I woud write to Mrs Midleton but that I thought haveing you was plesure enough to her. I am sure I envy her and every body ells that has the happness to have my dear mamas good companey when I have it not." [50] The next three letters are embellished with translated passages from French texts [51] in which lovers' quarrels are fervently described. The subject matter evidently appealed to Henrietta, who in one instance remarks: "I thinke this letter very pritty, if you do too pray let me know it." [52] Besides the quotations, there are a few personal items of interest, such as a request for "ovids epistles" and suggestions regarding the replenishing of her sister Anne's wardrobe in preparation for a visit to Althorp.

Henrietta's marriage and the birth of her son, "Willigo," did not divert her from the insistent topic of these letters: her love for her mother. She has made "a kind long letter . . . as much longer as I could by reading it a hundred times over and with more Satisfaction then I can express because I think it looks as if you loved mee as much as I can wish for, which is Saying a good deall"; yet she is disturbed to discover "by Som parts in it that you are not as easie as can be." On another occasion she reflects: "I can never know for any long time together any thing like true Satisfaction till I See my Dear Angell Mama again." When her sister has a letter from her mother and she does not, she confesses: "my Dear Mama knows I 'cant help being jealous and indeed 'tis impossible for one not to bee So when one loves any body to Such a degree as I do you." [53]

The next group of letters extends to 1716, at least. It is apparent that during these years there was increasing friction between an exacting mother, who wished to govern her daughter's life, and a high-spirited child, who resented interference and whose love chilled under parental discipline. One affectionate letter bears Sarah's annotation: "This letter was from Lady Godolphin before she was ruined by the very bad company she keeps." When Sarah was satisfied with her, Henrietta cherished her mother's letters, reading them over the last thing at night and the first thing in the morning. In a compliant humor she begs: "my Dear Mama do but allways love mee as much as I shall deserve from you, by my love to you, and I ask no more." She quickly detects the undertones of reproof, as when she expostulates: "your letter to mee was not neer so kind as the others, and when one wishes so much to allways have a kind one, one cant help being more nice in finding any thing out, then if one were indifferent." Once, after "afflictions both of them quite fresh" had resulted in a mood which her mother interpreted as unresponsive, the daughter urges: "pray dear Mama beleeve mee, and let us both bee as happy as wee can, for indeed I meane mighty well, and love you dearly." Again she writes:

I am but iust a wake, or I woud have thanked my Dearest mama much sooner for her kind letter, which I can deserve no way, but by loveing you, and whenever you think I 'dont, make mee so happy, as to tell mee so, and if affter that you dont find I do most tenderly, I never desier you shoud care for mee, and I am sure my

Dear Mama if it was but from last night, must see how misarable that woud make mee.[54]

The feud that was to bear such disastrous consequences seems to have begun when Sarah remonstrated against Henrietta's dancing country dances at Lady Fitzhardinge's house. Henrietta explains at some length that her husband felt it would be rude to decline without any apparent reason an invitation received "here in the country when I could have no other inyoyment." She sees Lady Fitzhardinge seldom, only out of deference to her mother's wishes, since "indeed when people are agreable I can not help Seeing it." Her mother's dissatisfaction can be "but for one reason and that is because no body must bee quite happy." Unable to let the matter rest, Sarah continued to object to this and other friendships which her daughter enjoyed, with the result that Henrietta "allmost wished my Self dead." She declines Mrs. Lowther's invitation to Newpark and describes again her position regarding Lady Fitzhardinge. As "for Saying I don't love countrey dances when I really do I could not think off deneying Such an inclination as that," and she advises her mother to remember that "She was once off my age her Self." The controversy goes on until Henrietta, losing patience, complains: "having you perpetually taking things ill off mee really makes mee very unhappy." She is willing, however, to offer the following terms:

I do hope still to bee quite upon an other foot then a visseter for what ever you are to mee I will bee still the same to you and you shall hear every morning where I go that day and with who. Mr Godolphin intended to come to you yesterday and see you alone to Say what he liked I shoud do in all this for I told him every thing iust as you told mee, and he would have me go into the drawing room as I used to do twice a week and if it happens that I have a mind to it to a play once a week and both off these in such company as my Dear Mama shall certainly aprove off and he hopes you wont take it ille he gives his opinion.[55]

After this, Sarah nursed Henrietta through an illness and obtained the reward:

I must bee the greatest brute in the world not to love you, if it was for only the kindness you showed me a very little while ago which indeed I think of very offten. . . I am never any thing like happy when I think you are not quite easie with mee, for upon my word I love you sincerely and wish for nothing more then that you knew exactly the truth of my heart, which you will ever have a prodigious share in as long as I live, and if you will beleeve it, I shall be very happy, and if not, extreamly otherwise indeed.[56]

One step which the daughter took won the mother's un-qualified approval: Henrietta's resignation in 1712, following her father's dismissal, of her office as Lady of the Bedchamber to Queen Anne. Sarah copied out in her own hand the letter which Henrietta sent to the Duchess of Somerset on this occasion, adding a note to the effect that she was gratified by her daughter's action. Her ten years' service as a lady in waiting had perhaps never been a source of much pleasure to Henrietta. In one letter to her mother she had regretted: "next Munday I go in to waiting and lye at Kensenton, which I fancy, will not be very agreable." [57]

After Sarah had gone abroad in 1713, Henrietta proposed that her mother send for her grandchild, Henrietta's eldest daughter, as soon as she was in some place where she could have her.

She Speakes french now, to bee of great use to you, and the longer She is a broad the better it will be for her, for it will make it, So young as She is, like her naturall langage. which will bee very prittey and useful to her. any roome in the world, for Such a child is good enough, and as well, as what, She has here.

The letter ends with the news: "wee was all last night at a mighty fine Ball at the Dutchess of Boltons." The next letters are short notes. Once Henrietta thanks "my Dear Angell Mama" for a gift and hopes to come to her "when all the horrid vissits are over." [58] Then hostilities were resumed. The intervention in 1715 of the Duke of Marlborough and Lord Godolphin induced Henrietta to send to her mother two rather formal notes of apology.[59] In the second she insists: "it was impossible to love you, and not take it ill that you shoud make me So many unkind reproaches." On the back of another letter (1716) of only a few lines, Sarah wrote: "Lady Go. when her Sister dyed." The last letter in the group was written to the Duke of Marlborough in November 1716, to inform him that Henrietta and her sister were starting out to visit him "when mama's letter came to forbid it." In a footnote Sarah observes that Lady Godolphin had asked a servant to deliver this letter "when I was not by" and that "nothing could be more offensive then such a leter to bee delivered in such a manner, & at a time that I would have been glad to have given my own life to have saved her father." [60]

The letters of the third group, all of which are dated, cover the period from 1721 to 1732. In a letter written in July 1721, Henrietta states briefly that she has done what her mother ordered and that she has known for some time "that Mr Walters is a very great Rogue." A year later, soon after she had become Duchess of Marlborough, she wrote to Sarah a stiff apology, because she had opened a letter addressed to the Duchess of Marlborough which was intended for her mother. Two years later, when the situation was reversed and Sarah had forwarded to Henrietta a note intended for the younger Duchess, the latter replied coldly: "indeed I can not help being Surprised Since your Grace woud take the Superscription to be for you, that you shoud change your opinion upon reading it." Below the text of the second letter, Sarah wrote, in bitterness of spirit: "Chrissmas eve 1724." [61]

In the last years of her life, Henrietta may not have corresponded with her mother. Copies, in Sarah's handwriting, of two letters written by her daughter the year before her death to her friend, Mrs. Mathews, indicate that Henrietta had ceased to ask favors directly of her mother. In the first letter Henrietta writes:

I hope you are pritty well Dear Mrs Mathews wee are both so here. you are acquainted with Mrs Harbury I know, & it would oblige me if you will tell her, that her Grace promised my Aunt tyrconell that when she went to St Albans she would give her a gold bottle for her to give to me, it is a thing poor Lady Ross [62] gave to me, when I was a child. if Mrs Harbury will be so good to do this, I shall take it as a favour. the man is just going that carrys this I am ever your sincere humble servant

Marlboroughe

Sept: 29, 1732

I dare say if Mrs Harbury will be so good as ask her as if she has a mind to have it, She will give it her, I allways gave her grace all my things as Soon as I had 'em if they were what I liked, & I loved my Lady Ross.[63]

The second letter concludes the subject:

Thank you Dear m^rs Mathews for your kind leter I am very sorry to find you have been so much out of order. wee are both very well. pray present my humble serviss to m^rs Harbury & say that I think my self much obliged to her, as to the bottle if her Grace can not recolect haveing given it away to any body, I dare say at some time or other in some place unthought of her Grace will find it, & I beleive where I saw it last in the closett at St Albans. my lady Rosses picture will please me extreamly & queen mary's box that her Grace has don me the honour to offer I shall vallue. I hope soon to hear you are better, & am allways Dear m^rs matthews your humble servant

Marlborough [64]

On the back of this letter Sarah comments: "This ridiculous letter was writt for things she had given me when She was A child, & desired them again." The statement, like most of Sarah's observations, is caustic. It is significant, however, that the mother was at pains to make and keep copies of letters which imply that her daughter, too proud to make concessions, thought of her with some kindness before death ended the long relationship.[65]

It was a relationship about which Sarah had more to say than could be expressed in footnotes to her daughter's letters. Among the private papers in Blenheim Palace is a narrative of over one hundred pages, entitled "An Account of the Dutches of marl. & montagus behaviour before and after their fathers death." The manuscript is dated September 19, 1722, and includes an appendix of five pages dealing with items of a later date. Sarah wrote this document only to show to her "particular Friends," to illustrate the "Barbarous Treatment" that she had received

74

from two of her children and to vindicate her treatment of them. Most of the first thirty-five pages are devoted to Mary, Duchess of Montagu; in the remainder of the essay Henrietta is the central figure, except in a long digression of sixteen pages on the conduct of the Duchess of Newcastle.[66]

The principal charges against Henrietta are that she neglected her mother and formed friendships of which her mother disapproved. Every incident of major importance stands out in sharp relief and is related with dramatic emphasis. Small vexations fill in the background, like a relentless dull ache which precedes and follows moments of intense pain.

Sarah begins her account of Henrietta by contrasting her daughter's devotion in the earlier years of her life with the indifference which she displayed after she had ceased to live with her mother.

When She was married, which was a Match extreamly to Her own Satisfaction Their Settlements not being great I contrived it so as to make it easy for them to live with me, and gave them my best appartment in my Lodgings at St James's, where She lived with me till She had had three children, Two of Which were the present Lord Blandford,[67] & ye D^{ss} of Newcastle, & they also were in my Lodgings, and one thing I can say that is very extraordinary, That in the whole time, we never had the least dispute or uneasiness, of any Sort, but liv'd like sisters: After this, She was with child of Her last son, & the Family was so large that Her Father had a mind to have them live with the late Lord Godolphin,[68] where She soon fell into very ill company, My Lady Oxford & Her daughters, Mrs Ramsey & Mrs Hamond, Afterwards my Lady Sandwich, & at last having a great mind to be thought a Wit Mr Congreve & several Poets, and in short the worst company that a Young Lady can keep, but for many years this produc'd nothing worse to me than a cold and careless behaviour: I saw it, & dreaded the consequences of such company, but I never spoke to *Her* but once upon that Subject, and in the softest manner imaginable, saying only, That I wish'd *She* would not go often to my Lady Fitzharding, for tho' she had a great deal of wit and Humour that was diverting, Her house was a dangerous place for Young people, and that all the world knew, that there was not upon Earth so vile a woman as my Lady Oxford; That

I knew *She* was good but that some time or other these people would wound Her, and that I was sure She would come to see That what I said was true. She did not seem angry at this, & we parted very good friends, but She went on in Her way, and came to me now & then, in Her usual manner: And I can be very positive That in Her whole life She never ask'd me once to go abroad with Her, but once I desir'd Her to carry me with Her to Hyde-park, which She did in Her chariot; but she had so little pleasure in it, That She did not call me till it was almost dark, & I remember we met the company coming out of the ring, However I never reproach'd Her, loving Her, & seeing her of a careless temper, and we sung all the way.[69]

After this Henrietta would never go with her mother on little parties of pleasure, and for some years she would never come to St. Albans, although her husband was often there for weeks at a time. Sarah cured Henrietta's second son of an illness and might have prevented his death,[70] had she been informed [71] when he fell ill again. When Henrietta had the smallpox, Sarah "flew from Woodstock" and scarcely left her daughter's bedside until she recovered; but these exertions were unappreciated. Before she went abroad in 1713, she invited Henrietta's children, Lord Rialton and Lady Harriot, to tea, and merely because she gave them a second cup of tea, diluted with milk, received an indignant letter from their mother. Another evidence of Henrietta's ingratitude was her failure to thank her mother for the gift of the little lodge in Windsor Park. Sarah took a good deal of pains in furnishing it, so that Henrietta "did not want so much as an Ombre Table." [72]

A letter from her daughter in May 1713 [73] was kind only because Sarah was considering having Henrietta's eldest daughter sent abroad to her. "She was so desirous to part with Her daughter that She thank'd me for it before I had her, which was the only thanks I ever had." [74] Eventually Sarah adopted this child, cared for her tenderly, negotiated her marriage, and assumed all the expenses of the wedding.

Sarah reports a conversation which she had with Henrietta before Lady Sunderland's death. On this occasion she reproached her daughter for never inviting her to dine at her house, and for refusing to go abroad with her and treating her like a stranger when they met in the houses of others. In conclusion, she reminded her of this incident:

When I came into England, Did not I come to Your House with all the kindness imaginable, but You always look'd as if You wanted to have me gone, and once I remember, I came in a very easy way, telling You that it was to consult You About Lady Harriot, Whether She should have pinners with lappets or without, for tho' we thought it was better without, because She was low, we would not determine a thing of that consequence without Your consent, (And in this manner I endeavour'd to be merry.) You were at Ombre with Mr Congreve & a Woman that I did not know: I thought He look'd out of Countenance but Shew'd more willingness to talk to me than You did; I soon put You at ease, by going away; and after that I came to You in a Morning: The porter told me You were abroad, but an old Servant of the Family, thinking it was impossible You could be denied to me run after my chair, & fetch'd me back: It was so quick that I am sure it was not by Your order, Upon which I went back: You were above stairs in Your dressing room writing: To this You Answer'd, that One may be denied to one's Second self. Being resolved to bear every thing in hopes of bringing Her to reason I did not quarrel with Her even upon these answers, but continued still expressing my kindness; and when She rise up to go away I took Her & hugg'd her in my Arms & wept over Her, begging Her still that She would love me, but all that I could get in Answer to This was, That she gave me a little squeeze with Her hand at parting, but I did not see her in some days after.[75]

When Sarah was recovering from an illness in 1715, another quarrel occurred; this time Henrietta was accused of having lost all shame and was told that the company she kept had corrupted her morals. The daughter gave her father a strange account of what had happened, whereupon Sarah explained to him her own position and he persuaded Henrietta to apologize.[76] The apology was a failure, serving only to convince Sarah that her daughter had become quite hardened. Lord Godolphin also labored with Henrietta and induced her to write a more civil letter. Sarah's rejoinder was an outburst of fine rhetoric:

I will end this letter with what I remember in a Play. I will trouble thee no more my child, Farewell, we shall meet sometimes I hope in a decent way, let shame come when it will I do not call it, I do not bid the Thunder-bearer strike, nor tell Tales: Mend when Thou can'st; be better at thy Leisure; I can be Patient.[77]

When the Duke was very ill in 1716, after sending him a letter which she did not wish her mother to read, Henrietta visited her parents in Woodstock. On her arrival, she refused to speak to her mother, taking "no more notice of me than if I had been the nurse to snuff the Candles." Sarah made every effort to prevent the Duke from perceiving such unkindness. The morning that Henrietta departed, "I went thro' the rooms with my Arm in Her's to hide this matter even from the Servants; & when She came into Her own Chamber as I was talking to her without disguise She seem'd mighty easy & indifferent, & look'd in the Glass; upon which I said You're extream pretty, & so left her."[78]

Henrietta grew increasingly careless as to the impression which her rudeness might make on other people. Sarah cites examples:

I remember last winter [1721] upon my asking Her if my Lord Ryalton was at Rome She said Yes, with an angry air; I hope He is well. (continued I) Yes, very well. She answer'd with a snap; which one of my poor little Grandchildren observing look'd surpriz'd. And another time this Winter, having been abroad I found her in the room when I came home sitting by a Table, where they were playing at Ombre, She look'd upon me with a great deal of fierceness, and then took a pinch of snuff without so much as rising up to make me a Curtsy.[79]

The final break with Henrietta occurred on the evening of her father's death, June 16, 1722. When the Duchess of Montagu and Lady Godolphin called, Sarah sent word by Mrs. Kingdom that they were not to stay a long time with their father. The Duchess of Montagu replied that "She did not understand Her, but if She meant that they were not to see their Mother, they were very well used to That." They remained, however, for some time and when Sarah entered, curtsied but did not speak to her. After the Duke was moved to his own room, they followed, and the Duchess of Newcastle joined them. At last, the Duchess of Newcastle left, and the sisters went into the drawing room, where they waited until four o'clock in the morning.

When they went to London They & their Creatures reported to every body That I had turn'd them out of my House, & that I had order'd that no body should give them any thing to eat or drink; That I had told the Dutchess of Newcastle That I was glad it was over, for now I should never see Her again; and that as soon as I had put the two Sisters out, I took Mrs Kingdom in, & that they heard us talk a great deal and laugh as they sat in the next room; That the D^{rs} & Surgeons all knew every thing that had pass'd, and therefore there was no keeping it a Secret, and that after such a Behaviour as I had had to their Father, they would never any more take any notice of me.[80]

Sarah quotes Henrietta's most recent letter, commenting on the pleasure that her daughter obviously took "in signing Marlborough, which I believe is ridiculous without an H." Her last thrust is directed against that "very great Hypocrite," Dean Jones, who pretended to sympathize with Sarah, while remaining on friendly terms with Henrietta and with Sir John Vanbrugh. The Dean's treachery was brought to light when, by accident, Sarah received one of his letters to Henrietta, "in which there was something like blasphemy in comparing her to God." [81]

From time to time, a few people dared to contest Sarah's assertion that she had been the most patient of mothers. Henrietta's gentle sister, Anne, Countess of Sunderland, assured her mother: "I am so sencible of my own misfortunes that I must say all I can for my sisters, which is that I never saw what you think in eather of 'em." [82] By saying a good word for Henrietta and the Duchess of Montagu, Mrs. Kingdom ran the risk of losing Sarah's friendship. In a letter to Sarah (November 7, 1722), Mrs. Kingdom pleads:

I cannot see how it c'd be wrong to y^r Grace to wish y^u might yet be happy in one another, nor that, it c'd ever be disagreable to y^u, to hear it said, that I beleiv'd those ladys (& perticulerly L^{dy} Go.

whom I had formerly loved extreamly & who had done a thousand obliging things to me) had a great many vertues, & that I hop'd at last they w'd see their errors, & be every thing y^u c'd wish them.[83]

Sarah's conduct, in the eyes of her romantic friend, had been like that of Augustus Caesar, who made public the faults of his daughter, Julia, but confessed afterwards that if Maecenas or Agrippa had been alive, he would never have done it. Sarah promptly replied (November 8, 1722) that she failed to be "convinced by this argument that at three score I should be contented to live and Die with such injurious aspersions thrown upon me." [84]

Sir John Vanbrugh sought to refute Sarah's contention that Henrietta was aggrieved [85] by the last will which the Duke of Marlborough made. On July 19, 1722, Vanbrugh wrote to Lord Carlisle: "This Will was made, but in March last; and hurts nobody but her. I don't find however that either She, or my Lord Godolphin have the least disposition to dispute it; and I hope nobody else will." He adds: "Her Grace has by this Will (for to be Sure that was her doings) made my Lord Blandford independent of his Father and Mother, Depriv'd her Daughter of the Jewells, and Cater'd bravely for herself." Lord Godolphin will have less than was expected; yet both he and his wife "Seem well content." Henrietta has been pleased by Lord Carlisle's remark that this fortune has fallen "into such Generous hands." She has observed that "Covetousness has happen'd to appear to her so very odious in some other people, that she is sometimes frightened, lest she shou'd have seeds in her blood, that may Spring up one time or other." [86]

Four years later, Dr. Francis Hare [87] appeared as the champion of the Duchess of Montagu and her sister, although he had "no degree of acquaintance with either of these ladies." In a letter to Sarah (October 7, 1726), he explains that a lady had recently spoken to him of her Grace in an unmannerly fashion.

But one thing she mentioned, in which I am afraid she has every body with her, that is the excluding your own children from seeing Blenheim[88] and going through the Park. I am so far from defending

FRANCIS GODOLPHIN, SECOND EARL OF GODOLPHIN

them that I think they are exceedingly to blame, but yet I must own I always thought this was carrying things to too great an extremity.

He has read Sarah's manuscript and wishes that some things had not been said. He will always feel that a reconciliation is desirable.[89]

Regarding Henrietta's relations with her husband and children, there are more reliable sources of information than Sarah's narrative. To be sure, the additional evidence that is available is not abundant and is often rather negative, but it softens the tones of the picture. Especially persuasive, when weighed against Sarah's extravagant statements, are the occasional reflections of her patient son-in-law, Francis, Earl of Godolphin. If Lord Godolphin did not disprove, he never affirmed Sarah's charge that Henrietta was a bad wife. He wisely accepted life as he found it, making the compromises which, in view of obstinate facts, kindness and tolerance dictated.

Although he may have lacked intellectual curiosity and political astuteness, Lord Godolphin was certainly not "that cypher"[90] which the Earl of Chesterfield was pleased to call him. Congreve respected him enough to make him executor of the will in which he bequeathed to Henrietta the major part of his estate. Sarah, possibly to her own surprise, was unable to quarrel with so just a man and for many years found him indispensable as her business adviser. Letters to his daughter, Henrietta, Duchess of Newcastle, written over a period of nearly forty years, reveal his sweet temper, his satisfaction in country air, and his mild enjoyment (which he shared with his daughter) of poor health. His love for this child was the strongest passion of his life. For long years his first concern was her welfare; and the hardest trial of his philosophy was the last letter of valediction to "Ma tres Chere."[91]

Sarah's only permanent grievance against her son-in-law was that he could not compel his wife to love her mother. It was some comfort to her to recall that once, when she had asked him if he thought that she had been an ill mother, he replied "with His eyes full of tears that I had been the best in the world

in all Respects. And so we parted much to my Satisfaction." [92]
When she quarreled with her daughter, Lord Godolphin served
as mediator; but, as she confided to her grandson, he loved quiet
too much [93] to take the decisive stand which she recommended.
Although good-humored and tactful, the Earl of Godolphin did
not hesitate to speak his mind to his formidable mother-in-law
when he considered it necessary to do so. When Sarah, wishing to
offer a country house to Lord Blandford, sought to recover possession of the little lodge in Windsor Park which she had formerly
given to Henrietta, she asked Lord Godolphin to use his influence to prevent his wife from making some other disposal of
the property. Courteously but firmly he refused to interfere. In a
letter dated November 8, 1724, he explains:

That I have not comply'd with what y^r Grace thinks so reasonable
for you to require of me, I confess; but, that I have declin'd it (or
at least intended to do so), in the most inoffensive terms I could
think of, is as certain. Y^r Grace will take it for granted that the D^s
of Marlborough (my Wife) has a design to part with her interest in
the little lodge, and that it will be a prejudice to the second life upon
it, Mr Charles spencer, if She does so. To this I answer, I have no
such design my self, nor do I know, or believe, that she has; nor do
I think, if She had, I should very easily consent to it; yet at the same
time, if she hereafter should happen to be so inclin'd, I, as She is
my Wife, am not willing to put it absolutely out of my own power
to agree with her in such a disposition; especially since I have very
good reason to believe that, as long as the king lives, it would not
be any manner of prejudice to the interest of the second life now
upon it.[94]

During the years 1728 and 1729, Lord Godolphin wrote to
Sarah with equal candor regarding the conduct of his son, Lord
Blandford. While not condemning her lenient treatment of her
grandson, he sums up the situation with a quiet impartiality, the
justice of which Sarah could hardly have failed to perceive:

As I take it for granted that Ld Blandford is unalterably bent upon
his marriage, I the less wonder y^r Grace has had no answer to the
last letter you honour'd him with, because I take the arguments,
contain'd in it ag^t his design, to have been such as would puzzle

a wiser man than himself to refute. All I can say is, his best friends have done what they could to divert him from this weak, improper, ill-judg'd step: Since that can have no effect, (tis a coarse & vulgar proverb to make use of, but) as he has baked so he must brew.[95]

Her son-in-law's tendency to form independent judgments that conflicted with her own irritated Sarah, who reminded herself on the wrapper of one of his letters that she had labored "like a pack horse" in his interests. Ordinarily he ignored her strictures, which irritated her still more. He made no reply, for example, when Sarah, ungraciously generous, informed him (February 13, 1722) that she had decided to settle Marlborough House on Henrietta, despite her shameful conduct, since "it would do me no good when I was dead to have the reasons given why I passed by her in the settlement & it would be a prejudice to her."[96] On one occasion, the year after his wife's death, Lord Godolphin's patience failed him. In a letter of December 9, 1734, he writes:

Your Grace has been pleased to send me in a Servants hand a most severe, not to say cruel, recapitulation of the faults of every one of my family, whether living or dead. Many of them I had never before heard of, none of them had I been able to prevent, tho from the beginning I ever endeavour'd it all I could; and for such of them as can properly be call'd my own, Your Grace had, for a great while now past, given me all the reason in the world to hope & believe they had been both forgiven and forgot.

Yet Lord Godolphin was too amiable to cherish resentment and a few months later was offering to wait on her Grace, as usual, at her pleasure.[97]

In the Earl of Godolphin's letters to his daughter there are very few and very brief references to her mother. There was complete understanding between father and daughter, and both may have preferred to avoid a subject which had painful aspects. Lord Godolphin may have been saddened, as Sarah implies, by his wife's conduct. At any rate, he chose to be indulgent and discreet. He announces the birth, on November 23, 1723, of Lady Mary Godolphin. He writes on July 7, 1727: "In the last letter

I had from y^r Mama, My Dear child, she desir'd you would get her a black fan. If you send one to my house, I'll take care of conveying it to her." In letters written on the 22nd and 24th of October, 1733, he describes, with proper solicitude and with his usual concern for exactness in such matters, the details of Henrietta's last illness. There is nothing to indicate how the loss of his wife really affected him. What he felt for his daughter, however, as her mother lay dying, emerges in the tenderness of the phrase: "God send you a good night My Dear." [98]

There is no very impressive evidence to support Sarah's contention that Henrietta was a bad mother. The only one of Henrietta's children whose opinion of her can be ascertained from primary sources is her eldest son, Lord Blandford; and his judgment in this, as in every other respect, cannot be taken seriously. His tutor said that Lord Blandford's ill health was due to indulgence in bad liquors and regretted his lack of ambition, his superficial way of traveling, his aversion to letter writing, and "great laziness." [99] His marriage was a bitter pill for everyone. Three years before his early death, his reasonable father gave up trying to reason with him and admitted: "I have hardly courage enough to wish him in England." [100] The Duchess of Newcastle, usually charitable, called him "Ld Worthless." Writing on February 2, 1731, to her aunt, Mrs. Henry Godolphin, she describes a recent occasion when her brother dined at her house, confessing: "you may be Sure I satt in a good deal of pain till t'was over, nothing extraordinary happened, but a few of his agreable Laughs, which dispos'd me much more to cry, than to Join with him in his mirth." She also gives an account of a dinner at his own house, when he kept his guests waiting for him two hours, while he dined with Lady Meadows. When he finally appeared, his grandmother inquired if he had been at the House of Commons. On his answering in the negative, she observed: "I wish I was nearer to you, that I might beat you." "Then I am very glad you are not," he replied. In about an hour, he went to the theater, and merely looked in on the company for a moment, later in the evening, as they sat at quadrille. The day was spoiled for every one except Sarah.[101]

Among Sarah's papers is a copy of a letter which Lord Bland-ford wrote to his mother from Paris in July 1724. Being cordially disposed towards her at the time, he remarks: "I believe I shall stay somewhat longer than I thought, the Italian Singers being come, & they are all in raptures with your Grace's bounty to Bononcini, as a Lover of the art, I think my self obliged to return your Grace my Hearty thanks for this encouragement of Italian musick." [102]

It was Sarah who quickened the flame of whatever ill feeling arose between Lord Blandford and his mother. Without the knowledge of his parents, she paid bills which he could not meet. She persuaded his grandfather to make him a liberal settlement and points out the fact that "if it had not been for me, you must have depended upon your mother for every shilling, perhaps till you had been past the Enjoyment of a great Estate for she is not I think twenty years older than you are." Lord Blandford, readily adopting Sarah's point of view, concludes as to "A Certain Lady, that her exceeding anger at a settlement's being made by Any One besides Her self, upon her son, looks as if She had not design'd his revenue should be extraordinary, as farr at least as She could hinder it." By 1725 Sarah had won the unprofitable allegiance of a grandson who remained obdurate whenever she opposed his wishes. Writing to her from Paris on August 18, 1725, Lord Blandford reports: "Sr J. Evelyns Second Son Who is here & at present out wth My Mother, has giv'n Me such an account of things at home, that I've all the reason in ye world to think, if it had not been for this distribution of things I shou'd have been left in a very uncertain state as to my income." [103]

Lord Blandford knew very well that his grandmother would welcome any critical reflections that he might make against his mother. On October 5, 1725, he writes to Sarah: "Lord Walgrove who is likewise here upon a complement from the King, told me ye other day that before his leaving England, he had seen My Father, but not My Mother, so that I suppose He and She are out, at present." [104] Another time, rebelling against his father's charge of "Indecent Omissions toward my mother," he notes, with ironical emphasis, "how Good a Daughter she has made to you, A Wife to My Father, & a Mother to Me." In letters to her grandson, Sarah reflects that his mother "is in so ill hands that she finds new ways every day of surprizing the world with her behaviour or rage against me," and that "she could have found nobody of her side, but such low flatterers, as have been the occation of all her misfortunes." Writing at some length on March 27, 1730, Sarah dwells upon the ill usage which she had received from Henrietta. She begs Lord Blandford not to bury himself in Utrecht but to return home and go through the formality of trying to see his mother. It is probable that she will refuse an interview; "in that case your father can have nothing to take ill of you, for tis not possible to believe that my lord Godolphin with his sence, & good nature can refuse to see, & live well with his only son, because he has the misfortune of having a madd woman for his wife." In several letters Lord Blandford discusses these problems with his grandmother. Then, unwilling to be bothered any longer, he ends the controversy with the statement (April 4, 1730):

Madam, I fear, I did not sufficiently explain my self in my last wth regard to the Circumstance of seeing my Mother; which I have so determind a Resolution, *not to do,* that as My Father persists, y^t I should see Her, as the condition of my living well with him, I sh^d (notwithstanding the Honour I ever had for Him, think my self acquitted from the Obligation of seeing either of them.[105]

There are no references to her mother in the correspondence of Henrietta, Duchess of Newcastle. "Her Mother," Sarah maintained, "never lov'd Her when She was a child, never let Her eat with Her, but shut her up in a Garret" and "affected to go often abroad with Her," after her marriage, only "to make people think She was a good mother and that She would have been a good daughter, if it had not been my fault." [106] On her return from the Continent, Sarah adopted the little girl, gave her every advantage, and made it possible for her to marry, with a favorable settlement, the man whom she loved. But the Duchess of Newcastle sided with her mother [107] against her grandmother. Sarah objected that she was alone with her granddaughter only once after the latter's marriage, and that when the Duchess of Newcastle was ill and she made a journey of twenty-four miles to see her, she was denied that privilege.[108] When she called on her grandmother, the Duchess of Newcastle "sat in a dead way," answering only "yes" or "no," if questions were asked; "and if I met her elsewhere, she only curtsied and did not come near me." Whenever she called with her mother, "they sat and whisper'd to one another as if they had no other business there." [109]

The Duchess of Newcastle frankly describes her relations with her grandmother in the following letter to her aunt, written from Tunbridge Wells on August 19, 1730:

the D[s] of Marlborough keeps altogether in one Room upon the walks, where She plays at hazard from morning till night. which I avoid going into, So only meet her sometimes upon the walks by chance, as She is going along in her chair, for she can't walk, I always make her a curtesy which she returns with a Bow, I hear She Says I behave my Selfe much better, than that great Lady, the D[s] of Montague, for that I curtesy to her when I happen to meet her, & dont come close to her at other times, to shew all the world, I dont know her.[110]

In a letter to Sarah, Lord Blandford's tutor once ventured to observe:

But God bless the Gentleman, who had the good nature to labour a reconciliation between Your Grace and the D[ss] of N. and wish him as much success, as I did once to my self in the same affair, when I found her, as he has done, with an excellent understanding and most lovely temper, yet still strangely bound and captivated with an excess of filial aw and respect, which has hung upon her from her cradle like an enchantment.[111]

We infer that the attachment of the Duchess of Newcastle to her mother must have been more reasonable than prejudiced observers considered it. Henrietta must have had some qualities, which Sarah refused to acknowledge, which occasioned the loyalty of her eldest daughter. In her will (July 11, 1732) Henrietta bequeathed to the Duchess of Newcastle "my Yellow Brilliant Diamond Ring and Wm Congreves picture by Knellar." [112]

To her youngest daughter, Lady Mary Godolphin, Henrietta appears to have been a most indulgent mother. According to Margaret, Duchess of Portland: "She order'd that Lady Mary G. shoud never see the moon for if she wish'd to have it she coud not give it her." [113] In her will, [114] which is a significant companion piece to that of Congreve, Henrietta made the most careful provision for "my dearly beloved Daughter." She left to this child for her "sole seperate personal and peculiar use," her jewels, her plate and Congreve's, her Japan cabinets, etc., which she lists with obvious satisfaction, mentioning particularly "my fine Brilliant-Diamond Necklace which cost five thousand three hundred pounds and also the fine diamond Ear Rings with Diamond Drops to them which cost two thousand pounds." Her own fortune and "all Wm Congreve's Personal Estate" she assigned to Lady Mary, requesting that the Earl of Godolphin should use the income "to pay for all his and my said Daughters Cloaths Servants wages and whatever else is suitable for the Education of a person of her Quality untill She attains the Age of One and Twenty Years or marries." She directed that Lady Mary should "go and live with her Sister the Dutchess of Newcastle" and that Mary Ferland should "be always her Nursery Maid." In a codicil to this will (March 15, 1733), Henrietta provided very generously for Mary Spencer and proposed that she should remain with Lady Mary, even after the latter's marriage, "if she is well and pleases my daughter."

The recently published correspondence of Lord Hervey throws some light on Henrietta in the years that followed Congreve's death. On September 4, 1730, she received attentions from the Prince of Wales [115] at a Court party. Lord Hervey observed: "Every body was gay, easy, and seemed pleased; but particularly the P. and Duchess of M., who are so taken with one another, that I am not sure it will not end in a flirtation." Subsequently, Hervey supped and dined with the Prince at Henrietta's house. With Sarah Lord Hervey had one notably harsh encounter, when that "old Beldam of Bedlam" used him "like a dog" and proceeded to air her opinion of her daughter's character "till her nose worked, her cheeks flushed, and her whole fabric trembled." [116]

Henrietta's reaction to Lord Blandford's death in 1731 struck Hervey favorably:

she is neither so unaccountable, as [not] to feel any affliction, nor so ridiculous as to affect it. She very truly says that his behaviour towards her must justify her being at least indifferent to his death; and that anybody who had any regard to *Papa's* memory must be glad that the Duke of Marlborough was now not in danger of being represented in the next generation by one who must have brought any name he bore into contempt. The death of her son makes a very great change in her present circumstances, and a much greater still in what must devolve upon her at her mother's death: but to do her justice, I believe that consideration of interest affects her (though daughter to the Duke and Duchess of Marlborough) as little as it would anybody I know. [117]

On the other hand, Hervey was amused by Henrietta's taste for "squeezing out sentiments," [118] when her guests were men of literary pretensions. Lady Mary Godolphin, so often her mother's companion, was treated by Hervey with good-humored indulgence. On December 25, 1731, he wrote to Stephen Fox:

Lady Mary was talking so fast, so incessantly, and so loud, at my elbow the whole time that I was writing my last letter, that I shall not be at all surprised if you are not able to understand, when you read, what I did not understand as I wrote. [119]

Throughout the summer of 1733, Henrietta lay ill in Harrow of a fatal malady. Dr. Arbuthnot kept the Duchess of Newcastle informed as to her condition, for, to her regret, Henrietta could not write to her daughter "with her own hand." Lord Godolphin also sent reports of his wife's illness to the Duchess of Newcastle and supplied the detail: "Mary spencer sits behind y^r poor Mama in the bed night and day to support her and can therefore neither read nor answer your letters." Henrietta died on October 24 and was privately buried on November 9 in Westminster Abbey, in the grave of Sidney, first Earl of Godolphin. [120]

Such are the records, fragmentary enough, of the life of the younger Duchess of Marlborough. They assist in building up several family portraits, but contribute little, it must be confessed, to our knowledge of Congreve's mistress and the mother, we may suppose, of his child. Henrietta was separated from her own mother by prejudice, from her husband and eldest daughter by differences of taste; and her youngest daughter, for whose future she planned so affectionately, could have remembered her but vaguely.

Congreve, no doubt, knew her best. It is clear that Henrietta was flattered by the great dramatist's friendship, that he enlivened a milieu which her romantic temperament found tedious, and that she gave him readily the devotion which had been so jealously exacted by and consequently withheld from her mother. It is disappointing that Congreve left no comment on the personality of the Duchess. Her wealth and the comforts which she could give him must have nourished his aristocratic tastes. Her beauty must have charmed him. Volatile and pleasure-loving, she provided a relaxation from the sobriety of middle age which none of his bookish friends could offer. Nor is it unlikely that the creator of Lady Froth recognized in his younger companion shy graces which the unsympathetic and the indifferent could not discern.

Mary, Duchess of Leeds

On November 23, 1723, the Earl of Godolphin wrote to
his daughter, Henrietta, Duchess of Newcastle: "You
will, I dare say, my Dear Child, be glad to hear that y^r Mama is
very well, after having been brought to bed, about two hours ago,
of a little girl, who is likewise in a prosperous way."[1] The baby
was named Mary, possibly in memory of Congreve's mother.

The shadow which fell across the life of the younger Duchess
of Marlborough seems not to have touched Lady Mary Godolphin. The following anecdote, written down for Sir Walter
Scott by Lady Louisa Stuart, indicates very well Mary's igno-
rance, even after she had become Duchess of Leeds, of the gossip
which had preceded and followed her birth:

The Duchess of Portland[2] once borrowed [the Duchess of Leeds's]
jewels to wear at a masquerade, and as they were examining them
together, the other, taking up [her] massive necklace, asked her
whether she could guess why the letters W.C. were engraved upon the
back of every collet? "I have often puzzled myself to divine what
could be my mother's meaning in it," said she, "do you think it was
the name of the jeweller?" "Oh yes, it must have been so," replied
the Duchess of Portland, well knowing the cypher meant William
Congreve, and in a hurry to get rid of the subject.[3]

With one exception, no family letters have survived which
imply that the Earl of Godolphin may not have been Lady
Mary's father. Although he obviously found her less congenial
than the Duchess of Newcastle, he thought of her "perpetually

... with the most tender affection"; [4] and in his will he made equal provision for his two "Dearly beloved Daughters." [5]

During the Duchess of Marlborough's last illness, Lady Mary was in Harrow. On July 11, 1733, Henrietta's physician, Dr. Arbuthnot, wrote to the Duchess of Newcastle: "Lady Mary is very well, & the only pleasure we have in this place." [6] After her mother's death, the child was sent to London, "without the least suspicion," wrote Lord Godolphin, "of the cruell loss that has befall'n her." [7]

With uncommon vehemence, the Duke of Newcastle opposed the Duchess of Marlborough's wish and the entreaties of his wife that Lady Mary should live with her sister. In an undated letter he wrote to Lord Godolphin:

The D[s] of Newc[l] has this moment desired I would write to your lordship upon a subject y[t] has already given Me the greatest pain. She has acquainted me wth her Mother's desire y[t] Lady Mary might live wth her. There is nothing in this World y[t] I would not do to shew My Duty to y[r] lordship & My Affection & Tenderness to her but My Lord I know My Self & My own Manner of Life is such y[t] I apprehend if this was to happen, Uneasinesses Might arise, w[ch] by y[e] Blessing of God have now never happend for above sixteen years ... I hope you know me too well to imagine, any thing but a firm persuasion of unavoidable inconveniences could suffer me to give so much pain to One I do sincerely & tenderly love, or a trouble of this kind to Your Lordship. [8]

Replying to this letter, Lord Godolphin, also with a forcefulness not characteristic of him, begged the Duke of Newcastle "not to come to any such hasty, positive, & unalterable resolution," but to consider at his leisure "such arguments as may be offer'd on both sides o' the question, and see which of them have the most weight, before you determine absolutely not to comply with a request of this kind." [9]

The Duke of Newcastle remained firm in his decision. It is possible that he acted from the selfish but understandable motive of seeking not to interrupt the tranquil routine of a childless household. He was, however, fond of children. He carefully supervised the education of various young relatives and was never happier than when they spent their holidays at Claremont. It is possible that, cautious and timid by nature, and keenly ambitious regarding his political career, he sought to avoid the breath of scandal by not adopting a child who was believed to be Congreve's daughter. The fact remains that for the first and apparently only time in his life he refused a request from his wife, disappointing her in the desire which was closest to her heart.

Thus the responsibility of Lady Mary's education fell upon Lord Godolphin. In his first letters, after her mother's death, he refers to her always as "the poor Child." Soon she became for him and remained "Dear Minos," to (or by) whom he wished "never to be forgott." [10] He petted the little girl and worried over her delicate health. Following her mother's death, Lady Mary resumed her lessons on the harpsichord and in dancing and writing, but "since she likes French least," was "respited that till after her birthday." [11] Three years later, the Earl of Godolphin was pleased when her Italian master recovered from an illness, so that Lady Mary might have "an opportunity of improving her self in the Italian She seems so desirous to be perfect in." [12] Her high spirits, so like her mother's, constantly surprised the aging Lord Godolphin, who had never possessed any vivacity of temperament. On one occasion he left her ill in bed, very cheerfully "playing upon her spinette." [13] She was made happy by being permitted to see a play once a week, provided her sister could go to the theater with her.

The Duchess of Newcastle called on Lady Mary nearly every day when she was in town and took an active interest in her welfare. She preserved over two hundred childish letters in English and French which Lady Mary wrote to her between 1735 and 1737. The brief daily epistles were clearly a task. Once Lady Mary hopes that her sister will think that her writing is "pretty strait." She signs one letter "Mary Worker." She thanks *une si Tendre Soeur* for taking her to the opera or "treating" her with the jugglers; relates her progress through the sonatas of Corelli; and laboriously copies quatrains about betrayed maidens and faithless swains [14] and "the gloomy state of mortals here." [15]

At twelve she realizes that "every thing relating to me gives you either pain or Pleasure."[16]

In the spring of 1737, to her great satisfaction, a visit to Bath was prescribed for Lady Mary, who was suffering from a stomach disorder. Her sister accompanied her, and Lord Godolphin fretted in London over the absence of his "Bath-friends." Chaperoning a lively young companion must be an act of penance, he was sure, for the Duchess of Newcastle, and he warned Minos not to let her amusements make her inconsiderate of her sister. He reflected that "a little Rhubarb & Carduris . . . might have been had without the assistance of Mr Nash."[17]

A tribute to the beauty and charm of Lady Mary at the age of thirteen was paid by her very young cousin, Thomas Pelham.[18] Writing to the Duchess of Newcastle on May 7, 1737, he expressed the hope that Bath would agree with Lady Mary, adding: "I wish her health from the bottom of my heart; that being, in my opinion, the only thing She wants, that is worth her desiring."[19] A few months later, he wrote to his aunt from Bath on October 21, 1737: "I have been at the Dutchess of Leeds's, the Dutchess of Kents, where I cannot deny, that I saw Lady Sophia Grey; but wonder how You could suspect that either she, or any Person whatever could make me forget Lady Mary Godolphin."[20]

Her sister's future became a matter of grave concern to the Duchess of Newcastle. In September 1739, when the Duke's financial embarrassments made a retired life in Sussex seem almost unavoidable, she reminded her husband:

there is one thing . . . that Sitts heavy indeed upon me, which is, the Leaving my poor Sister at the time in her whole life, when I think she will want me the most. young, as She is, unexperienc'd Iust going to be her own Mistress, without any friend in the world to advise her upon any occasion, is, to me, a most dreadful thought. I had Figur'd out, too much happyness, in Seeing her, & contributing towards, making her Happy. God knows, how it may turn out now.[21]

Actually, things turned out very well. In February 1740 plans were being made for the marriage of Lady Mary, not yet seventeen, and Thomas Osborne, fourth Duke of Leeds. Ten years

older than Lady Mary, like her he was motherless, although
he had been tenderly nursed through an ailing childhood by two
successive stepmothers.[22] He had become Duke of Leeds in 1731;
had received his D.C.L. from Christ Church, Oxford; had made
the "grand tour" of Europe; and was hoping, in spite of indifferent health, for an honorable post in the King's service.

The wedding occurred on June 26 and was a grand affair.
Mrs. Elizabeth Montagu wrote to her mother: "The Duke of
Newcastle's entertainment upon the occasion was 15 dishes in a
course, 4 courses . . . The Duchess had a diamond necklace
from her Mother worth £10,000, she was very fine in cloaths
and jewels."[23]

It was a love match on both sides. In a letter of congratulation from his college friend, Lord Romney,[24] the Duke of Leeds
was informed: "if you are not happy I believe I shall forswear
marriage, for I cannot expect to be more happily matched; so
that not upon your own account only, am I constantly wishing
that you may every day discover new Beauties in the Dutchess."[25]

Her granddaughter's marriage was gratifying to Sarah,
Duchess of Marlborough. In November 1740 the Countess of
Hertford wrote to the Countess of Pomfret:

The dowager Duchess of Marlborough has prepared a set of diamond
buttons on black velvet arm-gloves, which cost a thousand guineas
for the Duchess of Leeds. She is at present so fond both of her and
the duke that she says if any thing could make her wish to live,
it would be the desire of being longer a spectator of two young persons
so different from all others of the age.[26]

The Duchess of Newcastle made the wedding journey with
the young couple to Kiveton,[27] the Duke of Leeds's country residence in Yorkshire, where she remained for some weeks. She sent
back to her husband and father accounts of guests at Kiveton:
Lady Kinnoull [28] and her daughters, Robert Hay-Drummond,[29]
and Lord Dupplin,[30] by whom she expected "to be talked, down
to the Stumps Sometimes." [31] Wearisome distances must be
covered to return visits—ten Yorkshire miles, at least, for a
"dining visit." She was bored by the lack of interest in politics and

complained: "nobody would think (by this place) that there was ever Such a thing as an Election for parliment men, I have never heard the least word of it mention'd, either for this County, or Nottinghamshire, tho there passes few days, that more, or fewer, of the neighboring gentlemen are not here." [32]

The Earl of Godolphin was pleased by the Duchess of Newcastle's report that her sister was "so happy & well pleas'd . . . especially as the case is the same on the Duke of Leeds's part." His pleasure would be still greater "if I could be sure she behav'd towards You particularly in the manner I'm sure you deserve from her." [33] "I hope time & more experience," he concluded, "may produce a proper change." [34]

The young Duchess was popular in Yorkshire. Mrs. Pendarves, writing to her sister, Mrs. Dewes, from Bulstrode on December 12, 1740, observed:

The Duchess of Leeds is very much commended, she has behaved herself with great civility and complaisance in the country amongst the Duke's friends and neighbors, and I hope she will appear as well in a crowd as she has done in the shade. Such examples are wanting, and if the Duchesses of Portland and Leeds with the charms of youth and every other attraction *cannot* bring *virtue into fashion,* I am afraid we must not expect to see her tread the stage in our days.[85]

The Duke and Duchess of Leeds spent the winter months in London, in the large house which the Duke had rented on the east side of St. James's Square. Her first London season following her marriage was a gay one for the Duchess. On January 3, 1741, Lord Godolphin wrote to the Duchess of Newcastle: "Y^r Sisters cloaths, I hear, were violently comended o' Thursday both at Court and, (to my great surprise) at M.[arlborough] house no less." [36] Two weeks later, he commented: "Your sister was perfectly well to-day, only a little accablèe with the prospect of being to do the honours to morrow to their Graces of Montagu, L^d & L^{dy} Cardigan & My Ld Lovell." [37]

In May the Duchess lost her first son at birth. She visited her sister at Claremont in October. In December she was ill in London. Lord Godolphin, who believed in coddling oneself,

MARY, DUCHESS OF LEEDS

FRANCIS GODOLPHIN OSBORNE, MARQUIS OF CARMARTHEN

lamented her love of a crowd and her carelessness about her health.[38]

Country air refreshed her. The Earl of Godolphin was relieved to note that her husband "seems very watchfull of her Dyet, & carefull of her observing her D^{rs} prescriptions."[39] Part of the next winter was spent at Kiveton, where, wrote the Duke of Leeds, "she bears the cold weather very well."[40]

In the summer of 1743 the Duchess of Newcastle visited her sister at North Mimms,[41] the Duke of Leeds's country house in Hertfordshire. Mary was only too eager to display the beauties of Mimms; and Lord Godolphin felt obliged to caution his eldest daughter: "pray, My Dear, don't let Her walk you to death."[42] That August the Duke of Leeds received a welcome gift (not the first) of three thousand pounds from the Dowager Duchess of Marlborough, which her granddaughter acknowledged with a formal but very civil letter of thanks.[43]

"Old Sarah" (as the Duke of Newcastle privately called her) continued to take an affectionate interest in this delightful and tractable grandchild. About a month before her death, she received a letter from her granddaughter thanking her for "the China you have sent me, which is charming."[44] In her will Sarah left to Mary her diamond solitaire and to the Duke of Leeds three thousand pounds and properties in Hertfordshire and Kent.[45]

Mary's second child, Lady Harriot, was born in November 1744 but lived only a few days. The infant was buried in Harthill, Yorkshire, on the 16th of November.

The Duchess made her will on July 24, 1747, not long before the birth of her third child. Repeating the language of her mother's will to the effect that she might have the disposal of all her jewels, "as fully as if I was sole and unmarried independent of my Husband," Mary bequeathed them to any child of hers who might be living at her death, or, if she should have no child then living, to her "Dear Husband." To Francis, Earl of Godolphin, she left Congreve's enameled portrait of her mother, "which is sett in a Gold Frame in the form of a Spread Eagle and has some hair under the chrystal in the back thereof."[46]

It was a great joy to both parents when their first surviving child, Thomas Osborne, Marquis of Carmarthen, was born on October 5, 1747. The proud father wrote to the child's godfather, the Duke of Newcastle: "I hope the little boy would send you his best Respects if he could speak." [47] The Princess of Wales honored the Duchess of Leeds with a royal visit of congratulation.

Unhappily, financial worries intruded. In June 1748 the Duke of Leeds sent a long letter to the Duke of Newcastle, imploring his assistance in obtaining a Government post:

my Dear Lord to confess the Truth times are very bad on the east side our Square, what with the Taxes, the low Price of Land and the high Interest of money, which has hindred my selling estates to pay off mortgages . . . at present both your little Friend (who is absolutely the best Creature that ever Lived) & myself have but very unpleasant Hours.[48]

The melancholy letter bore fruit, for, before the year was out, the Duke of Leeds had been appointed Lord of the Bedchamber to George II and Warden and Chief Justice in Eyre of the Forests south of the Trent; and the Duke of Newcastle was congratulating the Duchess of Leeds on the turn of events.

Mary spent a pleasant summer and autumn at North Mimms. She wrote jokingly to her sister about "my own *Perfections*" and confessed herself "an *inadvertent* Creature." [49] She worked with enthusiasm on a scarlet and white shell vase, played the harpsichord, and found riding double a good medicine. She reported to her sister: "The Child is pure well & says Mamma quite plain, kisses me violently at Night, at no other time without he is bid." [50] As the Earl of Godolphin had regretted, she had often been "too heedless" to write letters; but just now she was very happy, and she had much to say to her dear sister. Like her mother, she wrote hastily and impulsively, without much reflection. Her health improved, although Lord Godolphin remained anxious about it. During a visit at North Mimms, supersensitive in the matter of ailments, he detected that she had "a little headache" and seemed "a little feverish," [51] and had his physician, Dr. Monsey, prescribe for her.

The life of a town lady was still more to Mary's taste. She

"thinks nothing else is *Living*," [52] objected Lord Godolphin. In June 1749 the Duke of Leeds was made a Knight of the Garter. He bombarded the Duke of Newcastle pretty steadily with requests for any court posts that might be available. Delays and rebuffs discouraged him; and he ruffled the vanity of his patron by alluding to his "many disappointments."

On January 29, 1751, Mary gave birth to another son, Francis Godolphin Osborne. The following spring the little Marquis had an illness, which was diagnosed as a light case of smallpox. That summer Lord Godolphin and Dr. Monsey were guests at North Mimms, where they found the Duchess "extremely well," said Dr. Monsey, and with "a much more florid Countenance than her own milk maid." [53]

It was in the course of this visit that her Grace outwitted Dr. Monsey quite handsomely, as he afterwards admitted in an amusing epistle to the Duchess of Newcastle, who had been mystified by receiving an unfinished letter from him. Having been accused by his hostess of having become "an old, gross stupid fellow," without a single grain of humor, he came down to breakfast early the last morning, and "to retrieve my Character," wrote part of a letter, in which he made facetious remarks about a certain lady, her "cruel Indulgences" to her children, and other foibles. He took counsel with the Duke and pretended to mislay the letter, leaving it in the Duke's paper case, where the Duchess was sure to find it.

She did, but was too cunning to bite, & cried out. oh! says She Mr Monsey intended to forget this,—Her resolution after being diverted with the immense wit of it was to burn it, but her Grace thought better of it, tumbled it into her pocket, shamm'd my Hand upon the outside of it, & very graciously sent it [to] Hanover without taking the least notice of it to his Grace that She had done so, till a week after.—I presum'd her Grace had sent a key with it, but she assur'd me this Day she had not, so I find ye unlocking it was left to your Grace's own Art of Penetration, which I hope you have done favourably for me.—I own her Grace is fully reveng'd on me for my folly, I told her I was now in her Debt & so hoped to pay her soon. She said the sooner the better, and so matters stand between us. [54]

In August 1754 the Duchess of Newcastle received the following letter, written in a large, round hand, from the Marquis of Carmarthen, then six years old:

Dear Aunt

I hope you, the Duke of Newcastle, Mrs. Spence & the Egg-Tea are well.

 I am

 your affectionate Nephew

   Carmarthen [55]

The child's aunt was devoted to him. Two years later, after he had entered his father's old school, Westminster, she sent him frequent presents of strawberries. These gifts he acknowledged very prettily. "I enjoy a perfect state of Health," he assured her, "and like School better and better every day." [56]

In a more familiar vein the young Marquis wrote to his brother, Francis:

Dear Panky

I hope your Flea continues safe under lock and key; I have inclos'd a silver penny, which I desire you'd accept of, it being given me as a reward for getting Captain of my fform,

  I am your affectionate Brother

    Spansy [57]

A few months later, he wrote again:

Dear Panky

I desire your acceptance of the inclos'd, they being what I receiv'd as an Encouragement for my Holidays task being well done: pray my Duty to Papa and Mama, and tell them I am in great expectation of being in the first Form to-morrow.

  I am

  Dear Panky

  your affectionate Brother

    Carmarthen [58]

On the back of Tom's letters to Francis, the Duke of Leeds afterwards wrote: "Brothers."

Meanwhile, the Duke of Leeds continued to propose himself to the Duke of Newcastle for any vacant posts of which he heard and to feel dejected when the best plums fell to others. He was, however, made Cofferer of the Household in January 1756 and a Privy Councillor in March 1757.

In the summer of 1758 the Duchess of Leeds visited Claremont. Lord Godolphin confessed his misgivings to the Duchess of Newcastle and hoped that Lady Lincoln [59] would soon "take your youthfull sister off your hands; for I cannot help fearing that Her vivacity may have but ill agree'd with your weak nerves & Low spirits." [60] The next summer Lord Godolphin and the Duke and Duchess of Leeds with their "charming children" spent some time at Claremont, and the Duchess of Newcastle returned with them to Mimms.

By 1759 "the good Snow" had joined his elder brother at Westminster, or "Hell," as Tom preferred to designate their school. Among their school friends were the future philosopher, Jeremy Bentham, Lord Edward Bentinck, and Thomas Bagot.

Jeremy Bentham shared Tom's unflattering views of Westminster. In later life, he remembered the school as "a wretched place for instruction" [61] and censured the inefficiency of the masters. The boys had to learn by heart Archbishop Williams's *Comments on the Catechism*. "Tappy" Lloyd (son of a tapster) taught them prosody, "a miserable invention for consuming time." [62] The headmaster [63] was a formidable person:

Our great glory was Dr. Markham; he was a tall, portly man, and "high he held his head" . . . He had a large quantity of classical knowledge. His business was rather in courting the great than in attending to the school. He had a great deal of pomp, especially when he lifted his hand, waved it, and repeated Latin verses. If the boys performed their tasks well, it was well; if ill, it was none the less well. We stood prodigiously in awe of him; indeed he was an object of adoration.[64]

Bentham recalled that the Duke of Leeds came to the school "once or twice" to see his sons, and the Duchess "more frequently."

One day, as the Duchess of Leeds was traversing the playground where I was amusing myself with other boys—one little boy amongst

many great ones—the duchess called me to her, and said—"Little
Bentham! you know who I am." I had no notion she was a great
lady and answered—"No, madam, no! I have not that honour." I
found that some strange tale had been told of my precocity, and my
answer was thought very felicitous; and, not long afterwards, I was
invited to go home with her sons to the duke's . . . A short time
before dinner, I was summoned up stairs to the duke's apartment,
where was a physician,[65] to whom he said:

"This is Bentham—a little philosopher."

"A philosopher!" said the doctor. "Can you screw your head off
and on?"

"No, sir!" said I.

"Oh, then, you are no philosopher."

Earl Godolphin, I remember, came in . . . He was a thin, spindle-
shanked man; very old . . . Many times I dined there afterwards.[66]

During these school days Tom dispatched to his aunt letters
which were masterpieces of youthful ingenuity, proposing visits
to "Heaven" (Claremont). On October 9, 1760, he wrote:

Dear Aunt

I hope this will find you well in *Heaven* as it leaves us here in
Hell & as we are Devils I hope you will for once excuse the ill-
writing of my black Claws: Saturday the 18th being a whole Holiday
is very convenient for us to go to Heaven, & I hope will be convenient
for you also; if it luckily is I hope you will send me word before
hand; & I think if Convenient it will be the best way to send the
Post-Chaise & 4 horses on the Friday Evening, because it will hold
us three better than the Coach, & besides that is more expeditious;
it does not signifie one straw whether we lay in the same room that
we did before or no because we don't care where we lay so we have
but a bed, as we are never in our room but at night; Pray give my
Duty to Uncle, burn this as soon as you have read it; & believe me to
be Dear Aunt your affectionate

Beast.[67]

Tom's ambitious father longed to introduced him at Court. He
requested that the boy might be permitted to carry the King's
train at the coronation; and His Majesty graciously promised
that he "certainly would not forget my Son." [68]

The Duchess of Leeds's good friend, Lady Lincoln, died in

childbirth on July 31, 1760. Commenting on this sad event, Mrs. Elizabeth Montagu remarked: "I think Death seems of late to be grown an epicure, and to feed on pea-fowl and singing birds." [69] Fourteen years later, the Duke of Leeds reminded the Duchess of Newcastle of Lord John Clinton's "melancholy meeting with your Dear Sister soon after the Death of his poor Mother, at Claremont, which I dare say you remember, I am sure I shall never forget it." [70]

In March 1761 the Duke of Leeds had to relinquish to James Grenville his post of Cofferer and content himself with the post of Warden and Chief Justice in Eyre of the Forests north of the Trent. "To break the fall," said Horace Walpole, "the Duke is made Cabinet Counsellor." [71]

That summer brought to the Duke and Duchess of Leeds an overwhelming tragedy in the loss of their eldest son at the age of thirteen. Less than a month before his death, Tom paid another visit to Claremont, preceded by a merry letter from Westminster School:

Dear Aunt

I hope this will find the sweet Canary-Bird well, as it was when it went from me; Friday is a Vigil & therefore as school will be up early, the Coach or one of the Post-Chaises may be with us at 6 o Clock; Mr. Cooper thinks that will be the best time; I mean in the Evening; I wish You much Joy of the good hens, that is, that there is a Pound of cherries taken. If you can, pray give my Duty to Uncle who is (I dare Say) in a violent splutter for joy of the good hens and believe me to be, dear Aunt,

ever Your most Dutiful

Beast

P.S.
Brother desires his Duty to the *Duke of Newcastle.*[72]

On August 11 Tom lay desperately ill with smallpox at Westminster, and the Duchess of Newcastle was in an agony of apprehension. She wrote to her husband on August 12 that she would be thankful all her life to Sir Edward Willmott for staying in town "to attend this dear boy. few things can Lye heavyer upon my heart, than his danger." [73] Tom died on August 15 and was buried on the 23rd in the church of All Hallows in Harthill. Under his name, in the entry in the parish register, are the words: *praecipe lugubres cantus.* In a sympathetic letter of condolence, Juliana, Dowager Duchess of Leeds, wrote to her stepson that she hoped

you will both endeavour to summon all y^r resolution to bear up under so severe a Tryall. . . I have gone threw it, therefore know how to pitty you, remember you have still one Left, who will require your Care, & consideration. . . I have mett with the Greatest hardships of all kinds, God almighty has strengthen^d me to bear them, I Pray he may do so by you. . .
I beg no answer.[74]

A tribute was paid to Lord Carmarthen's scholarship and character in some elegiac verses written by a Cornish cousin, Thomas Lambe. The gifted lad is praised as one who

> at such an early age,
> Delightedst in the classick page.

"The pride of all our youth" now makes "the brightest cherub" in Heaven.[75]

A depression of spirits settled upon the Duchess of Leeds which scarcely lifted, except for fleeting moments. When her sister was with her at North Mimms the following August, she was cheerful enough to write to the Duke of Newcastle a coaxing letter, urging him to join them. She promises him, if he will come, his favorite dish of stewed eels and a new mattress for his bed. Her steward, "with great dignity & proper deliberation," [76] has inquired when the Duke may be expected to arrive, since directions must be given about the small beer. The Duke of Newcastle, who had a gloomy conviction that North Mimms was "low & damp," [77] seems not to have been tempted. For the Duchess he had a genuine affection, and he nearly always referred to her in his letters as "my little friend."

In the spring and summer of 1763, Mary sent frequent letters to her sister, chiefly to beg for visits. On May 6 she wrote: "Panky is, thank God, a very good Boy, in all respects, & look'd so like his poor Brother this morning, as made me burst into

Tears; he was dress'd in a new Frock, & his waist was very long." [78] Later in the month, apropos of the death of Dr. Fanshaw, she confided:

you may guess, what a total alteration my misfortune has made in my Nature; poor Dr Fanshaw's Memory, I shall ever revere, as long as I live; two years ago, I should have been truely afflicted at his death, & should not have got over it for some time; but if you will believe me, I was not *at all* affected with his death *now,* just had the Tears in my eyes, did not fairly shed one, & was just as if I had never known him to say the Truth I don't believe I've shed a single Tear, since my misfortune but what has been for *that,* or *relative* to it. I don't think it *right* or *kind* to dwell upon this subject to you . . . tho' I'm inscensible to things, that I was not some time ago, I feel disapointments as much as ever, & have set my heart upon seeing you here at B.[artholomew] Tide & you seem to hope only a^{bt} it; for indeed as I told you before 'tis the most comfortable part of my Life & what I look forward to with the greatest pleasure.[79]

Knowing how much her sadness grieved her sister, Mary tried to be cheerful. "As I made my dear sister cry wth my last Letter, 'tis but fit I should make her laugh with this," she promised.[80] Then a wave of dejection swept over her once more.

Panky fell ill at school, was anxiously nursed in the house in St. James's Square, and was taken to the country to recuperate. His mother wrote from Mimms on July 26:

here we arriv'd safe & sound yesterday, at one o'clock, or a little after. Panky, quite fresh, & not the least fatigued with his journey. . . I was so much so, that I burst into Tears, after dinner, being quite spent & worn out, but am quite well to-day. I believe 'twas oweing, to having cry'd so very little before; & after such a flurry is over & one's spirits come to subside, one feels the effect of it. . . 'tis such dreadful Weather, this evening, one can't set one's foot out of Doors.[81]

Mary fell ill herself of a rheumatic fever, from which she recovered very slowly. A letter from the Duchess of Newcastle, announcing her approaching visit, was "really a Cordial" to "y^r *expecting* & *desiring* Sister." [82]

With this visit only a week away, Mary's spirits soared, and she wrote with a touch of her old vivacity: "you know, we can never want conversation, for you know, there's poor Mrs Elliot, M^r —— &.&.&.&.&. wch to be sure as you settled it, will last us our lives, be they never so long. I've not felt so heart-happy a long while, as I do this morning."[83] And she signed the letter, in a burst of gaiety:

M Leeds, Carmarthen
Danby, Latimore, Dumblein Osborne.

A "cholicky complaint" kept the Duchess of Newcastle at home until, in her husband's opinion, the season was too far advanced for her to pay a country visit. Quite unreconciled, Mary wrote reproachfully on November 9:

Dear Sister.
I've often heard, that nothing is sure, but Death; & do now verily believe that 'tis the only thing certain, for I had not only depended my self upon seeing you *here* this year, but flew in a Passion wth any body, that doubted it. the first passion of *crying* I've had, for above these two years (but upon *one subject*) was upon thinking I should *not* see you here, before I went to Town; & a very violent one it was, I assure you. as to *somebody's* being *afraid* of your coming here, so late in the year, I can easily believe; but as to their hindering your doing any thing you had in *the least degree* set y^r heart upon, is not in their nature; & that I know, & have known, ever since I knew any thing of them. so that I am not to be impos'd upon wth that; & will still (however vainly) flatter my self wth the hopes of seeing you, before I go to Town (the middle of Ianuary). . . I've a thousand things to say to you, & never injoy you so much as here (not even in y^r dressing room when we're not interrupted, for ages by Ly. Betty Germain,[84] or any body.) I remember the same Person (who has been so *dreadfully* successful, against y^r coming *here*) begging you very earnestly not to go to see the fire-works in the Green-Park; but you snap'd him up, & *went*. . . miserable as I am, all the harm I wish you, is that you may never have any *distress,* but what will be in y^r Power, to remove as easily as this. . . do write a comfortable Letter to y^r disapointed Sister.[85]

In an affectionate and more resigned mood, Mary wrote again, on November 24:

I'm vastly sorry, my dear Sister was so much griev'd; at any expressions in my Letter. I was so sincerely disapointed at not seeing you, when I so fully expected it, that I could not help expressing my self, as I did. I don't blame you, for not coming here, after what pass'd between you & Papa about it. I was very sorry to find Papa, had been represented so well to you; as I found by his Letters, & by those that had seen him, that his Spirits were very bad, & consequently we both dreaded your finding him, as I'm afraid you did. pray write me a *kind Letter* for I do think you owe it to

yʳ cruel Sister.

M Leeds.

you did say (*tho' kind*) & so I am.[86]

No letters of a later date by the Duchess of Leeds have been preserved. At the age of forty, she died suddenly at North Mimms on August 3, 1764. When the bitter news reached Claremont the next day, Horace Walpole was dining there for the first and only time in his life and reported:

I had been half round the garden with the Duke [of Newcastle] in his one-horse chair; we were passing to the other side of the house, when George Onslow met us, arrived on purpose to advertise the Duke of the sudden death of the Duchess of Leeds, who expired yesterday at dinner in a moment: he called it apoplectic; but as the Bishop of Oxford [Hume],[87] who is at Claremont, concluded, it was the gout flown up into the head. The Duke received the news as men do at seventy-one: but the terrible part was to break it to the Duchess [her sister], who is ill. . . It is a heavy stroke too for her father, poor old Lord Godolphin, who is eighty-six.[88]

The Duke of Leeds survived his Duchess by a quarter of a century. His favorite residence continued to be North Mimms, "this Dear old Seat of Tranquility"; [89] but he also made annual pilgrimages to Tunbridge Wells and to Bath, "according to custom." [90] He corresponded regularly with the Duke and Duchess of Newcastle and with his old friend, Dr. Monsey. He was grateful to the Duchess of Newcastle for her kind expressions "regarding my shattered frame," [91] and his attitude towards her was always sympathetic. In February 1765 he sent her a reddish gold lock of Panky's hair.[92]

He encouraged Panky to write a letter in Latin to Dr. Monsey, which the boy signed: *Maridunum*.[93] His ill health was a recurrent topic in his letters to the old doctor, whom he reminded:

tis true you are nineteen years older than me, but our good old Friend the late Ld Godolphin often said in my hearing, that his Hand shook by the Time he was forty years of age, & that was much younger than I am, but years are not what Break me down, it is having been a thorough Invalid Thirty years, & having suffered severe Shocks of mind in that Time. . .[94]

Francis Osborne, Marquis of Carmarthen, considered his father "the most affectionate of Parents & the best of friends." [95] With a number of kindred spirits, father and son enjoyed membership in the Plushing Society, of which the Duke was vicepresident and the Marquis secretary. When the Marquis and his young companions were with him, his father told the Duchess of Newcastle, "we have laugh'd most Hours of the day." [96] He assured her: "he is very good to me, & Dear you know he must ever be." [97]

The Duke was much pleased by his son's marriage in 1773 to Lady Amelia D'Arcy, daughter of Robert, fourth Earl of Holdernesse. His daughter-in-law charmed him; and he rejoiced when "my dear children" decided to "eat their michaelmas goose with me at Mims." [98] He wrote to the Duchess of Newcastle:

it is Inconcievable to me how I can possibly feel my Affection still increasing for them, considering how much I have always loved, but my Dear Madam my Sons Behaviour to me *is* & *has* been for many months, what it was *not*, but what I have ever wish'd it to be, this is the Greatest Blessing I can have upon Earth, in short he is a new Man since his Marriage with that Excellent Girl,[99] she has made him appear what I believe he ever has been, by inducing him to show his real self, which till now, he has from shyness, or God knows what, concealed.[100]

On the occasion when he saw for the first time "the little Sweet Boy," his grandson, the kindness of his son gave him "Happyness

not to be Described, in short he is the Greatest of Blessings &
Comforts to me his Poor old adoring Father." [101]

When the Duke of Leeds died in March 1789, Lord Carmarthen succeeded to the title. He was a handsome man, popular
in society. His political career, while not brilliant, was successful,
his principal post being that of Secretary of State for Foreign
Affairs, an office which he held for nearly eight years. Like his
father, he had scholarly tastes; and he was the author of two
unpublished comedies of no very great merit.[102] He died in
January 1799 at the age of forty-eight.

Thomas Osborne, had he lived to maturity, would probably
have outshone his younger brother. Thus, perhaps, reflected the
Duchess of Newcastle, who in one of her letters had sent "my
best love to dear Ld Carmarthen, and my next best to L^d
Franciss." [103] Before his early death, Mary's eldest son had
already displayed a keenness of mind, sweetness of temper, and
gifts of humor and perception such as, one fancies, distinguished
Congreve's boyhood, of which so little is known.

Dr. Messenger Monsey

*E*nter Dr. Monsey, and he sends his compliments to you." So wrote Catherine Talbot to her friend, Elizabeth Carter, in a mood of gentle expectancy. For wherever Dr. Monsey entered, the unpredictable happened. The ordinary tedium of life was lifted, and the lively wit and nonsense of this minor Swift delighted all observers. Even the doctor's unorthodoxy failed to alienate Miss Talbot, herself "a perfect pattern of evangelical goodness." She was flattered by his gallantry and would have been pleased had it been more marked and persistent. What might have given offense in others, she found "in *him* . . . very right and rational." [1]

Dr. Johnson, whom in some ways he resembled, dismissed Monsey as "a fellow who swore and talked bawdy." [2] Elizabeth Carter believed that he was only "an excellent harlequin" and objected to his "long succession of tricks." [3] But on the whole, even the most polite circles accepted the "unpossible Doctor" [4] with wonder and without reservations. His uniqueness was prized. Mrs. Elizabeth Montagu regaled Mrs. Vesey with an account of his extraordinary appearance at the Prince of Brunswick's wedding: "Of all the figures in the drawing room . . . the most conspicuous was our friend Monsey; he was unhouzel'd, disappointed, unaneal'd, he look'd like a felo de se corpse in the Highway; there was a dispute whether he got his wig off a gibbet or took it from a cherry tree." [5]

A friend once discovered on the doctor's table at Chelsea Royal Hospital an odd assortment of such miscellaneous objects as a basin of dirty water, an old wig half full of macaroons, dirty linen stockings, a pair of old leather slippers, and a half-eaten plum cake.[6] Monsey seldom washed his hands; and, if one may rely on Mrs. Montagu, "never had his face known the touch of water"[7] from his baptism until the day when he washed it, at the age of seventy-four, in honor of a visit from the King of Denmark.

Such idiosyncrasies did not dismay the doctor's contemporaries. He attracted high and low; the fastidious and the indecorous; the pious and the irreverent; the gay and the grave; the witty and those who loved wit in others. "No power of face" could resist his sarcasm.[8] The Dowager Viscountess Townshend much admired him and was said to have resembled him in conversation, "as far as was compatible with being a well-bred woman."[9] From Tunbridge Wells Mrs. Montagu wrote to Lord Lyttelton[10] in August 1760: "The great Monsey came hither on Friday and stays till Thursday. He is an excellent piece of Tunbridge ware. He is great in the coffee-house, great in the rooms, and great on the pantiles. Bucks, divines, misses, and virtuosi, are all equally agreeable to him." On another occasion she declared: "I am very happy in having Dr. Monsey with us; he is in fine spirits and amazes my country neighbors with his wit; I see that the most stupid of them are in doubt, whether he makes them laugh by being more witty or more foolish than they."[11]

Dr. Monsey was a north Norfolk man, whose family was descended from the Norman house of De Monceaux. He scoffed at family pride and remarked with satisfaction that the first of his ancestors "of *any* note" was a baker and a dealer in hops, who supported his large family with difficulty. Once, when he needed a sum of money, the hop dealer removed and sold the feathers of his feather beds, filling them with unsaleable hops. In a few years, when a blight had made hops scarce and expensive, he ripped open his beds, sold the contents at a good price, "and thus our family *hopp'd* from obscurity."[12]

The doctor was the grandson of Thomas Monsey of Hackford, Norfolk, and Elizabeth Barber, granddaughter of Augustine Messenger.[13] Elizabeth's uncle, Augustine, dying unmarried in 1680, left Whitwell Manor and Ross' Manor to her son, Robert (1656–1737).[14] Robert's second wife was Mary, daughter of Roger Clopton, rector of Downham in the Isle of Ely, by whom he had a large family of sons and daughters. Messenger, the eldest son, was born at Whitwell Manor in Whitwell, Norfolk, and baptized on October 30, 1694, in Whitwell Church in Reepham. He told the Duke of Leeds that he was born on the same day (September 22), as well as in the same year, as the Earl of Chesterfield. To Mrs. Elizabeth Montagu, whose birthday fell on October 2, he sent birthday letters for many years, giving her the impression that his own birthday was on the same day. Messenger's mother lived to be eighty-six. His brother Thomas died in 1720, his brother Clopton in 1762.[15]

In 1683 Robert Monsey became rector of the parish church of the small village of Bawdeswell, near Whitwell. Following the Revolution of 1688, he lost his living by refusing to take the oath of allegiance to William and Mary; but as a man of property, he was able to live comfortably in retirement. He had literary tastes and wrote verses, which he circulated among his friends. He was an eccentric man, if one may judge by his will, with its lengthy preamble in Latin and curious provisions to prevent his wife and his housekeeper from making illegal claims upon his estate. No doubt, there was a spiritual kinship between him and his eldest son, whom he made sole executor of his will and to whom he left his Whitwell property, his books, and his papers.

From his father Messenger received the foundation of a good classical education. He was one of a group of six Norfolk boys who, in 1709, entered the Grammar School of Woodbridge, Suffolk, where he remained for two years.[16] He was admitted as a sizar at Pembroke College, Cambridge, his father's college, on May 23, 1711, and received his B.A. degree there in 1714–15. His favorite classical authors were Horace and Juvenal. Among modern writers Swift and Pope pleased him most; he knew Swift by heart and had a high opinion of Pope, especially of his "Essay on Criticism."

After leaving Cambridge, Monsey studied medicine for some time in Norwich, under Sir Benjamin Wrench, who for over fifty years was a distinguished physician of that city. Monsey always regarded his old "blooding master" as one of the wisest and most amiable of men and one of the ablest of physicians. In later life, he kept a portrait of Sir Benjamin in his drawing room in Chelsea Hospital and often looked at it with great reverence.[17] On September 23, 1723, he was admitted extra licentiate of the College of Physicians, after being examined by Sir Hans Sloane.[18]

Medicine was but one of Monsey's many interests. He was a capable doctor, careful and accurate in diagnosis, addicted to such old-fashioned medicine as contrayerva and ptisan, but acquainted with modern theories. Common sense was very likely a strong ingredient in his successful career. The physicians' motto, said Monsey, should be: "Thou, Nature, art my Goddess." He wrote no medical treatises. He won fame, however, with his Rheumatic Powder, the recipe for which he bequeathed to his family and which was publicly sold. His device for drawing teeth was original, appealing only to himself. He fastened one end of a piece of catgut around the tooth to be extracted and the other end to a perforated bullet. A pistol was charged with the bullet, the trigger touched, and the operation concluded in an instant. His patients had to bear with his blunt manner and caustic wit. A squeamish man once said to him: "We are afraid of you, Doctor; you come from a sick room." "You often make me sick," replied Monsey, "but never afraid."[19]

Alone among his biographers, John Taylor claims that at one time Monsey had "an extensive practice" in Swaffham.[20] According to the parish register of St. Mary's in East Carleton, near Norwich, Monsey was "of Walton" at the date of his marriage; and he may have had a practice there. On September 21, 1725, he married in East Carleton Mrs. Ann Dawnay (or Dawney) "of Norwich,"[21] a widow with "a handsome jointure."[22] She died, leaving him an only daughter, Charlotte, to whom he was deeply devoted.

It is not known at what date Monsey settled in the "bright little town" of Bury. He practised in Bury for some years and, but for a strange coincidence, might have ended his days there in relative obscurity. "With a rusty wig, dirty boots, and leather breeches, he here might have degenerated into the hum-drum Country Doctor, with the common-place questions by rote, the tongue, the pulse, and the guinea; his merits not diffused beyond a country chronicle, and his fame confined to a country church yard." [23]

The accident that completely altered his fortunes and translated him to a milieu of wealth and fashion was a sudden illness of Francis, second Earl of Godolphin, who in October 1736, when on his way to his country seat in Gogmagog, was seized with a stroke of apoplexy in Newmarket. Dr. Monsey was hastily summoned and saved the Earl's life. As soon as he was able to take pen in hand, Lord Godolphin wrote from Newmarket to Henrietta, Duchess of Newcastle: "here is, no farther off than at Bury, a very able & skillful Surgeon, & very capable of performing operations." [24]

Throughout the following November, Dr. Monsey sent frequent letters to the Duchess of Newcastle, describing her father's illness and assuring her of his gradual recovery. Monsey wrote to Sir Benjamin Wrench for advice, not caring to have the life of "so valuable a man" under his sole direction. As Sir Benjamin suggested, appropriate remedies were tried: several bleedings, a vomit, a glyster, a blistering plaster, doses of hiera picra, and "two Fontanells" between the shoulders which were opened with caustics. [25]

As his patient began to mend, Monsey's spirits mounted. Lord Godolphin lost his daytime drowsiness, and the doctor hoped that he would be "no more a companion for Bats & Dormice." [26] Monsey wrote to the Duchess:

We have taken great care not to Spoil my L^d's Bowling and I hope one day or other to see him at Maribone with his bowls running close to ye Jack and all his Sorrows left a mile behind him . . . you will have great joy in ye recovery of a father and I shall rival you in that for a Patient. We Physicians are suppos'd to have little Religion, and so the Divines I fear will allow but little Efficacy in our Prayers, but if hearty and Sincere ones can avail any thing from me, my Lord Godolphin must do well, and if mine don't, sure the Prayers of Thousands will.[27]

In another letter Monsey observed: "I hope for your Grace's satisfaction we have now so repair'd my Lord that he is just setting out for another half Century or to give him a much longer time till all his Friends are tir'd of him." [28] The doctor reflected: "I don't know how it is but the small acquaintance I have had with my Lord has given me a strong attachment to him & his Welfare tho' indeed were it not so, I must be very singular since all yᵉ World that knows him and almost that which does not esteem and adore him." [29]

On November 30 Monsey thus ended the correspondence:

Had I the genius of a Voiture or a Pope I shou'd strive to continue my self in the agreeable scituation I am in. and even without this happiness I believe the account of my Lords progress toward health from my dull pen gives you more Joy than their most lively wit & turns upon indifferent matters.—but my Lord I hope will shortly show his Building amended, & then I must be contented to have my Self & Letters thrown by as all other scaffolding usually is.[30]

In July 1738 Lord Godolphin fell ill again. Monsey, considerably perturbed, wrote from Bury to the Duchess of Newcastle:

His goodness to me makes me look upon him almost in the same degree of relation with yʳ Grace.—I am sure if he was my Father I cou'd not feel more anxiety for him than I do.—and I wish to God I was at Liberty to see him, if I cou'd justify it to my Friends here no consideration upon Earth shou'd keep me from him in order to pacify my own mind, and if I were wanted & cou'd do him the minutest Service even that shou'd not restrain me, for he deserves from me as much as all Mankind . . . you are a great Woman but then you are a good & humane one, which makes me hope you will favour me with a line containing yʳ own Sentiments of my Lord.

The Duchess might guess, Monsey added, his feelings by her own and then "be angry if you can." [31]

Lord Godolphin was similarly attracted to Dr. Monsey. By 1740 he had persuaded Monsey to leave Bury and become his resident physician, living in comfortable apartments in his London house in Stable Yard, St. James's. Monsey watched over his elderly patient attentively. Whenever the Earl became ill, he took prompt measures to restore his health and wrote detailed accounts of his symptoms and convalescence to the Duchess of Newcastle, endeavoring to quiet her fears. When Lord Godolphin moved his chair hastily and thought his hold not quite so firm, Monsey saw to it that he was bled immediately. For a slight indisposition the doctor prescribed two teaspoonfuls of hiera picra, and rejoiced when his patient slept "as if he had taken Laudanum instead of Hiera picra." [32]

Lord Godolphin regarded Monsey more as a friend than as a physician. He admired his frankness, his literary talents, and his wit, and often said that he was "the solace and comfort of his life." [33] Through his influence Monsey was appointed Physician to Chelsea Royal Hospital in June 1742, with the understanding that he should not be required to reside there but should visit the Hospital when his services were needed. Monsey was frequently the Earl's traveling companion. It may be assumed that they spent many an evening at backgammon, which was the favorite game of both.

Being the least exacting of men, Lord Godolphin did not expect to absorb an unreasonable amount of Monsey's time and attention, and the doctor had ample leisure to busy himself "about his own inventions." [34] Monsey became the esteemed physician of various Whig statesmen and socially prominent persons to whom his patron introduced him. He allowed himself many "rambles" into Norfolk or elsewhere to visit friends. Sometimes his absences were prolonged; and Lord Godolphin never knew when to expect his return.

In some of the many amusing anecdotes which have been related of Monsey, Lord Godolphin figures in a quiet role. His Lordship, who preferred a retired way of life, enjoyed dining alone with Monsey at the Thatched House in St. James's Street. On one of these occasions, Monsey left him there over a newspaper, sauntered up the street, and met old Lord Townshend, who inquired where the Earl was and announced that he would dine with him. Monsey regretted the accident, but Lord Townshend was a determined man. Bursting in upon Lord Godolphin, Lord Townshend exclaimed: "Now, my Lord, I know you don't like this intrusion." "Why, my Lord, to say the truth, I really do not," said Lord Godolphin mildly, "because I have only ordered a dinner for Monsey and myself, and have nothing fit for your Lordship unless you will wait." "No, no," replied Lord Townshend, "anything will do for me"; and he sat down and indulged in "noisy gaiety." Presently he inquired: "My Lord, does Monsey flatter you?" "I hope not," said the Earl. Monsey at once demurred: "I never practised flattery, because I think none but a knave could give it, and none but a fool receive it." "That may be," said Lord Townshend, "but by G—— we all like it!" "I wish I had known your lordship's opinion," said Monsey, "before I had made my foolish speech." [35]

When Monsey's odd conduct led him into difficulties, Lord Godolphin was prepared to straighten out the tangle. The doctor, having lost a good deal of money in unwise investments, on the eve of a Norfolk holiday decided to leave a large number of bank notes buried in the ashes in a corner of the Bath stove in his sitting room. A month later, he came home to find that his housekeeper had just lit a fire in this room and was treating some friends to a cup of tea. He ran madly across the room and proceeded to pour the contents of the teapot and a pail of water from the pump over the fire and over "the retreating company." The half-drowned housekeeper exclaimed: "For God's sake sir, forbear; you will spoil the steel stove and fire-irons." "Damn the stove, irons, you, your company and all!" replied the doctor; "you have ruined and undone me for ever: you have burned my bank notes." He pulled out the coals and cinders and the remains of his notes, which had been wrapped in brown paper and twice folded and were still legible.

When informed of the mishap, Lord Godolphin, after a hearty laugh, offered to go to the bank with Monsey the following day and get the money for the damaged notes. He could not refrain from telling the story to the King, who came to the Earl's house the next morning and concealed himself in a closet in order to hear Monsey repeat the tale. The second version was so diverting that the King, trying to suppress his laughter, stumbled, and the closet door opened. "God," cried Monsey, adding hastily, as he saw the King emerge, "bless your Majesty! this may be a joke with you and his lordship, but to me a loss of near 400 *l.*"

It was arranged that Monsey should meet Lord Godolphin at the bank. The doctor went down the river by boat, and on the way pulled out his pocketbook to have a look at the notes, at which moment a sudden whiff of wind blew them into the river. "With a volley of oaths" he bade the boatmen turn back and managed to fetch them up in his hat, with half a hatful of water. He insisted on being put ashore at once and walked to the bank.

Carrying his dripping hat, Monsey was shown into the room where the directors of the bank were assembled. "What have you under your arm?" said Lord Godolphin. "The damned notes," replied Monsey, throwing the hat and its contents in the midst of the books and papers on the table "so forcibly that the water flew in the faces" of his auditors. "There, take the remains of your damned notes, for neither fire nor water will consume them." There was an interval of general amusement over Monsey's predicament. Then an order was made out for the full amount of the notes.

When Monsey went out to Lord Godolphin's carriage, the boatmen were clamoring for their fare. They laid hands on the doctor. Forgetting that he had not paid them, he knocked one of them down with his cane. Realizing the situation, Lord Godolphin gave the men half a crown for their fare and a crown for the mistake.[36]

The Earl of Godolphin's family and closest friends made much of Dr. Monsey. He was always a most welcome guest at Claremont, at North Mimms, and at Wotton. He corresponded with the Duke and Duchess of Newcastle and with the Duke and Duchess of Leeds. Although he did not presume to write to the Duchess of Newcastle, except during her father's illnesses, it is evident that she would have been glad to receive more of his spirited letters, so unlike the pedestrian, though affectionate, ones of her other correspondents. Her sister, of whom Monsey was certainly fond, was better qualified to appreciate his gaiety.

The Duke of Leeds regarded the doctor as one of his best friends. To him was dedicated the biographical sketch of Monsey published the year after the doctor's death. A modest but thoughtful man, the Duke of Leeds seems to have understood very well his friend's unusual qualities, making ample allowance for their defects. Regretting his own limitations, he confessed: "I wish I could write anything entertaining, but you know that was never my gift." He exerted himself to obey "your Princely Commands," conceding: "I am, I can't tell why, Dear Sr Your Sincere Friend." "Your nonsense," he assured the doctor, "is always agreeable to me." He delivered one of Monsey's love letters to Mrs. Montagu "without reading it," and at all times showed a solicitous interest in Monsey's health, his family, and his affairs. In the last of his letters to Monsey, of those which have been preserved, dated October 16, 1778, the Duke expresses the hope of seeing Monsey in town in about ten days and "having a Laugh with you as usual." He concludes:

in the mean Time I wish you well. I am, Dear Doctor,
> Your
>> Olde Friend &
>> Humble Servant
>>> Leeds.[37]

Monsey was the friend and physician of Sir Robert Walpole and the Earl of Chesterfield. Sir Robert often played billiards with his "Norfolk Doctor," who was a better player. "How happens it," said Sir Robert, "that nobody will beat me at billiards or contradict me but Dr. Monsey?" "They get places," said Monsey. "I get a dinner and praise." [38]

Chesterfield was grateful for Monsey's "voluntary and unwearied attentions" in regard to his deafness. He took Monsey's powders and recommended them to his son, and felt that the doctor's "little blisters" gave him "more relief than anything else." He believed that Monsey could do for him "more than other people; but then give me leave to add that I fear that *more* is not a great deal." When they were both seventy-three, he teased Monsey for pretending to be a year younger. For his own part, he bore with resignation the "gradual depredations upon myself . . . and so good night, dear Doctor." [39]

Monsey's courtship of Mrs. Montagu brought him in contact with members of her circle. He enjoyed the bountiful hospitality of Lord Lyttelton at Hagley. His relations were somewhat less cordial with Lord Bath,[40] his favored rival in love. Lord Bath was over seventy-five and Monsey only ten years younger, when they paid mutual homage to Mrs. Montagu, who was nearing forty. They were in agreement, at least, on the lady's charms. Dr. Monsey wrote to Lord Lyttelton of the warmth with which Lord Bath talked to him of Mrs. Montagu:

"She is the most extraordinary woman in the world" with a nod of the head and a grave face, "she beats a french Duchess with an hard name all to pieces, upon my word, Doctor, she is—" "Ay, so she is my Lord, but neither I nor you know what." "Suppose we say angel." "No," says I, "Devil, for she leads us all into temptation." [41]

The following passage from one of his letters to Monsey indicates Lord Bath's slightly patronizing view of his rival:

All I fear, Dr Doctor, is, that when this correspondence of hers with you comes to be printed, unless some friend who knew you both was to write explanatory Notes on the letters, she would be blamed by the Prudes of Posterity, for having been too forward in the tenderness of her expressions towards you, and you might be blamed by the future fraternity of Physick for writing too much Nonsense, to prove the Sincerity of your Passion. But believe me Dr Doctor a Man must have a great deal of good Sense, that is able to write pretty Nonsense.[42]

It was out of curiosity that David Garrick sought the acquaintance of Monsey. The famous actor often went to the court at the Old Bailey to study the facial expressions of the prisoners. On one of these occasions, he heard a gentleman ask a man who stood in front of him to move aside so that he might see the bench. To this and to a second request, the man, who was "a stout fellow," paid no attention. In a louder tone, the gentleman said: "If I were not a coward I would give you a blow even in the court." Garrick longed to meet this odd stranger, found out that he was Dr. Monsey, and managed to get introduced to him.[43]

For many years Monsey spent much time in the company of Garrick and his "sweet wife." [44] Both men relished practical jokes, which were often at the doctor's expense. One afternoon, when Garrick should have been dressing at the theater to play King Lear, Monsey found him in bed, wearing a nightcap, with the quilt drawn over him. Garrick explained that since he was too ill to act, an actor named Dagger Marr was to take his part and resembled him so closely that the audience would never know the difference. He begged Monsey to attend the performance and tell him how things went. As soon as Monsey, rather incredulous, had departed, Garrick, fully dressed, jumped out of bed, hurried to the theater, and played King Lear with his usual success. Puzzled by the satisfaction of the audience, Monsey half suspected a trick; but finding Garrick in bed after the play was over, he remained deceived, until he was disabused and laughed at the following day.[45]

Garrick's snobbishness was always distasteful to Monsey. When he had his revenge by being rude at his friend's table, the doctor's incivilities caused embarrassment but were tolerated. Garrick could not, however, endure being laughed at; and the friendship of years was destroyed by a bit of witty jesting in which Monsey indulged.

In a letter to a friend Monsey gave his version of the quarrel. One day Lord Bath said to Monsey that he thought "Mob" would drive Garrick from the stage. Monsey replied that he thought not and made the comment: "a Doctor & a Manager have not Virtue eno' to turn their Backs upon a Guinea . . . G—— knows a Guinea is *Pile on one Side, & Cross on the other.*"

A third person who was present misrepresented the episode to Garrick, who

without a *why* or a *wherefore* pleased to write me a Letter which
I would not have sent to a Footman or a Porter—The Marrow of it
was Horace's famous "Absentem qui rodit" &c with an application
to me, written in a feigned Hand. Upon which I began to reflect
whose Wife I had attempted, or whose daughter I had ravished.

Monsey laid the letter aside. A fortnight later he called at
Garrick's house, and Garrick was out.

I found his Wife just washing up her Tea-things with a very coy
Countenance, not a word of Dr Doctor! as usual, will you have any
Tea? Grave and gloomy I threw myself down in a great armed Chair
tried to force something of a Conversation, but found her very shy
of her breath, so for want of something better, says I, M^{rs} G——
I have had an odd sort of Letter. By her look or something I began
to surmise she knew a little about it. Can you, says I, tell me any
thing? yes—why the Devil your husband did not send it! But he did
tho', & I think for sufficient Reason—& then, as folks say, she up
and told me the d——d Lie which had been told him, & said Why
—love money! why we are now employing 20 or 30 Men at Hampton,
—that does not look like the love of money!—and dwelling upon it,
I could not forbear saying a man may love money, & pleasure as well
or better; and as to your workmen, never call paying them for their
work generosity which is but an act of Justice—you are more obliged
to them than they are to you—try & do what they do for you yourself
& that will shew you on which side the favor lies—and after a very
little more we parted.

Garrick and Monsey never exchanged another word. About
a year later, the two former friends met at Lord Bath's. Both
bowed slightly, and Garrick left. Monsey explained the situation
to Lord Bath, who wondered why the doctor had not mentioned
the matter before. "Why truly my L^d," said Monsey, "I thought
it much beneath your dignity to trouble you with the squabble
of a merry-andrew & a quack-doctor."

Time reconciled Monsey to this loss, although "it hurt griev-
ously at first, & . . . I bewailed it more than once with my
Eyes not quite dry." The doctor was philosopher enough to recog-
nize that "great friendships once broken are seldom soldered up
so as to hold tho' little ones may." [46]

DR. MONSEY

During the course of Garrick's last illness, when a number of physicians were called in, Monsey wrote some satirical stanzas on the subject. A friend who remembered the substance of the poem gave the following account of it:

> Seven wise physicians lately met
> To save a wretched sinner:
> Come, Tom, says Jack, pray let's be quick,
> Or I shall lose my dinner.

The consultation began, and, after various proposals, the remedy selected was "the famous chink of guineas." Having empty pockets, each physician declined his services, out of deference to those of superior age or rank. At last, one came forward with a purse of guineas which he had weighed, found heavy, and not returned his patients as light. He solemnly approached the bedside and shook the gold at the sick man's ear, with fatal consequences:

> Soon as the fav'rite sound he heard
> One faint effort he tried;
> He op'd his eyes, he stretch'd his hand,
> He made one grasp, and died.

Garrick did die, as Monsey had not expected, and he at once destroyed the verses; nor would he ever repeat them.[47]

His friends in Norfolk, whom he often visited, contributed a good deal to Monsey's enjoyment of life, as he did to theirs. To William Wiggett Bulwer of Heydon Hall he wrote: "I do assure you I have pass'd no moments of my life with more satisfaction than at Heydon." [48] Another Norfolk friend was William Windham of Felbrigg Hall.[49] The whole Windham family seems to have been both perplexed and tantalized by Monsey's quaint letters, seasoned with coarse and fantastic burlesque verses. Ashe Windham announced in a letter to William Windham:

Dr Monsey has writ another letter to Jos: lately of 4 sides of quarto paper. I never did see such crazy, Bedlamite, unconnected prose, & poetry in my Life. Wee (none of us) . . . can make head, nor tail of it—before this there was another as long, proving ye Windhams older than Adam's family—and ye Monseys older than ye Windham's.[50]

Among Monsey's medical friends, one of the "earliest and warmest" was Dr. John Taylor.[51] In a letter to William Windham, dated December 30, 1756, Monsey described some preposterous satirical verses which he had written about Taylor. They represented, said Monsey, "the very marrow & quintessence" of wit, but had made Taylor "damnatiously mad." [52] Taylor attended Lord Godolphin as an occulist and was also summoned, on occasion, to bleed him. When the Earl was ill in May 1755, Monsey turned to Taylor for advice. "I think him a very good physician," he assured the Duke of Newcastle, "& [he] has a good heart as well as a good head." [53]

There is a manuscript collection in the British Museum of letters covering a period of sixteen years written to Monsey by another medical friend and an able physician, Dr. Benjamin Gooch. These letters are in the somewhat florid style characteristic of many of Gooch's contemporaries. He speaks of "turbulent Boreas," "glorious Sol," and the "salubrious fountains" of Bath, and refers to the King of Denmark as "the rambling Hyperborean Monarch." A pious man, he trusts that Monsey will be "as happy as you can be, till you arrive at the beatific vision, wch I hope we shall view together." Despite their formality, the letters reveal Gooch as a kind and sympathetic friend.[54]

Gooch sent Monsey accounts of his most interesting cases and the papers that he was preparing for the press, and begged Monsey, at his convenience, to "bestow some medical news upon me, it will be very acceptable; you are in the place for it, I am not." He condoled with Monsey when his daughter and her "olive branches" were ill; suggested a remedy for Monsey's gouty thumb; and advised "moderate equitation" (quoting a phrase of Sir Benjamin Wrench's) for his legs. Like Monsey he had a profound admiration for Wrench. Having come across a print of Wrench, "a striking likeness," he had it hung "behind where I constantly sit." He rejoiced in the flourishing condition of the new Norfolk and Norwich Hospital: "I wished to live for nothing more than to see it perfected, & in the reputation it now is . . . I verily believe, in many respects, it excells any in Europe . . . Thank God for its prosperity." [55]

Gooch was concerned over Monsey's quarrel with Dr. Ranby, the Surgeon of Chelsea Hospital. But Monsey had acted in the affair "like an upright, honest man, true to his trust," and therefore, in his friend's opinion, would not suffer "that cruel sentence, self-condemnation." Once when Monsey was silent for nearly nine months, Gooch feared that the irascible surgeon might have sent him "by a *cutthroat* to happier regions." Ranby's death was reassuring news: "We were comforted with your letter, written in the gaiety of your heart, now you have conveyed your inveterate and implacable enemy over Styx." [56]

Monsey and Gooch were of one mind as to the "fine county" of Norfolk. Gooch looked forward to seeing and talking with his friend at Shottisham, "under the finest Oake in England, a magnificent Residence for a Druid." One of his letters he closed with the comment: "I know you'll make allowances for my writing in a hurry, the pudding being brought unto the table; & consider I am a Norfolk man, & very hungry." [57]

We can only make conjectures concerning Monsey's letters to Gooch. The latter was a good deal of an invalid and was grateful for "your tender & affectionate concern for my health and safety." Comforted in his turn, he observed: "It is some ease, to minds not at ease, to open them to true & sincere friends." In reply to some extravagant proposal by Monsey, he wrote: "When you are exalted to the post of Prime Minister, you'll find it, I fear, too hard a task to cleanse the Augean Stable, despite your boasting of what you will do." Gooch, his wife, and daughter all duly appreciated Monsey's letters, delighted by his "inimitable strain." The little granddaughter, who was five years old, objected to one letter about the devil, but admitted: "I like him well enough for all this, & if he don't write any more such stuff I'll forgive him." [58]

Monsey always enjoyed feminine society and perhaps feminine adulation. His wife appears to have been not the only rich widow whom he courted. Gooch wrote to him in jesting vein in November 1764: "It is said, that your widow is already bespoke; but don't let it break your heart; drink rattle-snake wine & you'll be fit for any thing; it will make you young again." [59]

Monsey was in later middle age when his heart was really smitten by Mrs. Elizabeth Montagu. Critics have had some sport over this "absurd" and "nauseous" courtship. Mrs. Montagu certainly encouraged the doctor, although there is some evidence that she regarded his suit chiefly as an agreeable exercise for two clever pens. Monsey, also, welcomed the literary possibilities of this attachment; but, as Benjamin Stillingfleet declared, he was at seventy capable of all the tenderness of a young man of twenty. [60] When Mrs. Montagu preferred Lord Bath, he was jealous and miserable.

The terms of this courtship were well defined by Mrs. Montagu in a letter to Stillingfleet, dated September 15, 1757:

You must know, Sir, Dr. Monsey is fallen desperately in love with me, and I am most passionately in love with him, the darts on both sides have not been the porcupine's, but the grey goose quill. We have said so many tender things to each other by the post, that at last we thought it would be better to sigh in soft dialogue than by letter. We agreed to meet, and the rather, as all the lovers we had read of (and being in love with each other only *du coté de l'esprit,* you may suppose we woo by book) had always complained of absence as the most dreadful thing imaginable. He said, nay he swore, he would come to Sandleford, and twice had named the day, but each time his grand-daughter fell sick, and I know not whether he will keep the third appointment, which is for next Monday. These disappointments have made me resolve, and I really believe it will not be difficult to keep the resolution, never again to fall in love with a man who is a grandfather. In all other respects the Doctor is a perfect Pastor Fido, and I believe when we get to Elysium, all the lovers who wander in the Myrtle Groves there will throw their garlands at our feet. [61]

Mrs. Montagu was flattered by the compliments of the "sage doctor" and told him: "I attribute your extraordinary admiration of me to a more than usual degree of penetration; and you may rest assured that I shall think you the wisest man in the world, till I meet with another that admires me as much." She once thanked Monsey "for all the wit and the wisdom, and the Latin and the Greek in your letter; for though I have no skill in these matters, it looks as if you thought I had, and the presumption does me some honour."[62]

She could and did take advantage of Monsey's enduring devotion. In a teasing, provocative tone, which he found irresistible, she wrote to him:

It is apparent from the contention of various goddesses for you, that you resemble Paris in features, complexion, air, and mien, and, as I flatter myself I am not less like Venus than you are to that beau garçon, I do not doubt your decision in my favour; and I will have a picture made of it. Hogarth will hit the subject better than Apelles could do. You have written me one letter to prove you are in love with me, another to prove I am in love with you: indeed you seem to have taken most pains, and given more arguments to demonstrate the latter, which was certainly unnecessary, and it was the natural consequence of the former; however, thanks to the probability of the fact, and the force of your logic, it is now so fully made out, we may expect our names should be inscribed in that small niche of the temple of fame that is consecrated to the memory of constant lovers. I know the charms of my rivals, but I think it is impossible they should disturb so tender and mutual a passion.[63]

The lady was not averse to observing the effects of jealousy on so singular a character. She wrote to Lord Lyttelton in October 1760: "Dr. Monsey is revenging my coquetry with Lord Bath by an assiduous courtship of Miss Talbot, but he can no more be untrue to me, than the needle to the pole."[64]

A discerning, although not warmhearted woman, Mrs. Montagu commended the doctor's humanity and admired his knowledge of the world, gained by close observation and long experience. In honor of his sixty-third birthday, she wrote to him on October 2, 1757, in a more serious mood:

My Climacteric Friend,
Good morrow to you, Sir! and many years and happy! How do you find yourself? Are you tired with your journey of 63 years? or are you in spirits to go forward to the stage of 64. Does Hope lead you

by the hand, and Philosophy support you under the arm?—You are a wise man, and therefore not to be cheated by hope; you are a mortal man, and of mere flesh and blood, therefore not absolutely to be sustain'd by philosophy. I will tell you therefore how you find yourself; why, alas! like one that has toil'd up to the top of a barren hill, and finds his pains ill paid, is unwilling to stay where he is, too wise to measure back the weary way, and afraid to proceed to the term and limit of his journey: be not ashamed of this; it is the quality of the road, not the infirmity of the traveller. . . March easily and indolently the rest of your way. . . In your sober walk, do not disdain to pick the few aromatics that grow on the declivity of the hill, and beguile the tediousness of the way; they will fade as you gather them; throw them away and gather fresh ones; don't seek them with impatience, don't part with them with regret; remember they are annuals.[65]

It was, however, his unflagging wit and raillery which Mrs. Montagu most enjoyed in Dr. Monsey. She commenced one of her letters to him:

Dear Doctor,
That is, because you have made me well.
Dear Sir,
Because you have made me laugh.

She wrote to Monsey in July 1757:

Have I not given you leave to entertain me out of any corner of your brain, and promis'd to read with equal complaisance what your wisdom or your wit shall suggest, nay even what you may say in your foolishness, if your wit should be at low ebb?

> Whether you choose Cervantes' serious air,
> Or laugh and shake in Rabelais' easy chair,

write like the sage Charron or the fantastical Hudibras, I am still your gentle reader.[66]

Monsey's variations of temper amused her. She wrote to Lord Bath in June 1762: "The great Monsey in his great manner, loves, hates, flatters, abuses, coaxes, and scolds me most nobly." She confessed: "I have often been puzzled to determine whether I loved him for his perfections or imperfections but I believe it is

DR. MESSENGER MONSEY

DR. MONSEY

for the Chequer of both in his character. He is certainly the greatest fool of a witt and the greatest Witt of a fool in the World." [67]

As a companion, Monsey was always diverting. In the course of a journey from Hagley to Hill Street, he related "a string of stories which it would take more time to reckon the number of, than the barleycorns that would reach from [London] to York." [68] Keeping pace with his moods, "from black to white, from red to blue," [69] was an almost impossible feat. When his friends were celebrating the birth of Prince George in August 1762, Monsey "was by his own account within half an hour of dying." He had written to his daughter a farewell letter, giving instructions about his burial, and advising her: "Do not grieve for me nor put on mourning, but be an honest girl, fear God, say your prayers constantly, and so adieu." All the while, he was "in perfect health, and yet swallowing asafoetida every 3 or 4 hours." Suddenly he recovered his spirits, put on his pea-blossom coat, and was ready to accompany Lord Bath to a ball.[70]

Excerpts give a very inadequate idea of Monsey's long love letters, written in his neat, cramped, "just legible" hand. Mrs. Montagu was his "dear Amadissa" and "Serenissima Principessa." When ill, she was "flimsey animal, puny insect, and other such opprobrious names." [71] One letter, written at the beginning of their friendship, he began a "minute past 12," as follows:

Dear Madame,

Now dead men's ghosts are getting out of their graves, and there comes the ghost of a doctor in a white sheet to wait upon you. Your Tokay is got into my head and your love into my heart, and they both join to club their thanks for the pleasantest day I have spent these seven years; and to my comfort I find a man may be in love and be happy, provided he does not go to book for it. I could have trusted till the morning to shew my gratitude, but the Tokay wou'd have evaporated, and then I might have nothing to talk of but an ache in my head and pain in my heart.

Two days later he ended the letter:

'Tis a sad thing to have to do with a fool, who can't keep his nonsense to himself. You know, I am a rose, but I have terrible prickles.

Dear madam, adieu. Pray God I may hear you are well, or that He will enable me to make you so, for you must not be sick or die. I'll find fools and rogues enough to be that for you, that are good for nothing else, and hardly, very hardly, good enough for that. Adieu, Adieu! I say Adieu, Adieu.[72]

When a guest at Wotton, Monsey was laughed at for the candles and fire billets which he consumed in writing nocturnal epistles to Mrs. Montagu and for being preoccupied with thoughts of her the rest of the time. If he picked up a book, "instead of the title-page, there stands Montagu in Roman capitals." If he came downstairs, a loud "gibble gabble" greeted him because he had written down for Lord Godolphin: "Take of Mrs. Montagu two ounces and a half," instead of his prescription for rhubarb and diagrydium. Yet why not? "There can be no harm for a polite man to take a little of the delicacy, sweetness, &c. of a lady . . . and make it up into a bolus or draught, with the essence of her judgment, the je ne scay quoi of her looks, and the syrup of her sweetness."[73]

After Lord Bath entered the picture, Mrs. Montagu paid less attention to Dr. Monsey. She grieved over the Earl's death and cherished her memories of "the most perfect character I ever saw." Yet her friendship with Monsey continued to the end of his life. In November 1783 she wrote: "I expect Dr. Monsey his Daughter and Grand Daughters to dine with me to day. He told me with great gayety that he was now in his ninetieth year. I congratulated him upon having kept all his Witt, and a great deal of his indiscretion. I was really rejoiced to see him so gay."[74]

Of Monsey's family life little is known. His only daughter, Charlotte, married a London linen merchant, William Alexander, the elder brother of James Alexander, who became third Earl of Caledon. When William Alexander died in 1774, he left his wife in comfortable circumstances financially,[75] but with eleven children, whom Dr. Monsey took under his wing. Monsey was a happy father and Charlotte a loving child. "My dear Daughter," wrote Gooch, "is . . . as good a child as yours."[76] Mrs. Montagu gives hints in one of her letters of the role played by Dr. Monsey as father and grandfather:

DR. MONSEY

I assure you I have always honoured you for your rational and well-founded love of a worthy daughter, and not less for your foolish instinct about your little grand children. . . I could weep for the poor grand-father approaching his grand child with a lancet in one hand and a blister in the other: so when you have any of these domestic distresses, you may bring them to me, and I will give them their due share of pity. . . I do not find any foolishness in your head, but there is a good deal in your heart, and pray keep it there; for it makes you a tender parent, a good friend, and a very indulgent correspondent. . .[77]

Sometimes accompanied by his daughter, Monsey was continually making journeys, most often into Norfolk. Travel always agreed with him. A humorist on holiday, he had quaint adventures, of a Shandean flavor. One day, when riding with a servant in his own county, he noticed a shepherd tending his flock, wearing a new coat. "Harkee, friend," said Monsey, "who gave you that coat?" The shepherd, mistaking the black-coated doctor for a parson, replied: "The same that clothed you—*the parish.*" Much pleased with this rejoinder, Monsey rode on a short distance, then sent his man back to ask the shepherd if he wanted a place, as the doctor wanted a fool. "Why, are you going away?" the shepherd inquired of the servant. "No." "Then tell your master, that his living, I am sure, cannot maintain three of us." The message was conveyed to the doctor, who sent the servant back once more, with a crown for the jest.[78]

On another occasion, Monsey was returning to London in the Norwich coach in the Christmas holidays. The inside of the coach was crowded with presents of game from country gentlemen to their friends in town, so that there was room for but one passenger. Unable to change his reservation, Monsey amused himself by altering all of the addresses on the game, taking care that good turkeys intended for titled gentlemen were redirected to tradesmen.[79]

The doctor's friends, growing older more sedately, marveled at his youthful spirits. When Monsey was sixty-six, Dr. Gooch congratulated him on parading through the streets of Bungay on one of Mr. Windham's horses "to the admiration of the beholders," and added: "You're a gallant youth indeed." [80] Mrs. Montagu found him at seventy-seven as lively as ever: "He tells me he is in high health, and by the fulness of his witty vein, and the strong pulse of his folly, I am sure he is so." [81]

Lord Lyttelton's letter in honor of the doctor's seventy-eighth birthday may surely be considered one of the most delightful compliments ever paid to a young old man:

Much Joy to my dear Monsey on his being arrived at his 78th Year in his way to a hundred. Ld Chesterfield, I fear, is a bright sun almost setting; but You are still in full Lustre, and must shine many years to make us amends for his Loss. Seventy eight is no Age for a stout fellow like You. Look up to Ld Bathurst, or come and read the Tombstones in my Church yard here at Hagley: You will see that a Man who happend to die at sixty was considered by the Clerk, who wrote his Epitaph, as an unfortunate Youth that had perished in the prime of Life. *Like as a Flower was I cutt down,* &c. Near to this stripling are the graves of two of his neighbours, one of whom lived to eighty eight and the other to ninety five. My Grandfather died untimely at eighty seven by getting a bruise on his shin, which hindered his usual Walk to the top of his Park Hill, and made him unable to digest the fat of a Ven'son Pasty, which he commonly eat with a Spoon: but one of his Gamekeepers, Old Paget, attain'd to more than a hundred years, notwithstanding a large Beer Glass of English Brandy, which he drank every morning for the last thirty years before his Death. Think then to what an Age your vigorous Constitution, Philosophical Temperance, and Medical Knowledge, ought to carry you, especially being cherish'd (as you are and ever will be) by the smiles of Mrs Montagu, which keep your heart always warm, and your Spirits in a quick and lively flow.[82]

When Lord Godolphin died in January 1766, at the age of eighty-eight, Monsey reluctantly took up permanent residence at Chelsea Royal Hospital. Realizing how great was the change in his friend's circumstances, Gooch wrote to him in April, reminding him: "Nunquam minus solus quam solus." And a few months later, he recommended: "Like a good philosopher be content with what you now have, without regretting the loss of a kind of paradise you long enjoyed." [83] Monsey's apartments were pleasant but drafty. He complained that the wind often turned the pages of his books, until he stopped his casements with paper and putty. At least, as he informed Mrs. Montagu, he was at no loss for occupations:

In writing you this long scribble-scrabble you will naturally suppose I don't know how to employ my time. There you are out, for I have my Bible, Grotius, Hammond, Butler, Sir Isaac, a saw, an Hammer, a Chissel, and an Hatchet, with which I chop off fools' heads when they begin to be too wise, though I now stand in need of a very wise one to teach me to go to bed before 2 or 3 ocl. in the morning, though I am very well with it at present.[84]

Monsey was considered parsimonious, although many stories of his charity have been recorded. One day John Barber, a watchmaker, was regulating for him a complicated clock, which was one of his most prized possessions. As Barber worked, Monsey sat by the fire, with his legs on the table (for he "courted," as he said, a horizontal position, so that his blood might circulate more easily). Presently Monsey remarked in a loud tone: "Barber, I don't believe you'll ever be able to pay the 100 $l.$ that I lent to you." Barber turned around, raised his spectacles on his forehead, and replied quietly: "Why really, Doctor, I believe I never shall." "Well," said Monsey, "if you cannot, I shall not ask for it."[85]

As Monsey grew older, his eccentricities became more pronounced and his geniality less so. His violent quarrels with Dr. Ranby and with his "old woman" were given considerable publicity by Monsey himself. He remained on the worst of terms with his eldest grandson, Monsey Alexander. In a letter dated April 1, 1775, to his grandson at Oxford, he upbraided the foppish lad for "unpardonable extravagance" and "consummate Impudence" and observed acidly: "I suppose you think you are making your Self a modern Gentleman, the most odious Character upon Earth."[86]

Monsey once gratified his taste for the macabre by a ride and a nap in a hearse, having persuaded the driver to give him a lift to Chelsea Hospital. Robert Adair, who was then Surgeon of the Hospital, was on his way thither in a carriage at the same time; and the carriage and the hearse were delayed, side by side, in a congestion of traffic. The driver of the hearse could not refrain from telling Adair's coachman that his "present fare" was no corpse but "the odd old Doctor at Chelsea." The coachman passed on the news to Adair, who sent his footman with his compliments to invite Monsey to share his carriage. The doctor was awakened with difficulty; damned the footman for disturbing him; and declined the offer, stating that he was so fatigued that he preferred his present mode of conveyance.[87]

Monsey lived on at Chelsea Hospital for more than a quarter of a century,[88] surviving enemies and friends, and also those strangers to whom the reversion of his grant had been promised. One day, observing one of his would-be successors examining the house and gardens, the doctor went out and greeted him with the gloomy reminder:

Well, sir, I see you are examining your house and gardens that *are to be,* and I assure you they are both very pleasant and very convenient; but I must tell you *one* circumstance, you are the *fifth* man that has got the reversion of the place, and I have buried them all; and what is more (said the doctor, looking very archly at him,) there is something in your face that tells me I shall bury you too.[89]

The doctor was a strange mixture of realism and idealism, of cynicism and faith. His unorthodox religious views shocked many people. On a certain occasion he was riding in Hyde Park with a Mr. Robinson, who denounced the impiety of the times, lamenting: "and Doctor, I talk with people who believe there is *no* God." "And I, Mr. Robinson," said Monsey, "talk with people who believe there are *three.*" Robinson set spurs to his horse and never spoke to the doctor again.[90] Yet Monsey was seriously interested in, at times preoccupied with, religious questions. He admitted: "I can't do without an intelligent agent." [91] In a fragment of a letter written in his old age, his longing is recorded for some "Acute country parson" to explain certain Biblical passages which have puzzled him. Why did St. Paul join foolishness to God and add weakness? "I want foolishness set as far

from God . . . as we are from the nighest fix'd Star—I shudder
at the Shadow of folly coming near God." He proposes: "Let us
mend our manners, be humble, & wait the Explication of things
too great for us snotty nosed animals to comprehend at present." [92]

Monsey never entirely lost his resilience; but he was not
spared the weariness, loneliness, and disillusion of extreme old
age. He grew "tired of life, but [was] like many fools and many
philosophers, afraid to die." [93] He became nearly blind and had
to dictate his letters, although he signed them, with a shaking
hand, to the end. In the last letter which he was able to write
himself to his friend Bulwer, he acknowledged:

I know it, Master Bulwer, I shall never see you more except you
come to Chelsea. Thank your son for his kind visit. This world is
trumpery at best, and now worserer and worserer to me. . . Farewell Heydon and the pleasures of it. I hope to have a better carcass
and a better situation in one of the fix'd stars, and, if I can, will get
you a good place there. My kind love and respects to all yr family,
and thanks for all their favours to a poor old man. I wish you free
from all Gout, Rheumatism and Stone, all which I thank a good
God for preserving me from daily, and ought to hourly, And so
    Mars, Bacchus, Apollo virorum.
                        Yrs affectionately
                        M. Monsey [94]

Most of his older friends having died, Monsey turned somewhat wistfully to their children. On February 20, 1786, he wrote
to young William Windham [95] to wish "all the comforts and
blessings of a world, of which you are so great an ornament" to
"the son of a man whom I so really, and truely loved." [96] The following August Windham made this entry in his diary:

. . . Had company to dinner; that is to say, Sir Joshua, Malone,
Courtenay, who came from Bath, and with him, not unwelcomely,
old Mounsey, at the age of ninety-three. I don't know that he improved the conversation much, but it was not for want of spirits
to talk, nor from any cause that might not equally have existed forty
years ago. To me his presence was a satisfaction, independent from
what he might add or take from the society.[97]

To the Marquis of Carmarthen Monsey wrote in 1787:

if you lov'd me half as well as I have do now and ever shall love you, you will in a morning walk, call upon an old friend before he drops into his Grave, I shou'd be very glad to see you once more before I dye which I hope & expect daily to do. . . When you write to your good Father present him my best Love and good wishes for his health & happiness here & hereafter.[98]

Young John Taylor often dined with Monsey. A few months before the latter's death, Taylor brought John Wolcot to Chelsea Hospital to paint the doctor's portrait. But the two men "did not harmonize," chiefly because Wolcot criticized some of Monsey's favorite quotations from Pope.[99]

Monsey had made arrangements to have Dr. Thompson Forster dissect his body, after his death. In his chambers in Chelsea he kept a large box, full of air holes, with poles attached to it, for the purpose of conveying his corpse to this surgeon.[100] On May 12, 1787, supposing that he was about to die, he wrote a letter to Dr. W. C. Cruikshank, requesting him to make the examination, in case Dr. Forster should not return in time from Norwich. Monsey discusses his symptoms and concludes: "I am now very ill & hardly see to scrawl this & feel as if I shou'd live ten days, the sooner the better."[101] He recovered, however, and lived on until December 26 of the following year. In accordance with his wishes, Dr. Forster dissected his body before the students of Guy's Hospital.

The epitaph which Monsey wrote for himself may be cited as a fair specimen of his doggerel verses:

Here lies my old limbs, my vexation now ends,
For I've lived much too long for my self and my friends;
As for church-yards and grounds which parsons call holy,
'Tis a rank piece of priestcraft and founded on folly.
In short I despise them; and as for my soul,
Which may mount the last day with my bones from this hole,
I think that it really hath nothing to fear
From the God of mankind whom I truly revere.

What the next World may be, never troubled my pate:
If not better than this, I beseech thee, oh Fate,
When the bodies of millions fly up in a riot
To let the old carcase of Monsey lie quiet.[102]

In the last year of his life, Monsey made a curious and complicated will, to which he added three codicils. He left to "my dear Daughter Charlotte Alexander" most of his estate of about £16,000, with the provisoes that she should "live and reside at some place at the least twenty five Miles distant from London and at least six Months in every Year" during the remainder of her life, and not "keep or cause to be kept at her own expense or jointly with others any Coach Chariot or other such like Carriage." But in a second codicil he made void these restrictions, in the belief that his daughter, "seeing the bent of my inclination will voluntarily pay some regard thereto."[103] He left legacies to his surviving grandchildren, with the exception of Monsey Alexander, and entailed his estate on four granddaughters: Catherine,[104] Jemima,[105] Elizabeth, and Ann.

Monsey showed his affection for young John Taylor by bequeathing to him fifty pounds "as a small Acknowledgment for the many and kind Civilities" he had received from him; an annuity of ten pounds; his Chambers Dictionary; and his black velvet coat and waistcoat, green laced waistcoat, and old shoe buckles. He gave to another friend the buttons of his velvet coat. To a Miss Jordan he bequeathed his old gilt snuffbox and a handkerchief, explaining:

The motives I have for taking this notice of Miss Jordan are because I think her the most far from all pride prudery and self conceitedness of all the young Women I ever knew in my life if she has any faults which is not the fault of this Age it is almost a total unconcerness about all sort of dress for she has no more pride about her than a Grasshopper.

After this final sally, regretting that he had left many things still unsaid, Monsey signed the third codicil on December 2, 1788, "with all my Senses about me thank God."[106]

Despite his odd ways, Monsey possessed that fundamental sanity by which men of his period are best remembered. For living nearly a century he paid a not uncommon price in the infirmities and crotchets of his old age, and he reaped uncommon benefits. In a long life, brimming over with friendships, little that was worth noting escaped his sharp and humorous gaze; little that was worth recalling was forgotten. The impression which Monsey made on those who knew him is summed up in the words of his first biographer: "He was a storehouse of anecdote —a reservoir of good things—a living chronicle of past times." [107] His contemporaries justly regarded him as a remarkable man, whose peculiarities, if sometimes exasperating, were delicious flights from the commonplace.

Notes

Bibliography

Index

Notes

The following abbreviations have been used: Add. MSS. (Additional Manuscripts, British Museum, London); HMC (Reports of the Royal Historical Manuscripts Commission); PCC (Prerogative Court of Canterbury Will Book, Somerset House, London); PMLA (Publications of the Modern Language Association of America); PROD (Public Record Office, Dublin); RDD (Registry of Deeds, Dublin); SO (State Papers, Domestic, Signet Office, Public Record Office, London); SP 44 (State Papers, Domestic, Entry Book, Public Record Office, London); SP 63 (State Papers, Ireland, Public Record Office, London); TCD (Trinity College, Dublin).

William Congreve

1. W. E. Henley, "Congreve," in *Works* (London, 1908), V, 241.

2. [John Dryden and others], *Examen Poeticum* (London, 1693), Dedication.

3. Thomas Southerne's notes on Congreve, Add. MSS. 4211, f. 61.

4. *The Letters of John Dryden,* ed. Charles E. Ward (Durham, N.C., 1942), pp. 59, 76.

5. *Ibid.,* pp. 62–63.

6. Edmund Gosse, *Life of William Congreve* (London, 1888), p. 56.

7. *The Double-Dealer, A Comedy . . . Written by Mr. Congreve* (London, 1694), verses prefixed to the play, "To my Dear Friend Mr. Congreve, On His Comedy, call'd, The Double-Dealer."

8. Dryden, *Letters,* p. 134.

9. *The Works of John Dryden,* ed. Sir Walter Scott (London and Edinburgh, 1808), II, 9–11.

10. *The Poems of Jonathan Swift,* ed. Harold Williams (Oxford, 1937), I, 44.

11. *Jonathan Swift, Journal to Stella,* ed. Harold Williams (Oxford, 1948), II, 396.

NOTES

12. *The Mourning Bride, Poems, & Miscellanies, by William Congreve,* ed. Bonamy Dobrée, World's Classics (London [1928]), p. 496.

13. *The Correspondence of Jonathan Swift,* ed. F. Elrington Ball (London, 1910–14), III, 276.

14. Swift, *Journal to Stella,* I, 75, 193, 70, 295.

15. Swift, *Correspondence,* III, 153.

16. *The Works of Alexander Pope,* ed. Whitwell Elwin and W. J. Courthope (London, 1871–1889), X, 417.

17. Swift, *Correspondence,* IV, 58.

18. Pope, *Works,* III, 251; VI, 412; VII, 430.

19. *The Letters and Works of Lady Mary Wortley Montagu,* ed. Lord Wharncliffe (London, 1898), II, 24.

20. Pope, *Works,* VI, 415; VII, 422, 434.

21. *The Iliad of Homer Translated by Alexander Pope, Esq.* (London, 1750), VI, Dedication.

22. [Thomas Babington] Macaulay, "Leigh Hunt," in *Critical and Historical Essays* (London, 1903), III, 44–45.

23. Joseph Spence, *Anecdotes* (London, 1820), p. 232.

24. Pope, *Works,* IX, 347.

25. *Ibid.,* 354, 364.

26. Montagu, *Letters,* I, 208, 214.

27. *The Mourning Bride,* ed. Dobrée, p. 535.

28. Montagu, *Letters,* II, 24.

29. Wortley MSS., Sandon Hall, Stafford, VIII. (In the eighth line, "breath" was revised by Lady Mary to "sigh.") This tribute does not imply that Congreve had been Lady Mary's lover. Her poem, "The Lover: A Ballad" (Montagu, *Letters,* II, 498–499), was addressed "To Mr. C———," long supposed to be Congreve. "Mr. C———" has been identified, however, as Richard Chandler (later Cavendish), eldest son of Edward Chandler, Bishop of Durham. See *Horace Walpole's Correspondence with Thomas Gray, Richard West and Thomas Ashton,* ed. W. S. Lewis, G. L. Lam, and C. H. Bennett (New Haven, 1948), II, 245 (vol. XIV in Yale Edition of Horace Walpole's Correspondence).

30. *The Poetical Works of John Gay,* ed. G. C. Faber (London, 1926), p. 166.

31. Swift, *Correspondence,* III, 153.

32. *Letters Upon Several Occasions,* ed. [John] Dennis (London, 1696), p. 98.

33. Charles Wilson, *Memoirs of the Life, Writings, and Amours of William Congreve Esq.* (London, 1730), p. 137.

34. *The Mourning Bride,* ed. Dobrée, pp. 518–519.

35. Dennis, *Letters,* p. 141.

36. *The Works of the Right Honourable Joseph Addison, Esq.* (London, 1721), I, 40.

37. *The Letters of Joseph Addison,* ed. Walter Graham (Oxford, 1941), p. 11.

38. *The Mourning Bride,* ed. Dobrée, p. 500.

39. *A New Miscellany of Original Poems,* ed. Charles Gildon (London, 1701), "Epistle to Mr. Congreve, Occasion'd by his Comedy Call'd, The Way of the World," p. 336.

40. *The Epistolary Correspondence of Sir Richard Steele* (London, 1787), p. 403.

41. *Ibid.,* pp. 501–502.

42. [Theophilus] Cibber, *The Lives of the Poets of Great Britain and Ireland* (London, 1753), IV, 92.

43. *An Apology for the Life of Mr. Colley Cibber,* ed. Robert W. Lowe (London, 1889), I, 173.

44. See *The Works of Mr. Thomas Brown* (London, 1707–8), III, 42–43; *Poems on Affairs of State, From 1620 to this present year 1710* (London, 1703–1710), IV, 49–50.

45. See *The Works of Nicholas Rowe, Esq.* (London, 1747), "Horace, Book II, Ode IV, Imitated, The Lord Griffin to the Earl of Scarsdale," II, 307.

46. *Animadversions on Mr. Congreve's Late Answer to Mr. Collier* (London, 1698), Preface.

47. [Charles] Gildon, *A Comparison Between the Two Stages* (London, 1702), p. 17.

48. T. Cibber, *The Lives of the Poets,* IV, 93.

49. See pp. 65–67 of this text.

50. [James Thomson], *A Poem to the Memory of Mr. Congreve, Inscribed to her Grace, Henrietta, Dutchess of Marlborough* (London, 1729).

51. Sir Richard Temple, Viscount Cobham (1669?–1749), eldest son of Sir Richard Temple, by Mary, daughter of Henry Knapp, was created Viscount Cobham in 1718. He distinguished himself as a soldier in the campaigns of Marlborough. He was appointed Privy Councillor (1716); Comptroller of the accounts of the army (1722); Governor of Jersey (1723).

52. *Cobham and Congreve. An Epistle to Lord Viscount Cobham, In Memory of his Friend, The late Mr. Congreve* (London, 1730), p. 7.

53. Rowe, "The Reconcilement between Jacob Tonson and Mr. Congreve," in *Works,* II, 313.

54. *The Mourning Bride,* ed. Dobrée, "Of Pleasing; An Epistle to Sir Richard Temple," p. 325; "Letter to Viscount Cobham," pp. 400, 401–402.

55. *A Description of the Gardens of Lord Viscount Cobham at Stow in Buckinghamshire* (Northampton, 1748), p. 26.

56. Charles Hopkins, *Boadicea* (London, 1697), Dedication.

57. Congreve speaks of Dryden's "very partial" verses. See Dryden, *Works,* II, 7.

58. *The Spectator* (London, 1744), III, 82.

59. *Ibid.,* I, 264–266.

60. [Edward Young], *Love of Fame* (London, 1728), Satire I, p. 5.

61. [Giles Jacob], *The Poetical Register* (London, 1719), p. 46.

62. Macaulay, III, 31.

63. Samuel Johnson, "Congreve," in *Lives of the English Poets,* ed. G. B. Hill (Oxford, 1905), II, 225.

64. Gosse, p. 174.

65. Macaulay, III, 45.

66. Leigh Hunt, "Congreve," in *Dramatic Works of Wycherley, Congreve, Vanbrugh, and Farquhar,* ed. Leigh Hunt (London and New York, 1866), p. xxix.

67. Charles Lamb, "On the Artificial Comedy of the Last Century," in *Essays of Elia,* ed. Alfred Ainger (London and New York, 1903), p. 195.

68. [François Marie Arouet] d[e] V[oltaire], *Lettres Ecrites Sur Les Anglois et Autres Sujets* (Basle, 1734), p. 175.

69. Johnson, II, 226.

70. *The Letters of Charles Lamb,* ed. E. V. Lucas (London, 1935), II, 50.

71. *The Mourning Bride,* ed. Dobrée, p. xx.

72. W. M. Thackeray, "Congreve and Addison," in *The English Humourists of the Eighteenth Century* (London, 1853), pp. 77–78.

73. Leigh Hunt, p. xxv.

74. Macaulay, III, 48.

75. Johnson, II, 227. Johnson had the sense to add that this legacy was made "for reasons either not known or not mentioned."

76. Gosse, p. 184.

77. See the MS. Notes of George Thorn-Drury in an interleaved copy of Gosse's *Life of William Congreve,* Bodleian Library, Oxford.

78. Gosse, p. 140.

79. Thorn-Drury, MS. cited.

80. Gosse, p. 175.

81. D. Crane Taylor, *William Congreve* (London, 1931), p. vii.

82. *Ibid.,* pp. 164, 175, 221, 173, 191.

83. John C. Hodges, *William Congreve The Man* (New York and London, 1941).

84. These interests are evident even in small matters. For example, the name of the hero (Mellefont) of *The Double-Dealer* is a reminiscence of Mellifont, a parish in a beautiful valley, partly in the barony of Upper Slane, county Meath, partly in that of Ferrard, county Louth, where the Moore family resided in an old abbey. Charles Moore was a member of the Irish Parliament from 1703 to 1714.

85. See K. M. Lynch, "Congreve's Irish Friend, Joseph Keally," in PMLA, LIII (1938), 1076–87.

86. *The Mourning Bride,* ed. Dobrée, p. 491.

87. G. D. Burtchaell and T. U. Sadleir, *Alumni Dublinenses* (Dublin, 1935), pp. 12 and 516.

88. See C. M. Tenison, "Cork M.P.'s, 1559–1800," in *Journal of the Cork Historical and Archaeological Society,* I, second series (1895), 524–525.

89. *The Mourning Bride,* ed. Dobrée, pp. 485, 501, 511.

90. It is possible that Mein was related to Benjamin Mayne of Charleville, county Cork, whose will was proved in 1686. He may have been related to the Southwell family of Kinsale, as he had a brother named Southwell Mein. See Charles Mein's will, PCC 1735, 128 Ducie.

91. See *Calendar of Treasury Books & Papers, 1735–1738,* ed. W. A. Shaw (London, 1900), p. 151.

92. Swift, *Journal to Stella,* I, 48–49.

93. Gay, *Poetical Works,* p. 167.

94. *The Mourning Bride,* ed. Dobrée, pp. 486, 487.

95. *Ibid.,* pp. 487–488.

96. *Ibid.,* pp. 498, 509, 514, 507.

97. See Edward Porter's will, PCC 1731, 75 Isham. A marginal note states that Porter was "formerly of the Inner Temple, London but late of the parish of Saint Clement Danes."

98. Taylor, p. 164.

99. See PCC 1729, 135 Brook. Congreve also left legacies to Anne Bracegirdle, Edward Porter, and Charles Mein. Both Congreve and Porter left legacies to Deborah Rooke. All of his legacies, except those to members of his family, Anne Jellet (to whom Henrietta, Duchess of Marlborough also left a legacy), and Anne Bracegirdle, Congreve canceled in a codicil added to his will on January 29, 1728.

100. Frances Porter was buried on November 27, 1727; Edward Porter in the same vault on February 9, 1731. See the Registers of St. Clement Danes for 1717 to 1728 and 1728 to 1737.

101. PCC 1731, 75 Isham.

102. *The Mourning Bride,* ed. Dobrée, pp. 522–524.

103. *Ibid.,* pp. 524–525.

104. *Ibid.,* p. 526.

105. See PCC 1748, 258 Strahan. Anne Bracegirdle died on September 12, 1748, at the age of eighty-five, and was buried in the East Cloister of Westminster Abbey.

106. C. Cibber, *An Apology,* II, 306.

107. See K. M. Lynch, "Henrietta, Duchess of Marlborough," in *PMLA,* LII (1937), 1072–93.

108. See PCC 1729, 135 Brook.

109. William Hazlitt, "Of Wycherley, Congreve, Vanbrugh and Farquhar," in *Lectures on the English Comic Dramatists* (London, 1819), p. 139.

NOTES

110. Bonamy Dobrée, "Congreve," in *Restoration Comedy, 1660–1720* (Oxford, 1924), p. 122.

111. *The Mourning Bride,* ed. Dobrée, pp. 401–402.

Joseph Keally

1. Gosse, p. 141.

2. Taylor, p. 210.

3. G. D. Burtchaell, *Genealogical Memoirs of the Members of Parliament for the County and City of Kilkenny* (Dublin, 1888), pp. 74–75.

4. *Pue's Occurrences,* XLVI, from Tuesday May 9 to Saturday May 13, 1749.

5. [W. R. Chetwood], *A Tour Through Ireland* (Dublin, 1748), p. 216.

6. *The Chronological Remembrancer* (Dublin, 1750), p. 75.

7. Burtchaell, pp. 74–75.

8. *Saunders's News-Letter,* January 8, 1783.

9. On December 1, 1689, Lancelot Stepney was appointed consul at Oporto, Portugal. See Narcissus Luttrell, *A Brief Historical Relation of State Affairs* (Oxford, 1857), I, 614.

10. James Butler, second Duke of Ormonde (1665–1745) was the second son of Thomas, Earl of Ossory, by Emilia, daughter of de Beverweert, Governor of Sluys. He was Gentleman of the Bedchamber to King William. His Irish estates, confiscated by the Act of Attainder of 1689, he recovered in 1690. In 1702 he commanded the English and Dutch land forces in the expedition against Cadiz, and in 1712 directed the campaign in Flanders. He served twice as Lord Lieutenant of Ireland (1703–06 and 1710–14). In 1715 he was impeached and fled to France; his honors were extinguished; and he died in exile. He married in 1682 Anne, daughter of Lawrence Hyde, afterwards Earl of Rochester, who died in 1684; and secondly, in 1685 Mary, daughter of Henry Somerset, first Duke of Beaufort.

11. Letter XXXIII, acquired in 1940; and letter XXIV and an address leaf marked "1702," acquired in 1941. Dobrée's numbering of the letters is followed in this text.

12. Letter XXXII. The date of acquisition was not recorded.

13. Letter V, acquired between 1917 and 1921.

14. Letter XXXVIII, in the library of Carl H. Pforzheimer, acquired in 1920; letter XVI, sold by Sotheby in 1937; and letter VII, recently acquired by the Bodley Book Shop, New York City.

15. Add. MSS. 39,311, f. 5, acquired in 1916.

16. Add. MSS. 28,888, f. 268.

17. Add. MSS. 39,311, f. 1 and f. 3.

18. Burtchaell, pp. 64–66.

19. PROD *Prerogative Will Book, 1664 To 1684,* ff. 309–310. Only a few

JOSEPH KEALLY

Prerogative Will Books were saved when the Public Record Office of Dublin was destroyed in 1922.

20. See T. U. Sadleir, "The Register of Kilkenny School," in *The Journal of the Royal Society of Antiquaries of Ireland*, LIV (1924), 155–156, 64, 159.

21. HMC, *Ormonde*, n.s., VII (London, 1912), 444.

22. *The Correspondence of Henry Hyde, Earl of Clarendon, and of His Brother, Lawrence Hyde, Earl of Rochester*, ed. S. W. Singer (London, 1828), I, 499.

23. HMC, *Ormonde*, page cited.

24. HMC, *Fifth Report*, part I (London, 1876), p. 345.

25. [William King], *The State of the Protestants of Ireland Under the Late King James's Government* (London, 1691), p. 192. King James replaced the Duke of Ormonde's school with a Royal College, in the charter of which, dated February 21, 1689, Dr. Hinton was declared attainted. See Walter Harris, *The History of the Life and Reign of William-Henry* (Dublin, 1749), p. 234.

26. HMC, *Ormonde*, n.s., VIII (London, 1920), 390.

27. Luttrell, I, 490, 500, 510.

28. See entry: "Elizabeth Kelly, widow, Kilkenny, 4 ch.," in TCD MSS. F.4.3, List of the Protestants Who Fled from Ireland—1688.

29. King, p. 288.

30. Burtchaell, pp. 89–91.

31. HMC, *Ormonde*, n.s., VII, 483.

32. Luttrell, I, 602.

33. *Ibid.*, II, 59, 74.

34. Burtchaell, pp. 89–91.

35. Admissions To House & Chambers, 1658 To 1685, Middle Temple, f. 589.

36. Letters I, VIII, X, XX, XXI, XXII, XXXIV.

37. Berkeley mistook (but questioned) Congreve's "97" for "07" in letter XXIV, which should be letter I. The manuscript letter, now in the Berg Collection, New York Public Library, is clearly dated: "7br 28: 97." In letter XXXI, which should be letter XVIII, Berkeley evidently read "08" for "05."

38. Berkeley placed at the end of the sequence as letter XLIII the undated letter from Northall, which belongs to the autumn of 1705 and should be letter XVII; and he left undated but misplaced letter XXXII, which must be assigned to the early spring of 1710. See Lynch, "Congreve's Irish Friend, Joseph Keally," PMLA, LIII, 1081, n. 44, and 1082. Another error is the dating of letter XXVII as August 3, 1708, although the context seems to require a date somewhat later than August 3. See Taylor, p. 203.

39. Letters XXI, XXII, XXIII, XXIV. Dobrée made this change be-

cause Berkeley placed four letters dated 1700 in the order: September, July, March, February.

40. Congreve's letter of July 7, 1711 (Add. MSS. 39,311, f. 5) first published by Taylor, should be placed in this group, making a total of four letters for 1711.

41. See Luttrell, III, 125, 351; IV, 188, 229, 263.

42. On Wednesday, October 6, the Duke of Ormonde "sett forward for Ireland." See Luttrell, IV, 288. Were such evidence needed, the references to the Peace of Ryswick, the Duke of Ormonde's approaching journey to Ireland, and the Duchess of Ormonde's sojourn in Kilkenny would clearly establish the date of this letter as 1697.

43. John Hartstonge (1654–1717) was the third son of Sir Standish Hartstonge, one of the Barons of the Exchequer in Ireland. He received his early education in Charleville and Kilkenny, and took his B.A. degree in 1677, his M.A. degree in 1680 at Trinity College, Dublin. He received an M.A. degree from Gonville and Caius College, Cambridge, in 1680 and became a fellow of that college. He was chaplain to both the first and the second Duke of Ormonde. In 1693 he was appointed Bishop of Ossory and in 1714 Bishop of Derry.

44. *The Mourning Bride,* ed. Dobrée, pp. 503–504.

45. For the earlier and later impressions of Kilkenny of Mary, Duchess of Ormonde, see Add. MSS. 28,927, f. 161, and HMC *Seventh Report,* part I (London, 1879), p. 769.

46. This fact was noted by George A. Aitken, *The Life of Richard Steele* (London, 1889), I, 65n.

47. *A List of the Claims as they are Entred with the Trustees At Chichester-House on College Green Dublin, On or before the Tenth of August, 1700* (Dublin, 1701), p. 121.

48. Add. MSS. 28,888, f. 268.

49. In the same year Congreve still writes "Keally." See the address leaf, inscribed "1702," of a letter which Congreve addressed "To Joseph Keally Esqre," in the Berg Collection, New York Public Library. Mein's manuscript letter of 1704 is addressed to "Joseph Kelly"; and all of Keally's manuscript letters (1705–7) to the Duke of Ormonde are signed: "Jos: Kelly."

50. Add. MSS. 39,311, f. 1.

51. *The Journals of the House of Commons of the Kingdom of Ireland* (Dublin, 1796–1800), II, 447.

52. *Impartial Occurrences, Foreign and Domestick* [later *Pue's Occurrences*], June 2, 1705.

53. Ormonde MSS. 164, f. 476. In 1711 Nutley became a Judge of the Queen's Bench. See *The Journals of the House of Commons of the Kingdom of Ireland,* II, 719.

54. Burtchaell, pp. 74–75.

55. *The Sixth Report of the Deputy Keeper of the Public Records in Ireland* (Dublin, 1874), p. 83.

56. Ormonde MSS. 167, f. 676.

57. Burtchaell, pp. 74–75.

58. *The Mourning Bride*, ed. Dobrée, p. 508.

59. *Ibid.*, pp. 514–515. This undated letter (XLIII) was obviously written in the autumn of 1705. There is a reference to the Porters of Arundel Street, who by June of the next year had moved to Surrey Street, where Congreve joined them.

60. Letter XXI, which must have been written on December 15, 1705, although Berkeley assigned it to December 15, 1708, indicates that Keally had recently arrived in Dublin. See *The Mourning Bride*, ed. Dobrée, p. 508.

61. Ormonde MSS. 169, f. 807.

62. *The Mourning Bride*, ed. Dobrée, p. 499. According to local tradition in the parish of Paulstown, county Kilkenny, Joseph Keally was a very corpulent man. When he drove up the long avenue (now a grass-grown lane between hedges) to Kellymount House and reached the rising ground near the house, another horse had to be sent down to assist in drawing the carriage the rest of the way.

63. *Literary Relics*, ed. George Monck Berkeley (London, 1789), p. 397.

64. See *The Mourning Bride*, ed. Dobrée, pp. 505 and 509. Taylor, p. 203, misinterprets the statement: "I hear you have increased your family by two" [a daughter and a brother-in-law] and infers that Keally's family was "enlarged by the birth of twins." Keally may have had a son, John, who died in infancy. In *The Register of the Parish of S. Peter and S. Kevin, Dublin, 1669–1761* (Exeter and London, 1911), p. 185, under christenings for November 1709, occurs the entry: "Jo^n, ye son of Joseph and Eliz. Kelly of Stephens Greene, bp^t 13th."

65. See "Autobiography of Pole Cosby," *Journal of the Co. Kildare Archaeological Society and Surrounding Districts*, V (1906–1908), 87.

66. Thomas Wharton, first Marquis of Wharton (1648–1715), was the third son of Philip, fourth Baron Wharton, by his second wife, Jane, daughter of Arthur Goodwin. He was a Privy Councillor and Comptroller of the Household under King William, and Lord Lieutenant of Ireland (1708–10) and a leading Whig in Queen Anne's reign. In 1715 he was created Marquis of Wharton. He married in 1673 Anne, daughter of Sir Henry Lee, fifth Bart. of Ditchley, who died in 1685; and secondly, in 1692, Lucy, daughter of Adam Loftus, Viscount Lisburne.

67. *The Mourning Bride*, ed. Dobrée, p. 508.

68. *Literary Relics*, ed. Berkeley, p. 384.

69. *Liber Munerum Publicorum Hiberniae . . . Being the Report of Rowley Lascelles of the Middle Temple, Barrister at Law* [London, 1824–30], I (parts I–IV), 136.

NOTES

70. *The Journals of the House of Commons of the Kingdom of Ireland*, II, 664.

71. Add. MSS. 39,311, f. 3.

72. *The Mourning Bride,* ed. Dobrée, pp. 509, 513–514.

73. *Ibid.,* pp. 495, 507.

74. *Literary Relics,* ed. Berkeley, pp. 402, 393–394.

75. *The Mourning Bride,* ed. Dobrée, p. 489.

76. *Ibid.,* p. 496.

77. A translation of Congreve's ballad, "Jack French-Man's Defeat." The poem and the translation were both printed in 1709 in Tottel's *Sixth Miscellany.* See Hodges, pp. 89–90.

78. *The Mourning Bride,* ed. Dobrée, p. 507.

79. Ormonde MSS. 172, f. 1000.

80. *Literary Relics,* ed. Berkeley, pp. 398–399.

81. *The Mourning Bride,* ed. Dobrée, pp. 495, 498.

82. *Ibid.,* pp. 491, 486.

83. *Literary Relics,* ed. Berkeley, p. 391.

84. Add. MSS, 39,311, f. 3.

85. *The Mourning Bride,* ed. Dobrée, pp. 486, 491, 506, 504, 497.

86. *Ibid.,* pp. 491, 492, 502, 505–506, 507.

87. *Ibid.,* pp. 507, 486, 494, 497, 511, 513.

88. *Ibid.,* p. 513.

89. With the Tories in power, Congreve was in some danger of losing his commissionership of wine licenses. But by December 27 of this year, Swift had intervened successfully in his behalf. See Swift, *Journal to Stella,* II, 589.

90. *The Mourning Bride,* ed. Dobrée, p. 514.

The Fitzgeralds of Castle Dod

1. Congreve matriculated at Trinity College, Dublin, on April 5, 1686, Robert Fitzgerald two months later, on June 14. See Burtchaell and Sadleir, pp. 168 and 286.

2. See Egmont MSS. I, f. 12a.

3. It is possible that Richard's grandfather was George Fitzgerald of Fitrongten, slain with two of his sons in the Queen's service before 1596. See SP 63.192–3, f. 185. Two of George Fitzgerald's surviving sons were William and Richard, in which connection it may be noted that the Richard of this memoir had a brother, William, to whom there are references in the Egmont MSS.

4. The Irish Court of Wards was established to educate minors who were tenants-in-chief of the Crown and to administer their estates.

5. Sir Philip Percivall (1605–1647) was the second son of Richard Percivall of Sydenham, by his second wife, Alice, daughter of John

THE FITZGERALDS

Sherman of Ottery St. Mary. He became Clerk of the Commission for Wards in Ireland (1624); Clerk of the Crown, Clerk of the Common Pleas, and Custos Brevium (1628); Collector of Customs in Dublin (1629); was sworn of the Privy Council (1638); became Commissary General of Victuals for the army (1642); served as a Commissioner to the King from the Irish Council of State (1644); was M.P. for Newport, Cornwall, in the English House of Commons (1647), where he defended himself against charges of disloyalty to the Parliament. He was knighted in 1636. In 1626 he married Katherine, daughter of Arthur Usher, by Judith, daughter of Sir Robert Newcomen.

6. Add. MSS. 27,988, f. 15.

7. *Ibid.*, f. 18.

8. Egmont MSS. I. In these manuscripts the folio pages are frequently not numbered.

9. *The Journals of the House of Commons of the Kingdom of Ireland,* I, 65, 66, 77, 137, 140, 142, 144, 145, 149, 155, 157, 159, 160, 164, 165, 293, 301.

10. Egmont MSS. I, f. 52.

11. *Liber Munerum Publicorum Hiberniae,* I, 171.

12. See *Journal of the Cork Historical and Archaeological Society,* III, no. 33 (1894), 199. Castle Dod is two miles southeast of the town of Charleville (Rathluirc), which is twenty-nine miles from Cork, on the highway leading from Cork to Limerick.

13. See Charles Smith, *The Ancient and Present State of the County and City of Cork.* ed. R. Day and W. A. Copinger (Cork, 1893), I, 302.

14. See SP 63.167, f. 44 III; SP 63.175, f. 157; and SP 63.202, Pt.3, f. 292.

15. Egmont MSS. II.

16. William Fitzgerald acted as agent for Lady Ann Docwra, a cousin of Richard Boyle, first Earl of Cork. See Egmont MSS. II.

17. Egmont MSS. II.

18. George Fitzgerald, sixteenth Earl of Kildare (1611–1660), was the third but only surviving son of Thomas Fitzgerald, brother of Gerald, fourteenth Earl of Kildare, by Frances, first daughter of Sir Thomas Randolph, Postmaster-General of England. He was educated at Christ Church, Oxford; was colonel of his own regiment against the rebels in the Irish Rebellion (1641–47); was Governor of county Kildare (1641); and deputy Governor of Dublin (1647). In 1630 he married Joan, fourth daughter of Richard Boyle, first Earl of Cork, by his second wife, Catherine, daughter of Sir Geoffrey Fenton.

19. Egmont MSS, VI, ff. 44–45. Sellunyin may be Killuntin, parish Ardnageehy, county Cork; Ardmaye may be Ardmayle, county Tipperary.

20. *Ibid.*, CCVIII, f. 57.

21. *Ibid.*, CCII, f. 363.

NOTES

22. *The Journals of the House of Commons of the Kingdom of Ireland*, I, 165.

23. *Ibid.*, 244.

24. Sir William Parsons, a relative of the Earl of Cork, and Sir John Borlase. Sir Henry Tichborne succeeded Parsons.

25. Richard Boyle, first Earl of Cork (1566–1643), was the second son of Roger Boyle of Preston, near Faversham, Kent, by Joan, daughter of Robert Naylor of Canterbury. He was admitted to Corpus Christi College, Cambridge (1583); then to the Middle Temple, where he was clerk to the Chief Baron of the Exchequer; emigrated to Ireland (1588) and became deputy to the Escheator General; was imprisoned, on charges of embezzlement, in both Ireland and England, but acquitted; became Clerk of the Council of Munster (1600); bought all of the lands of Sir Walter Raleigh in Ireland (1602); was made Privy Councillor (I. 1613, E. 1640); was appointed one of the Lords Justices (1629); Lord Treasurer of Ireland (1631); in the Rebellion of 1641, raised two troops of horse and opposed the rebels. He was created Lord Boyle, Baron of Youghal, county Cork (1616), and Viscount Dungarvan, county Waterford, and Earl of Cork (1620). In 1595 he married Joan, daughter of William Apsley of Limerick; she died in 1599. In 1603 he married Catherine, daughter of Sir Geoffrey Fenton; she died in 1630.

26. Richard Boyle, second Earl of Cork and first Earl of Burlington (1612–1698), was the first surviving son of Richard Boyle, first Earl of Cork, by his second wife, Catherine, daughter of Sir Geoffrey Fenton. He was knighted in Youghal (1624), being then styled Viscount Dungarvan. He raised a troop of horse for the King (1639); was Governor of Youghal (1641); Lord Lieutenant of the West Riding, Yorkshire (1667, 1679–87); and Recorder of York (1685–88). He was attainted by the Irish Parliament of 1689 but restored in 1690. He became Earl of Cork (1643); Baron Clifford of Lanesborough, Yorkshire (1644); and was created Earl of Burlington, in the county of York (1664). In 1634 he married Elizabeth, Baroness Clifford, daughter and heir of Henry Clifford, fifth Earl of Cumberland.

27. Roger Boyle, first Earl of Orrery (1621–1679), was third son of Richard Boyle, first Earl of Cork, by his second wife, Catherine, daughter of Sir Geoffrey Fenton. He was educated at Trinity College, Dublin, and traveled on the Continent. In the Rebellion, he defended Lismore and held a command at the battle of Liscarrol. He served the parliamentary commissioners (1647–49), but after the execution of Charles I, lived in retirement at Marston, Somersetshire; assisted Cromwell in the subjection of Munster (1649–51); was a member of Cromwell's council; assisted Sir Charles Coote in securing Ireland for Charles II; was appointed one of the Lords Justices and Lord President of Munster (1660); drew up the Act of Settlement; was impeached in the House of Commons, but cleared

THE FITZGERALDS

himself (1668); spent his last years at Castlemartyr. He was created
Baron Broghill (1627); Earl of Orrery (1660). In 1641 he married Lady
Margaret Howard, third daughter of Theophilus, second Earl of Suffolk.
He was the author of a number of heroic tragedies, a romance, *Parthenissa,*
and a *Treatise of the Art of War.*

28. Egmont MSS. CCIII, f. 38.

29. HMC, *Ormonde,* n.s., II (London, 1903), 27.

30. Egmont MSS. VI, f. 65.

31. Sir John Percivall, first Bart. (1629–1665), was the eldest son of
Sir Philip Percivall, by Katherine, daughter of Arthur Usher. He was educated at Magdalene College, Cambridge; admitted to Lincoln's Inn (1649).
He accompanied Henry Cromwell to Ireland (1655); settled in Kinsale
(1656); was knighted (1658); became Clerk of the Crown, Prothonotary
of the Common Pleas, and Keeper of the Public Accounts (1660); was
made a Privy Councillor and created a baronet (1661); became a member of the Council of Trade in Ireland (1664); and was appointed Regis-
trar to the Commissioners for the Settlement of Ireland (1665). In 1656
he married Katherine, daughter of Robert Southwell of Kinsale.

32. Elizabeth Fitzgerald married Captain Owen Lloyd (1633–1664).
She had three sons: Thomas, who became a colonel in the army and
took part in the Battle of the Boyne; Owen, who became Dean of Connor;
and Richard (b. 1662), who matriculated at Trinity College, Dublin, in
1677, in 1681 was sent to London to study law, and became Lord Chief
Justice of Jamaica.

33. Anne Fitzgerald married Colonel William Legge, son of William
Legge, Groom of the Bedchamber to Charles I, and brother of George
Legge, first Baron Dartmouth. Colonel Legge became Governor of Kinsale
(*c.* 1684). Anne's daughter, Alice, married as her second husband Sir
Robert Stewart of Castle-Stewart.

34. In December 1646 the house of John Fitzgerald's foster mother,
near Dublin, was burned by the rebels. The boy expressed a desire to live
with Sir Luke Fitzgerald, but was placed with a family in Fonts. His
father made plans to have him sent to England the following spring.
See Egmont MSS. XI, f. 126.

35. Egmont MSS VI, f. 57.

36. Thomas Morrice, *A Collection of the State Letters of the Right
Honourable Roger Boyle, The First Earl of Orrery* (Dublin, 1743), II,
5, 7, 4.

37. Egmont MSS. VI, f. 60.

38. HMC, *Ormonde,* n.s., II, 173.

39. *Ibid.,* 189.

40. Egmont MSS. XI, f. 115.

41. Murrough O'Brien, first Earl of Inchiquin and sixth Baron Inchiquin (1614–1674), was the eldest son of Dermod, fifth Baron Inchiquin,

by Ellen, eldest daughter of Sir Edmond Fitzgerald of Cloyne. He distinguished himself as a commander in the Rebellion and won notable victories against the rebels. In 1644 he served Parliament as President of Munster, but in 1648 declared for the King, and subsequently assisted Ormonde. Cromwell's conquest of Ireland forced him to seek asylum in France in 1650. He became Lieutenant General in the French army and Viceroy of Catalonia. After the Restoration, he was restored to his Irish honors and estates. In 1654 the exiled King created him Baron O'Brien of Burren, county Clare, and Earl of Inchiquin. In 1635 he married Elizabeth, daughter of Sir William St. Leger.

42. Egmont MSS. VI, f. 69.

43. "Rebellion 1641–2 Described in a Letter of Rev. Urban Vigors to Rev. Henry Jones," in *Journal of the Cork Historical and Archaeological Society,* second series, II, no. 19 (1896), 293.

44. "The Battle of Liscarroll, 1642," ed. James Buckley, in *Journal of the Cork Historical and Archaeological Society,* second series, IV, no. 38 (1898), 100.

45. In 1644 the Earl of Leicester had retired to Penshurst, out of favor with both King and Parliament.

46. In 1645 Sir John Temple made formal accusations against Sir Philip Percivall, which, however, came to nothing.

47. Egmont MSS. X, f. 16.

48. *Ibid.,* XI, f. 17.

49. *Ibid.,* ff. 18, 19.

50. SP 63.266, ff. 68–69.

51. Egmont MSS. XI, ff. 116, 126, 150, 160; XII, f. 67.

52. *Ibid.,* XI, f. 126; XII, f. 119.

53. *Ibid.,* XII, ff. 59, 111.

54. *Ibid.,* CLI.

55. James Butler, twelfth Earl and first Duke of Ormonde (1610–1688), was the eldest son of Thomas, Viscount Thurles, by Elizabeth, daughter of Sir John Poyntz. At his father's death, he became a royal ward. He was made Lieutenant General of His Majesty's forces in Ireland (1641); concluded with the rebels a Cessation of Arms for a year (1643) and a treaty of peace (1646); surrendered Dublin to the Parliament Commissioners (1647); effected a peace between the royalists and rebels (1649); was an exile in France and Belgium (1650–60). He was created Duke of Ormonde (1661). He was Lord Lieutenant of Ireland (1644–47, 1661–69, 1677–85). In 1629 he married Elizabeth Preston, Baroness Dingwall, only daughter and heir of Richard, Earl of Desmond.

56. Add. MSS. 27,988, f. 96. See the statement, in "Notes concerning my family," by Sir John Percivall: "In 1649 dyed Mr Fitzgerald of Castle Dod brother in Law to Sr P.P. while he was collector in Wales for the mony assessed for the releif of Irel^d."

57. Egmont MSS. XIII, f. 9.

58. *Ibid.*, XII, f. 58.

59. *Ibid.*, XIII, f. 9; CCV, ff. 201, 242.

60. *Ibid.*, XVI, ff. 28, 42. Judith Percivall, Sir Philip's eldest daughter, married in 1654 Colonel Randall Clayton, son of Lawrence Clayton of Mallow.

61. Egmont MSS., XVII, f. 22.

62. *Ibid.*, f. 37.

63. *Ibid.*, f. 46.

64. *Ibid.*, XVIII, ff. 1, 8.

65. *Ibid.*, XVII.

66. *Liber Munerum Publicorum Hiberniae*, I, 171.

67. SO 1.4, f. 625.

68. SP 63.142.

69. Morrice, I, 86.

70. *The Journals of the House of Commons of the Kingdom of Ireland*, I, Part II, 672.

71. Robert Southwell (1607–1677) was the son of Anthony Southwell, by Margaret, daughter of Sir Ralph Skelton of Norfolk. He was appointed collector of Kinsale (1631); sovereign of Kinsale (1657); governor of the fort at Ringcurran; and Vice-Admiral of Munster (1670). He married Helena, only daughter of Major Robert Gore of Shereton, Wiltshire.

72. *Admissions to the Middle Temple, 1501–1744.*

73. SO 1.8, f. 109.

74. Add. MSS. 38,015, f. 149.

75. Elizabeth Fitzgerald married the Rev. Simon Gibbings, rector of Mallow, in 1696. She had a son, Robert. Her daughter, Elizabeth, married Randall Clayton, eldest son of Lawrence Clayton, son of Colonel Randall Clayton, by his wife, Judith. See Egmont MSS. CLI.

76. Mary Fitzgerald married Hawes Cross in 1698. She had a son, Fitzgerald.

77. Sir Philip Percivall, second Bart. (1657–1680), was the eldest son of Sir John Percivall, first Bart. He was educated at Christ Church, Oxford; admitted to Lincoln's Inn (1675); traveled on the Continent (1676–79); and settled at Burton, county Cork (1679).

78. Sir Robert Southwell (1635–1702) was the eldest son of Robert Southwell of Kinsale. He received his B.A. degree at Queen's College, Oxford (1655). He was clerk to the Privy Council (1664–79); succeeded his father as Vice-Admiral of Munster (1677); was envoy to Portugal and Brussels; Commissioner of Customs (1689–97); principal Secretary of State for Ireland (1690–1702); and president of the Royal Society (1690–95). In 1664 he married Elizabeth, eldest daughter of Sir Edward Dering of Surrenden-Dering, Kent.

NOTES

79. Egmont MSS. XXXVIII.

80. Sir John Percivall, third Bart. (1660–1686), was brother of Sir Philip Percivall, second Bart. He was educated at Christ Church, Oxford; admitted to Lincoln's Inn (1678); became Clerk of the Crown, Prothonotary of the Common Pleas, and Keeper of the Public Accounts (1677); and settled at Burton (1682). In 1681 he married Katherine, daughter of Sir Edward Dering of Surrenden-Dering, Kent.

81. Egmont MSS. XL.

82. *Ibid.*, XLI.

83. *Ibid.*, XL.

84. *Ibid.*, XLIV.

85. *Idem.*

86. The Hon. Henry Boyle (d. 1693) was the second son of Roger Boyle, first Earl of Orrery. He married Lady Mary O'Brien, daughter of Murrough O'Brien, first Earl of Inchiquin, by Elizabeth, daughter of Sir William St. Leger. He took part in the Battle of the Boyne, and died during the Duke of Marlborough's campaign in Flanders.

87. *Calendar of the·Orrery Papers,* ed. Edward MacLysaght (Dublin, 1941), p. 337.

88. Egmont MSS. XXXI and XXXII.

89. *Ibid.*, CCVII, f. 1283.

90. TCD Senior and Junior Book, 1685–87.

91. Francis H. Tuckey, *The County and City of Cork Remembrancer* (Cork, 1837), p. 110.

92. TCD MSS. F.4.3, List of the Protestants Who Fled from Ireland—1688.

93. Lionel Boyle, third Earl of Orrery (1670–1703), was the eldest son of Roger Boyle, second Earl of Orrery, by Lady Mary Sackville, daughter of Richard, fifth Earl of Dorset. He married Mary, natural daughter of Charles, fourth Earl of Dorset.

94. Charles Boyle, Lord Clifford of Lanesborough (1639–1694), was the first surviving son of Richard Boyle, second Earl of Cork and first Earl of Burlington. He took his seat in the House of Lords in 1663 as Viscount Dungarvan. On the death of his mother in 1691, he became Lord Clifford. In 1661 he married Jane, first daughter of William Seymour, Duke of Somerset, who died in 1679; in 1688 he married Arethusa, sixth daughter of George Berkeley, first Earl of Berkeley. He died during his father's lifetime.

95. *Journal of the Very Rev. Rowland Davies, L.L.D.,* ed. Richard Caulfield, Camden Society Publications, no. LXVIII (1857), pp. 92, 98.

96. *Ibid.*, p. 98.

97. Lieutenant Congreve, the dramatist's father, whom Davies met in London on May 2, 1689 (see *Davies,* p. 13) may have sought the assistance of the Earl of Cork, whose estate agent he became in 1690.

THE FITZGERALDS

98. See SP 44.339, f. 410.

99. See Admission Register, 1670–1750, Inner Temple, f. 1223. This information was kindly supplied by E. A. P. Hart, Librarian of the Inner Temple.

100. Robert Fitzgerald may have chosen the Inner Temple because the Middle Temple was overcrowded, with over four hundred members. See J. Bruce Williamson, *The History of the Temple* (London, 1925), p. 558.

101. See Hodges, p. 56.

102. *The Mourning Bride,* ed. Dobrée, pp. 487–488, 491, 490.

103. *Ibid.,* p. 489.

104. See *The Council Book of the Corporation of the City of Cork, From 1609 to 1643, and From 1690 to 1800,* ed. Richard Caulfield (Guildford, Surrey, 1876), p. 311.

105. In 1677 nearly all of King's Bench Walk was destroyed by fire. An extensive building program was undertaken, which probably extended into the early 1690's.

106. *The Mourning Bride,* ed. Dobrée, pp. 493, 495, 508.

107. *Ibid.,* pp. 497–498.

108. *The Orrery Papers,* ed. Countess of Cork and Orrery (London, 1903), I, 215.

109. *The Mourning Bride,* ed. Dobrée, pp. 502, 505–506.

110. *Ibid.,* p. 509.

111. See *Liber Munerum Publicorum Hiberniae,* I, 71–72.

112. A child born in 1710 (see *The Mourning Bride,* ed. Dobrée, p. 509) must have died in infancy.

113. See RDD Transcript Books 53.416.36166 and 54.386.36167.

114. Richard Boyle, third Viscount Shannon (1674–1740), was the eldest son of Richard Boyle, son of Francis Boyle, fifth son of Richard, first Earl of Cork. He served three campaigns in Flanders and under the Duke of Ormonde in Spain. He was appointed Lieutenant General and Commander in Chief of His Majesty's land forces in Ireland (1720); one of the Lords Justices of Ireland (1721–24); and with John, Duke of Argyll, Joint Field Marshal of all His Majesty's forces (1738). He was of the Privy Council of George I and George II. In 1695 he married Mary, Dowager Countess of Orrery, widow of Roger, second Earl of Orrery; she died in 1710. By a second marriage, he had one daughter, Grace.

115. See Tuckey, p. 127.

116. *An Elegy On the much Lamented Death of Mr. Prime Serjeant Fitz-Gerald* (Dublin, n.d.).

117. To Catherine Fitzgerald he left an annuity of thirty pounds to be paid out of the "towns and lands of Castledod." See RDD Transcript Book: 85.41.58956.

NOTES

118. PROD Betham's Genealogical Abstracts, Prerogative Wills (Phillips MSS.), 79, f. 27.

119. PROD Prerogative Will Book, 1726–7–8, f. 200.

120. William Stewart, third Viscount Mountjoy and first Earl of Blesington (1709–1769), was the only surviving son and heir of William Stewart, second Viscount Mountjoy, by Anne, youngest daughter of Murrough Boyle, first Viscount Blesington. He succeeded his father as Viscount Mountjoy in 1728. After being educated in England, he returned to Ireland, and in 1731 took his seat in Parliament. In 1745 the King, pleased by "his great humanity and extensive charity," created him Earl of Blesington. In 1748 he became a P.C. and Governor of county Tyrone.

121. Martha, Viscountess Blesington (d. 1767), was the eldest daughter of Samuel Matthews of Bonnettstown, county Kilkenny, by Anne, daughter of Joseph Cuffe of Castle Inch, county Kilkenny. In 1709 she became the second wife of Charles Boyle, second Viscount Blesington.

122. Castle Dod was renamed Castle Harrison. Its tower was removed, and other alterations were made; but the thick walls and barred windows of the older part of the building bear witness to the dangerous times that this historic house has withstood. Castle Harrison has a pleasant demesne and beautiful views of the Ballyhoura Hills.

123. See RDD Transcript Book 85.71.59091.

124. Another son, Lionel Robert, was born on April 12, 1736, but died in infancy.

125. William Stewart, styled Viscount Mountjoy, died in Paris of smallpox on February 2, 1754.

126. John Forbes (1714–1796), Admiral of the Fleet, was the second son of George Forbes, third Earl of Granard, by Mary, widow of Phineas Preston and first daughter of William Stewart, first Viscount Mountjoy. He became Rear Admiral of the Royal Navy (1747) and Commander in Chief in the Mediterranean (1749); occupied a seat in the Admiralty (1756–63); and held the rank of Admiral of the Fleet (1781–96). In 1758 he married Lady Mary Capel, daughter of William, third Earl of Essex, by whom he had twin daughters, Catherine Elizabeth, who married in 1784 the Hon. William Wellesley-Pole, afterwards third Earl of Mornington, and Maria Elinor, who married in 1791 the Hon. John Charles Villiers, afterwards third Earl of Clarendon.

127. John Baptist Kelly, son of Joseph Keally's brother, John.

128. PCC 1774, 358 Bargrave.

Henrietta, Duchess of Marlborough

1. Leigh Hunt, p. xxvii.
2. Lady Barbara Clarges was the wife of Sir Thomas Clarges. She

was the youngest daughter of John Berkeley, fourth Viscount Fitzhardinge, by Barbara, first daughter of Sir Edward Villiers. Sarah, Duchess of Marlborough, objected because Henrietta went so often to the house of Lady Fitzhardinge, Lady Clarges' mother, "a dangerous place for Young people." See Blenheim MSS. FI. 35, f. 37.

3. Swift, *Journal to Stella*, II, 630–631.

4. Pope, *Works*, VII, 422.

5. *Ibid.*, 75–76.

6. Montagu, *Letters*, I, 349.

7. *Ibid.*, 361.

8. Wortley MSS. IV, f. 185.

9. See *The Tears of Amaryllis for Amyntas* (1703).

10. See "To the Right Honourable the Earl of Godolphin. . . Pindarique Ode," in *Poems Upon Several Occasions* (1710).

11. Blenheim MSS. FI. 35, f. 36.

12. William Villiers, second Earl of Jersey, Lady Fitzhardinge's nephew, married in 1705 Judith, only daughter of Frederick Herne, a London merchant.

13. *The Wentworth Papers, 1705–1739*, ed. James J. Cartwright (London, 1883), p. 214.

14. Soon after Sarah's return from the Continent (August 1, 1714). See Blenheim MSS. FI. 35, f. 61.

15. "The Secret History of Henrada Maria Teresa," in *The Court Parrot; A New Miscellany, in Prose and Verse* (London, 1733), pp. 13–22. According to *The Daily Journal*, November 23, 1733, *The Court Parrot* was published "This Day."

16. Swift, *Correspondence*, III, 153.

17. Pope, *Works*, VII, 422.

18. *Ibid.*, p. 78.

19. See the statement in *The Daily Post*, May 6, 1728, that on Saturday, May 4, "the Junior Dutchess of Marlborough, accompany'd by Mr. Congreve, set out for the Bath. For which Place the Lady Mary her Daughter set out the Day before." Gay had intended, at any rate, to be of the party, for on March 20, 1728, he wrote to Swift: "In about a month I am going to the Bath with the Duchess of Marlborough and Mr. Congreve." See Swift, *Correspondence*, IV, 16.

20. Montagu, *Letters*, II, 17.

21. Blenheim MSS. E. 8.

22. The day after her mother's death, Lord Godolphin wrote to the Duchess of Newcastle: "I rejoyce, My Dear, in the midst of my affliction, that you went from this dismall place at the time you did." See Add. MSS. 33,079, f. 19.

23. PCC 1729, 135 Brook.

24. For a detailed discussion of this will, see Hodges, pp. 117–120.

25. HMC, *Fifteenth Report, Appendix,* part VI (London, 1897), pp. 56–57.

26. Horace Walpole, *Reminiscences,* ed. Paget Toynbee (Oxford, 1924), p. 87. John Taylor in *Records of My Life* (London, 1832), I, 76, says that Sarah never mentioned her daughter "but by the name of Moll Congreve."

27. Spence, p. 376.

28. Pope, *Works,* III, 199.

29. *Ibid.,* 88. Sarah may have paid Pope to suppress this portrait, which he had intended for the 1735 edition of the *Essay on Man.*

30. From a comment by Sarah (see Mrs. Arthur Colville, *Duchess Sarah,* London, 1914, p. 312), it may be inferred that this gift was by way of reward for Gay's "An Epistle to Her Grace, Henrietta, Dutchess of Marlborough." See Gay, *Poetical Works,* pp. 169–170.

31. *The Female Faction: or, The Gay Subscribers; A Poem* (London [1729]), p. 5.

32. *The Amorous D[uc]h[e]ss Or, Her G[race] Grateful* (London, 1733), p. 8. The author asserts (p. 5) that a paragraph which had appeared in *The Daily Post* inspired his verses. *The Daily Post,* July 15, 1732, states: "We hear that the Effigies of the late ingenious William Congreve, Esq; done in Waxwork, at the Expence of 200 *l* and which was kept at a Person of Quality's house in St. James's, was broke to Pieces by the Carelessness of a Servant in bringing it down Stairs last Monday night."

33. T. Cibber, *The Lives of the Poets,* IV, 92.

34. Thomas Davies, *Dramatic Miscellanies* (London, 1783–84), III, 382.

35. Andrew Kippis, *Biographia Britannica* (London, 1778–93), IV, 75n.

36. Leigh Hunt, p. xxvi.

37. See *Letters To and From Henrietta [Howard], Countess of Suffolk, and Her Second Husband, The Hon. George Berkeley; From 1712 to 1767* (London, 1824), I, 330–331.

38. Add. MSS. 22,628, f. 87.

39. "Letters of Congreve to Tonson the Bookseller," in *The Gentleman's Magazine,* n.s. III (June, 1835), 610. The manuscript letter is in Malone MSS., Yale University Library. The portrait that Henrietta longed to have is reproduced as one of our illustrations.

40. Add. MSS. 22,627, ff. 59–60. Mary Bellenden, the youngest daughter of John, second Lord Bellenden, was a maid of honor to Princess Caroline. Her private marriage in 1720 to Colonel John Campbell, afterwards fourth Duke of Argyll, was resented by the Prince of Wales, who had courted her without success.

41. Add. MSS. 20,104, ff. 68–69.

42. Lady Anne Evelyn was the daughter of Edward Boscawen of

Cornwall and the wife of Sir John Evelyn (1682–1763), grandson of the diarist. Sir John Evelyn held the posts of Joint Postmaster-General (1708–15) and Commissioner of Customs (1721–63).

43. Add MSS. 15,949, ff. 73–74.

44. At the time of Henrietta's death, Sir John held a duplicate of her will, of which he was one of the executors. See Add. MSS. 33,079, f. 20.

45. Add. MSS. 15,949, f. 65.

46. For example, Sarah did not keep a letter concerning which she writes to Lord Godolphin as follows (November 12, 1724): "I sent your Lordship a Copy of her last letter to me which you were not pleased to take any notice of. she seems to think she is injured as to her fortune and that you are of the same oppinion, but I can't believe that." See Blenheim MSS. E. 21.

47. "An account of the Dutches of marl. & montagus behaviour before & after their fathers death," Blenheim MSS. Fl. 35, f. 7.

48. Blenheim MSS. E. 6.

49. In a postscript to the first letter, Henrietta announces: "The Princess is just come to Berkeley house and sent for us where we are now going." Princess Anne and the Prince of Denmark moved to Berkeley House in the summer of 1692. The last letter in this group was written on the day (October 24, 1701) when Robert Spencer, second son of Henrietta's sister, Anne, Countess of Sunderland, was born.

50. Blenheim MSS. E. 6.

51. Stuart J. Reid, who examined these letters when he catalogued the Blenheim MSS., remarks that in one of her letters "Henrietta tells her mother that she is prepared to 'go cheerfully to my martyrdom,' which is scarcely a pleasing allusion to the fact that the Duchess had expressed a desire to see her." But since the phrase in question occurs in a translated letter, it cannot refer to Sarah. See Reid, *John and Sarah, Duke and Duchess of Marlborough* (London, 1915), p. 420.

52. Blenheim MSS. E. 6.

53. *Idem.*

54. *Idem.*

55. *Idem.*

56. Blenheim MSS. E. 7.

57. Blenheim MSS. E. 6.

58. *Idem.*

59. Blenheim MSS. Fl. 35, ff. 63–66.

60. Blenheim MSS. E. 6.

61. *Idem.*

62. Lady Ross was Henrietta's cousin, Elizabeth, eldest daughter of Sir George Hamilton, by Sarah's elder sister, Frances (afterwards Duchess of Tyrconnel). She married Richard, first Viscount Ross.

63. Blenheim MSS. E. 6.

64. Blenheim MSS. FI. 33.

65. Sarah made a futile attempt to be reconciled to Henrietta, during the latter's final illness. In October, 1733, soon after Henrietta's death, she wrote of her to her granddaughter, Diana, Duchess of Bedford: "It is certain that her nature was tender and that she had many good things in her, with some oddness's. . . [She] had good nature and was the modestest young creature that ever I saw, till she was flattered and practised upon by the most vile people upon earth." See *Letters of a Grandmother, 1732–1735,* ed. Gladys Scott Thomson (London, 1943), p. 96.

66. Lady Henrietta Godolphin married in 1717 Thomas Pelham-Holles, first Duke of Newcastle-upon-Tyne (1693–1768). The Duke of Newcastle was the son of Thomas Pelham, first Baron Pelham of Laughton, by Lady Grace, youngest daughter of Gilbert Holles, third Earl of Clare. Among the posts which he held were those of Lord Chamberlain of the Household (1717–24); Privy Councillor (1717); Secretary of State for the South (1724–48) and for the North (1748–54); and First Lord of the Treasury (1754–56 and 1757–62). He was created Marquis of Clare and Duke of Newcastle-upon-Tyne (1715) and Duke of Newcastle-under-Lyne (1756).

67. William Godolphin, Marquis of Blandford (*c.* 1700–1731), was admitted to Clare Hall, Cambridge (1717); received the degree of D.C.L. from Balliol College, Oxford (1730); was M.P. for Penrhyn (1720–22), for Woodstock (1727–31). He was styled Viscount Rialton (1712–22); and became Marquis of Blandford (1722). He married (1729) Maria Catherina, daughter of Peter S. C. de Jong, Burgomaster of Utrecht, Holland.

68. In the letters of Sidney, first Earl of Godolphin, to Sarah there are many affectionate references to his daughter-in-law. When Henrietta was ill of the smallpox, he wrote of her (Blenheim MSS. E. 20): "I have just now near three, been kneeling by dear L^{dy} Harryett's bed side, and I find her pulse much slower, & not so Low as it was yesterday . . . She has not yett been told, she has the small pox, nor does she seem to suspect it, and if she did, I don't think she w^d bee much afrayd."

69. Blenheim MSS. FI. 35, ff. 36–37.

70. Henry Godolphin died in February, 1706. On February 29, 1706 Lady Wentworth wrote to her son, Lord Raby: "Lady Harryot Godolphin greeved soe much for the death of her youngist son . . . that she has throan herself into the smallpox by her exses of greef." See *The Wentworth Papers,* ed. Cartwright, p. 56.

71. Sarah's children and grandchildren perhaps grew weary of having her force upon them, when they lacked physical energy to object, such medicines as Russia Castor, liquorice and rhubarb, Dr. Lewis' bitter drink, and Sir Walter Raleigh's cordial.

72. Blenheim MSS. FI. 35, f. 40.

73. The original texts of this letter and the letter about the children's tea party have not been preserved.

74. Blenheim MSS. FI. 35, f. 42.

75. *Ibid.,* ff. 61–62.

76. In a letter to Sarah, written on June 24, 1703, the Duke remarks (Blenheim MSS. E. 2): "Upon your saying some thing to mee in one of your letters, of the Company 53 [Lady Harriet] keeps I write to her of my self, not taking any notice of what you had urged, that she Cou'd never find any lasting happyness in this world, but from the kindness of 27 [Mr. Godolphin] soe that she ought to omit nothing that might oblige him, you must not aske her for this letter, but I shou'd be glad to know if it has any effect, for I love her, and think her very good, soe that I shou'd hope if she Comits indiscresions, it is for want of thinking."

77. Blenheim MSS. FI. 35, f. 70.

78. *Ibid.,* f. 74.

79. *Ibid.,* f. 59.

80. *Ibid.,* f. 90.

81. *Ibid.,* ff. 95, 101. In a letter dated August 1 [1722] (see Blenheim MSS. E. 43) Dean Jones thanks Henrietta for a gift of one thousand pounds for mourning and concludes: "I shall constantly and earnestly beseech, The Infinite Goodnesse, wch only could Inspire so Divine a likenesse in y^r Graces breast, to give and continue to y^r Grace all the blessings of this life."

82. Blenheim MSS. E. 6.

83. Blenheim MSS. GI. 17.

84. *Idem.*

85. See n. 46.

86. *The Complete Works of Sir John Vanbrugh,* ed. Bonamy Dobrée and Geoffrey Webb (London, 1928), IV, 148–149.

87. Sarah had a warm regard for Dr. Hare, who had been the tutor of her son, John, Marquis of Blandford.

88. Henrietta stated in her will that "it is my desire and express Will that my Body be not at any time hereafter or on any pretence what soever carried to Blenham." See Add. MSS. 28,071, f. 35.

89. Add. MSS. 9120, f. 105.

90. Countess of Suffolk, *Letters,* II, 83.

91. Add. MSS. 33,080, f. 282.

92. Blenheim MSS. FI. 35, f. 66.

93. Blenheim MSS. E. 8.

94. Blenheim MSS. E. 21.

95. Blenheim MSS. E. 22.

96. Blenheim MSS. E. 21.

97. Blenheim MSS. E. 24.

98. Add. MSS. 33,079, ff. 1, 3, 17–19.

99. Blenheim MSS. E. 8.

100. Blenheim MSS. E. 23.

101. Add. MSS. 28,052, ff. 293, 295–296.

102. Blenheim MSS. E. 8. On May 16, 1723, Mrs. Pendarves wrote to Anne Granville: "The young Duchess of Marlborough has settled on Bononcini for his life £500 a-year, provided he will *not* compose any more for the ungrateful Academy, who do not deserve he should entertain them, since they don't know how to value his work as they ought, and likewise told him he should 'always be welcome to her table.'" See *The Autobiography and Correspondence of Mary Granville, Mrs. Delany,* ed. Lady Llanover (London, 1861), I, 79–80.

103. Blenheim MSS. E. 8.

104. *Idem.* James, first Earl Waldegrave (1685–1741), was sent to Paris as ambassador extraordinary in 1725.

105. Blenheim MSS. E. 8.

106. Blenheim MSS. FI. 35, f. 59.

107. One evidence of the Duchess of Newcastle's attitude towards her mother is afforded by the following item in *The Daily Post,* November 25, 1723: "On Saturday Night last, the young Dutchess of Marlborough was brought to Bed of a Daughter. A Messenger being sent Express with the News to her Daughter the Dutchess of Newcastle at Clermont, was handsomly gratify'd by her Grace, who came to Town immediately to attend her Mother on that Occasion."

108. Blenheim MSS. E. 9.

109. Blenheim MSS. FI. 35, ff. 49, 59.

110. Add. MSS. 28,052, f. 286.

111. Blenheim MSS. E. 8.

112. Add. MSS. 28,071, f. 35.

113. Longleat MSS., Note-Books of Anecdotes, Extracts, etc. of Margaret, Duchess of Portland, Box II, notebook 16.

114. Add. MSS. 28,071, ff. 34–42. See also PCC 1736, 113 Derby. Lord Godolphin is named first among the four executors.

115. Frederick Lewis, Prince of Wales (1707–1751), was the eldest son of George II by Queen Caroline and the father of George III. In 1717 he was created Duke of Gloucester, in 1727 Duke of Edinburgh, in 1729 Prince of Wales. He came to England in 1728. In 1736 he married Princess Augusta, daughter of Frederick, Duke of Saxe-Gotha; she died in 1772. His patronage of Bononcini and his friendship with Cobham were probably gratifying to Henrietta, Duchess of Marlborough.

116. *Lord Hervey and His Friends, 1726–38,* ed. Lord Ilchester (London, 1950), pp. 56, 67, 74, 92, 59.

117. *Ibid.,* p. 83.

118. *Ibid.,* p. 161.

119. *Ibid.,* p. 127. The "last letter" (p. 125) was dated "From the Duchess of Marlborough's Dressing-Room, December 23rd."

120. Add MSS. 33,064, ff. 475, 17. Henrietta had requested in her will that she might be buried "in the very same place" with her father-in-law.

DUCHESS OF LEEDS

Mary, Duchess of Leeds

1. Add. MSS. 33,079, f. 1.

2. Margaret Cavendish, Duchess of Portland (1715-1785) was the only daughter of Edward Harley, second Earl of Oxford, by Henrietta Cavendish Holles, only daughter of John Holles, fourth Earl of Clare, created Duke of Newcastle. She was the first cousin of Thomas Osborne, fourth Duke of Leeds. As a child, she was praised by Prior as "noble, lovely little Peggy." In 1734 she married William Bentinck, second Duke of Portland. Her mother was a great favorite of Lady Mary Wortley Montagu.

3. *The Private Letter-Books of Sir Walter Scott,* ed. Wilfred Partington (London, 1930), p. 345. Lady Louisa Stuart comments: "Congreve's contemporaries . . . were far from thinking the Duchess of Leeds . . . no relation to him." Boswell relished the account which he had from Mrs. Douglas, wife of Dr. Andrew Douglas, of Congreve's liaison with Henrietta. Boswell reports the story, relates the anecdote of the wax image of Congreve, and comments that the Duchess of Leeds "has turned out extremely well." See *Boswell's London Journal, 1762–1763,* ed. Frederick A. Pottle (New York, London, Toronto [1950]), p. 157.

4. Add. MSS. 33,079, f. 121.

5. PCC 1766, 16 Tyndall.

6. Add. MSS. 33,064, f. 447.

7. Add. MSS. 33,079, f. 20.

8. Add. MSS. 33,064, f. 481.

9. *Ibid.,* f. 482.

10. Add. MSS. 33,079, f. 161.

11. *Ibid.,* f. 28.

12. *Ibid.,* f. 128.

13. *Ibid.,* f. 90.

14. In mature life Mary, like her mother, had a taste for romantic literature. After she had become Duchess of Leeds, the Duke's librarian sent to her, probably at her request, thirty-two volumes, chiefly French romances and books of songs, from a collection which appears to have been Congreve's library. See a marginal note in a manuscript catalogue of books in the library of the Duke of Leeds, deposited with the Yorkshire Archaeological Society in Leeds, Yorkshire. The name "Congreve" in the heading of this catalogue, although crossed out, is legible. See also John C. Hodges, "Congreve's Library," in *The Times Literary Supplement,* August 12, 1949, p. 521.

15. Add. MSS. 33,081.

16. *Idem.*

17. Add. MSS. 33,079, f. 162.

18. Thomas Pelham, afterwards first Earl of Chichester (1728–1805). His son, Thomas Pelham, second Earl of Chichester (1756–1826), married in 1801 Lady Mary Henrietta Juliana Osborne, daughter of Francis Godolphin Osborne, fifth Duke of Leeds, by his first wife, Amelia, only surviving child of Robert D'Arcy, fourth Earl of Holdernesse.

19. Add. MSS. 33,065, ff. 181–182.

20. *Ibid.*, ff. 215–216.

21. Add. MSS. 33,073, f. 134.

22. Peregrine Hyde Osborne, third Duke of Leeds (1691–1731) married in 1712 Elizabeth, eldest daughter of Robert Harley, first Earl of Oxford; she died in 1713 at the birth of Thomas Osborne. He married in 1719 Anne, daughter of Charles Seymour, sixth Duke of Somerset; she died in 1722. He married in 1725 Juliana, daughter of Roger Hele, who survived him. She married in 1732 Charles Colyear, second Earl of Portmore, and died in 1794.

23. *Elizabeth Montagu, The Queen of the Blue Stockings,* ed. E[mily] J. Climenson (London, 1906), I, 51. According to Horace Walpole, the Duke of Newcastle possessed a set of gold plates "that would make a figure on any sideboard in the Arabian Tales." See *The Letters of Horace Walpole,* ed. Peter Cunningham (Edinburgh, 1906), I, 223.

24. Robert, second Baron Romney (1712–1793).

25. Add. MSS. 28,051, f. 327.

26. *Correspondence Between Frances, Countess of Hartford (Afterwards Duchess of Somerset,) and Henrietta Louisa, Countess of Pomfret, Between the Years 1738 and 1741* (London, 1806), II, 127–128.

27. Some years later, Horace Walpole described Kiveton as "an ugly neglected seat of the Duke of Leeds, with noble apartments and several good portraits." See Walpole, *Letters,* III, 31.

28. Lady Kinnoull was Abigail, youngest daughter of Robert Harley, first Earl of Oxford, by Elizabeth, daughter of Thomas Foley. In 1709 she married George Henry Hay, eighth Earl of Kinnoull. She had six daughters.

29. Robert Hay-Drummond (1711–1776) was the second son of George Henry Hay, eighth Earl of Kinnoull. He made the grand tour (1731–35) with his cousin, Thomas Osborne, fourth Duke of Leeds. He was royal chaplain to George II. In 1748 he became Bishop of St. Asaph; in June 1761, Bishop of Salisbury; in October 1761, Archbishop of York.

30. Lord Dupplin was Thomas Hay, afterwards ninth Earl of Kinnoull (1710–1787), eldest son of George Henry Hay, eighth Earl of Kinnoull.

31. Add. MSS. 33,073, f. 146.

32. *Ibid.,* f. 151.

33. Add. MSS. 33,080, f. 35.

34. *Ibid.* f. 39.

35. Mrs. Delany, *Autobiography and Correspondence,* II, 137.

36. Add. MSS. 33,080, f. 42.

37. *Ibid.,* f. 47.

38. *Ibid.,* f. 72.

39. *Ibid.,* f. 73.

40. Add. MSS. 32,992, f. 579.

41. For several drawings and water-color sketches of North Mimms Place (now North Mymms Park) see Add. MSS. 32,350, ff. 136–140. The property remained in the possession of the Leeds family until 1800.

42. Add. MSS. 33,080, f. 105.

43. Blenheim MSS. E. 9.

44. *Idem.*

45. PCC 1744, 259 Anstis.

46. PCC 1764, 395 Simpson.

47. Add. MSS. 32,713, f. 307.

48. Add. MSS. 32,715, f. 220.

49. Add. MSS. 33,066, ff. 78–79.

50. *Ibid.,* f. 104.

51. Add. MSS. 33,080, f. 154.

52. *Ibid.,* f. 190.

53. Add. MSS. 33,066, f. 298.

54. *Idem.*

55. *Ibid.,* f. 415.

56. Add. MSS. 33,067, f. 19.

57. Add. MSS. 28,050, f. 226.

58. *Ibid.,* f. 228.

59. Catherine, Countess of Lincoln (1727–1760), was the wife of the Duke of Newcastle's nephew, Henry Fiennes Clinton, ninth Earl of Lincoln, afterwards second Duke of Newcastle.

60. Add. MSS. 33,080, f. 280.

61. *The Works of Jeremy Bentham,* ed. John Bowring (Edinburgh, 1843), X, 30.

62. *Ibid.,* 34.

63. William Markham (1719–1807) was for eleven years (1753–1764) headmaster of Westminster School, where he was generally more highly regarded than by Bentham. In 1765 he was appointed Dean of Rochester; in 1767 Dean of Christ Church, Oxford; and in 1776 Archbishop of York. He named his youngest son, Osborne, for his former pupil, Francis Osborne, Marquis of Carmarthen. See Sir Clements Robert Markham, *A Memoir of Archbishop Markham, 1719–1807* (Oxford, 1906).

64. Bentham, *Works,* X, 30.

65. Undoubtedly Dr. Monsey.

66. Bentham, *Works,* X, 31. Bentham wrote some Latin couplets as a tribute to the Marquis of Carmarthen, on his recovery from an illness in December 1758. See *ibid.,* 32–33.

67. Add. MSS. 33,067, f. 232.

68. Add. MSS. 32,914, f. 431.

69. *The Letters of Mrs. Elizabeth Montagu,* ed. Matthew Montagu (London, 1809–13), IV, 274.

70. Add. MSS. 33,083, f. 59.

71. Walpole, *Letters,* III, 383.

72. Add. MSS. 33,067, f. 293.

73. Add. MSS. 33,076, f. 180.

74. Add. MSS. 28,050, f. 238.

75. [Thomas Lambe] *Lycidas, A Masque, To which is added Delia, A Pastoral Elegy; and Verses on the Death of the Marquis of Carmarthen* (London, 1762).

76. Add. MSS. 33,067, f. 339.

77. Add. MSS. 33,073, f. 230.

78. Add. MSS. 32,948, f. 244.

79. *Ibid.,* ff. 389–90.

80. Add. MSS. 32,949, f. 3.

81. Add. MSS. 33,067, f. 368.

82. *Ibid.,* f. 372.

83. *Ibid.,* f. 378.

84. Lady Elizabeth Germain (1680–1769), second daughter of Charles, second Earl of Berkeley, by Elizabeth, daughter of Baptist Noel, third Viscount Campden, married in 1706 Sir John Germain; he died in 1718. Her London house was in St. James's Square.

85. Add. MSS. 33,067, ff. 384–385.

86. *Ibid.,* f. 387.

87. John Hume was the brother-in-law of the Archbishop of York. He was appointed successively Bishop of Bristol (1756), of Oxford (1758), of Salisbury (1766).

88. Walpole, *Letters,* IV, 260.

89. Add. MSS. 28,051, f. 401.

90. *Idem.*

91. Add. MSS. 33,083, f. 131.

92. Add. MSS. 33,068, f. 386. Tied with a bit of thread, the hair remains pinned to the letter.

93. Add. MSS. 28,051, f. 362.

94. *Ibid.,* ff. 402–403.

95. Add. MSS. 28,059, f. 192.

96. Add. MSS. 33,082, f. 253.

97. *Idem.*

98. Add. MSS. 33,083, f. 54.

99. The marriage ended unhappily. Lady Carmarthen left her husband in 1778, and they were divorced in 1779. She subsequently married John Byron, by whom she had a daughter, Augusta, half-sister of Lord Byron,

the poet. The Marquis of Carmarthen married, secondly, in 1788 Catherine, daughter of Thomas Anguish.

100. Add. MSS. 33,083, ff. 95–96.

101. *Ibid.*, f. 158.

102. See Add. MSS. 27,917. One of the characters in *Don't Be Too Sure* quotes "my old Favorite Congreve."

103. Add. MSS. 28,051, f. 354.

Dr. Messenger Monsey

1. *A Series of Letters Between Mrs. Elizabeth Carter and Miss Catherine Talbot from the Year 1741 to 1770*, ed. Montagu Pennington (London, 1809), II, 21, 81, 36. Catherine Talbot (1721–1770), granddaughter of William Talbot, Bishop of Durham, was brought up in the family of Thomas Secker, who became Archbishop of Canterbury.

2. *Boswell's Life of Johnson*, ed. G. B. Hill (Oxford, 1889), II, 64.

3. *Letters from Mrs. Elizabeth Carter, to Mrs. Montagu, Between the Years 1755 and 1800*, ed. Montagu Pennington (London, 1817), I, 131.

4. *Ibid.*, II, 277.

5. *Mrs. Montagu, Queen of the Blues*, ed. Reginald Blunt (London [1923]), I, 90. Mrs. Elizabeth Montagu (1720–1800) was the elder daughter of Matthew Robinson of West Layton, Yorkshire, by Elizabeth, daughter of Robert Drake. In 1742 she married Edward Montagu; he died in 1775. In her later years, she presided over a famous salon at Montagu House, 22 Portman Square. In addition to her letters, she wrote *An Essay on the Writings and Genius of Shakespear* (1769).

6. Add. MSS. 28,051, f. 407.

7. *Mrs. Montagu*, ed. Blunt, I, 176.

8. *A Sketch of the Life and Character of the Late Dr. Monsey* (London, 1789), p. 79.

9. Reginald Blunt, *Paradise Row* (London, 1906), p. 148. Audrey (self-styled Etheldreda), Viscountess Townshend, was the daughter of Edward Harrison of Balls Park, Hertfordshire. In 1723 she married Charles, third Viscount Townshend. She survived her husband and died in 1788.

10. George Lyttelton, first Baron Lyttelton (1709–1773), a Whig politician, served as Cofferer of the Household, a member of the Privy Council, and Chancellor of the Exchequer. His works include *Dialogues of the Dead* (1760).

11. Mrs. Elizabeth Montagu, *Letters*, IV, 274, 235.

12. *A Sketch of . . . Dr. Monsey*, p. 63.

13. See the Monsey pedigree in Add. MSS. 19,142, f. 122.

14. Francis Blomefield and Charles Parkin, *An Essay Towards a Topographical History of the County of Norfolk* (Lynn, etc., 1739–1775), IV, 438 f.

15. There are memorial tablets to Robert Monsey and his wife (with an inscription by Messenger Monsey) and to Messenger and Clopton Monsey in Whitwell Church.

16. This information was kindly supplied by R. R. James of Woodbridge, Suffolk.

17. J. Taylor, I, 71.

18. On September 23 Monsey wrote to Sir Hans Sloane, requesting that his examination be postponed for a day or two and thanking the latter for his kindness to him. See Sloane MSS. 4047, f. 54. His college diploma entitled Monsey to practice medicine exclusively in the country, not in London or in a circuit of seven miles around it.

19. *A Sketch of . . . Dr. Monsey,* pp. 70, 56.

20. J. Taylor, I, 70. Taylor also says, incorrectly, that Monsey was born in Swaffham. John Taylor (1757–1832) was the eldest son of Monsey's friend, John Taylor. He was oculist to George III and George IV. Becoming interested in journalism, he was dramatic critic, then editor, of *The Morning Post* and was proprietor of other newspapers.

21. The name of Monsey's wife and the date and place of his marriage are now printed for the first time. It is highly probable that Ann Dawney was the widow of John Dawney of Roydon, Norfolk (near Bury St. Edmunds). In his will, proved on January 9, 1720, John Dawney appoints "Ann my Wife" sole executrix and provides for three minor children, John (b. 1706), Edward, and James. See Norwich Consistory Court 1719, Register Book 183. 291. John Dawney was buried in Roydon on December 11, 1719. He was probably the son of John Dawney, rector of Roydon (d. 1705).

22. *A Sketch of . . . Dr. Monsey,* p. 58.

23. *Ibid.,* p. 15.

24. Add. MSS. 33,079, f. 116.

25. *Idem.*

26. Add. MSS. 33,065, f. 112.

27. *Ibid.,* f. 108.

28. *Ibid.,* f. 113.

29. Add. MSS. 33,079, f. 118.

30. Add. MSS. 33,065, f. 112.

31. *Ibid.,* f. 295.

32. Add. MSS. 32,856, f. 423.

33. *A Sketch of . . . Dr. Monsey,* p. 18.

34. Add. MSS. 33,080, f. 165.

35. J. Taylor, I, 77. Charles, third Viscount Townshend (1700–1764), held the posts of Lord of the Bedchamber (1723–27), Custos Rotulorum and Lord Lieutenant of Norfolk, and Master of the Jewel Office (1730–38).

36. Henry Wilson, "Messenger Monsey," in *Wonderful Characters* (London, 1821), III, 139–142. If this story taxes the credulity of the reader,

it must be remembered that Dr. Monsey himself would not have objected.

37. Add. MSS. 28,051, ff. 365, 397, 386, 399, 405.

38. *A Sketch of . . . Dr. Monsey,* p. 49.

39. *The Letters of Philip Dormer Stanhope, 4th Earl of Chesterfield,* ed. Bonamy Dobrée ([London], 1932), VI, 2259, 2761–2762, 2259, 2260, 2783.

40. William Pulteney, Earl of Bath (1684–1764), like Lord Lyttelton a Whig politician, was a member of the Privy Council and Cofferer of the Household. He was a man of great wealth.

41. *Elizabeth Montagu,* ed. Climenson, II, 201.

42. Monsey MSS., Bedwell Lodge, Essendon, Herts.

43. J. Taylor, I, 83.

44. Monsey MSS., Royal College of Surgeons of England.

45. J. Taylor, II, 4–5.

46. Monsey MSS., Royal College of Surgeons of England.

47. Wilson, III, 135–136.

48. R. W. Ketton-Cremer, "Dr. Messenger Monsey," in *Norfolk Portraits* (London [1944]), p. 94; and, for an excellent account of this friendship, pp. 90–94.

49. William Windham (1717–1761) was the son of Ashe Windham of Felbrigg Hall, Norfolk, by Elizabeth, daughter of William Dobbins of Lincoln's Inn. In 1737 he made the grand tour with his tutor, Benjamin Stillingfleet. He was interested in literature and science and was a fine horseman, swordsman, and boxer. Towards the end of his life, he served as Lieutenant Colonel of the Norfolk Militia.

50. Monsey MSS., Felbrigg Hall, Norfolk.

51. J. Taylor, I, 11. This John Taylor (1724–1787) was the grandson of an eminent surgeon of Norwich, and the son of Chevalier Taylor, who was oculist to George II and the principal oculist of his time. He studied in Paris and under his father and became oculist to George III. See note 20 for an account of his son, John Taylor.

52. Monsey MSS., Felbrigg Hall, Norfolk.

53. Add. MSS. 32,855, f. 278.

54. Add. MSS. 24,123, f. 116. Benjamin Gooch (d. 1776) was for many years Surgeon of the first village hospital in England, founded in Shottisham by his patron, William Fellowes. He was Consulting Surgeon and a member of the Board of Governors of the Norfolk and Norwich Hospital, also founded by Fellowes. His publications include *A Practical Treatise on Wounds and Other Chirurgical Subjects,* 3 vols. (1767–73).

55. Add. MSS. 24,123, ff. 19, 139, 187–188.

56. *Ibid.,* ff. 151, 165, 178. John Ranby (1703–1773) was Sergeant-Surgeon to George II and first Master of the Corporation of Surgeons. In 1752 he was appointed Surgeon of Chelsea Royal Hospital. He was the author of a treatise on gunshot wounds.

57. Add. MSS. 24,123, ff. 172, 152.

58. *Ibid.*, ff. 88, 71, 136–137, 143.

59. *Ibid.*, f. 127.

60. *Elizabeth Montagu*, ed. Climenson, II, 185.

61. *Ibid.*, p. 117.

62. Mrs. Elizabeth Montagu, *Letters*, IV, 145, 120.

63. *Ibid.*, pp. 137–138.

64. *Ibid.*, p. 321.

65. *Ibid.*, pp. 175–176.

66. *Ibid.*, pp. 115, 134–135.

67. *Mrs. Montagu*, ed. Blunt, I, 22, 67.

68. *Ibid.*, p. 24.

69. Mrs. Elizabeth Montagu, *Letters*, IV, 347.

70. *Mrs. Montagu*, ed. Blunt, I, 32.

71. Mrs. Elizabeth Montagu, *Letters*, IV, 91.

72. J. Cordy Jeaffreson, "Messenger Monsey," in *A Book About Doctors* (London, 1860), II, 82–88.

73. Mrs. Elizabeth Montagu, *Letters*, IV, 154–159.

74. *Mrs. Montagu*, ed. Blunt, I, 56; II, 138.

75. William Alexander's will was proved on December 3, 1774. See PCC 1774, 419 Bargrave.

76. Add. MSS. 24,123, f. 170.

77. Mrs. Elizabeth Montagu, *Letters*, IV, 148–150.

78. Wilson, III, 147.

79. *Ibid.*, p. 145.

80. Add. MSS. 24,123, f. 124.

81. *Mrs. Montagu*, ed. Blunt, II, 250.

82. Add. MSS. 28,051, f. 395.

83. Add. MSS. 24,123, ff. 99, 114.

84. Blunt, *Paradise Row*, pp. 149, 150.

85. J. Taylor, II, 186–187.

86. Monsey MSS., Royal College of Surgeons of England.

87. [Jeremiah Whittaker Newman], *Memoirs of the Life of Robert Adair, Esq.* (London, 1790), pp. 33–35.

88. Monsey was indeed one of the "ornaments" of the Hospital. There are interesting references to Monsey in C. G. T. Dean, *The Royal Hospital, Chelsea* (London, 1950).

89. Wilson, III, 148.

90. *A Sketch of . . . Dr. Monsey*, p. 42.

91. J. Taylor, II, 186.

92. Monsey MSS., Royal College of Surgeons of England.

93. *A Sketch of . . . Dr. Monsey*, p. 79.

94. Ketton-Cremer, p. 94.

95. William Windham (1750–1810) was the only son of Monsey's friend, William Windham.

96. Add. MSS. 37,914, f. 38.

97. *The Diary of the Right Hon. William Windham,* ed. Mrs. Henry Baring (London, 1866), pp. 123–124.

98. Add. MSS. 28,062, f. 505.

99. J. Taylor, I, 90.

100. *Ibid.,* I, 91.

101. Monsey MSS., Royal College of Surgeons of England.

102. Ketton-Cremer, pp. 94–95.

103. PCC 1789, 40 Macham. Charlotte Alexander respected her father's wishes. She died in Mulbarton, Norfolk, and her will was proved on November 12, 1798. See PCC 1798, 691 Walpole.

104. On March 18, 1800, Catherine Alexander, of the parish of St. James in Bury St. Edmunds, married John Bedingfield Collyer of Aylsham, Norfolk.

105. Jemima Alexander married on July 4, 1789, the Rev. Edmund Rolfe, rector of Cockley Clay, Norfolk. Her only surviving son, Robert Monsey Rolfe, first Baron Cranworth (1790–1868), was called to the bar in 1816; was made Baron of the Exchequer in 1839; and Lord Chancellor in 1852.

106. PCC 1789, 40 Macham.

107. *A Sketch of . . . Dr. Monsey,* p. 83.

Bibliography

MANUSCRIPT SOURCES

Bedwell Lodge, Essendon, Herts.: Monsey MSS.
Blenheim Palace, Woodstock, Oxon.: Blenheim MSS. E. 2; E. 6; E. 7;
  E. 8; E. 9; E. 20; E. 21; E. 22; E. 23; E. 24; E. 43; FI. 33; FI. 35;
  GI. 17.
Bodleian Library, Oxford: MS. Notes of George Thorn-Drury in an inter-
  leaved copy of Edmund Gosse, *Life of William Congreve* (1888).
British Museum, London: Add. MSS. 4211; 9120; 15,949; 19,142; 20,104;
  22,627; 22,628; 24,123; 27,917; 27,988; 28,050; 28,051; 28,052; 28,059;
  28,062; 28,071; 28,927; 28,888; 32,350; 32,713; 32,715; 32,855; 32,856;
  32,914; 32,948; 32,949; 32,992; 33,064; 33,065; 33,066; 33,067; 33,068;
  33,073; 33,076; 33,079; 33,080; 33,081; 33,082; 33,083; 37,914; 38,015;
  39,311.
Sloane MSS. 4047; 4436.
Felbrigg Hall, Roughton, Norfolk: Monsey MSS.
Inns of Court, London: Inner Temple, Admission Register, 1670–1750, f.
  1223 (Robert Fitzgerald).
Middle Temple, Admissions To House & Chambers, 1658 To 1685, f.
  589 (Joseph Keally).
Kilkenny Castle, Kilkenny: Ormonde MSS. 164; 167; 169; 172.
Longleat, Warminster, Wilts.: Longleat MSS. Note-Books of Anecdotes,
  Extracts, etc. of Margaret, Duchess of Portland, Box II, notebook 16.
New York Public Library: Berg Collection, Congreve's letter to Joseph
  Keally, September 28, 1697.
Public Record Office, Dublin: Betham's Genealogical Abstracts, Preroga-
  tive Wills (Phillips MSS.), 38, f. 146 (Joseph Keally); 79, f. 11
  (William Fitzgerald) and f. 27 (Robert Fitzgerald).
Prerogative Will Books, 1664 To 1684, ff. 309–310 (John Keally);
  1726-7-8, f. 200 (Ellen Fitzgerald); 1728–29, ff. 98–99 (Thomas
  Amory).

BIBLIOGRAPHY

Public Record Office, London: Egmont MSS. (on temporary deposit), I–XLIV; LXI–LXVI; CL–CLII; CCII–CCVIII; CCXIII; CCXXIV; CCXXXV.
    SO 1.4, f. 625; 1.8, f. 109.
    SP 44.339, f. 410.
    SP 63.142; 167, f. 44 III; 175, f. 157; 192–3, f. 185; 202, Pt. 3, f. 292; 266, ff. 68–69.
Registry of Deeds, Dublin: Transcript Books, 53.416.36166; 54.386.36167; 85.41.58956, and 85.71.59091.
Royal College of Surgeons of England, London: Monsey MSS.
Sandon Hall, Stafford: Wortley MSS.
Somerset House, London: PCC 1729, 135 Brook (William Congreve); 1731, 75 Isham (Edward Porter); 1735, 128 Ducie (Charles Mein); 1736, 113 Derby (Henrietta, Duchess of Marlborough); 1744, 259 Anstis (Sarah, Duchess of Marlborough); 1748, 258 Strahan (Anne Bracegirdle); 1764, 395 Simpson (Mary, Duchess of Leeds); 1766, 16 Tyndall (Francis Godolphin, second Earl of Godolphin); 1774, 358 Bargrave (Elinor, Countess of Blesington) and 419 Bargrave (William Alexander); 1776, 325 Bellas (Henrietta, Duchess of Newcastle); 1789, 40 Macham (Messenger Monsey) and 208 Macham (Thomas Osborne, fourth Duke of Leeds); 1798, 691 Walpole (Charlotte Alexander).
Trinity College, Dublin: Senior and Junior Book, 1685–7.
    TCD MSS. F.4.3, List of the Protestants Who Fled from Ireland –1688.
Yorkshire Archaeological Society, Leeds: *A Catalogue of Books in the Leeds Library.*

PRINTED SOURCES

Addison, Joseph. *The Letters of Joseph Addison,* ed. Walter Graham. Oxford, 1941.
———— *The Works of the Right Honourable Joseph Addison, Esq.,* vol. I. London, 1721.
Aitken, George A. *The Life of Richard Steele,* vol. I. London, 1889.
The Amorous D[uc]h[e]ss Or, Her G[race] Grateful. London, 1733.
[Anderson, James]. *A Genealogical History of the House of Ivery.* 2 vols. London, 1742.
Animadversions on Mr. Congreve's Late Answer to Mr. Collier. London, 1698.
Bagwell, Richard. *Ireland Under the Stuarts and During the Interregnum.* 3 vols. London, 1909.
Bentham, Jeremy. *The Works of Jeremy Bentham,* ed. John Bowring, vol. X. Edinburgh, 1843.

BIBLIOGRAPHY

Berkeley, George Monck, editor. *Literary Relics*. London, 1789.

Blomefield, Francis, and Charles Parkin. *An Essay Towards a Topographical History of the County of Norfolk*, vol. IV. Fersfield, Norwich, and Lynn, 1739–1775.

Blunt, Reginald. *Paradise Row*. London, 1906.

Boswell, James. *Boswell's Life of Johnson*, ed. George Birkbeck Hill, vol. II. Oxford, 1887.

—— *Boswell's London Journal, 1762–1763*, ed. Frederick A. Pottle, Yale Editions of The Private Papers of James Boswell. New York, London, Toronto [1950].

Brown, Thomas. *The Works of Mr. Thomas Brown*, vol. III. London, 1707–1708.

Buckley, James, editor. "The Battle of Liscarroll, 1642," *Journal of the Cork Historical and Archaeological Society*, second series, vol. IV, no. 38 (1898), pp. 83–100.

Budgell, E[ustace]. *Memoirs of the Lives and Characters of the Illustrious Family of the Boyles*. London, 1737.

Burke, Sir [John] Bernard. *Burke's Peerage, Baronetage and Knightage*. London, 1939.

—— *A Genealogical and Heraldic History of the Landed Gentry of Ireland*. London, 1912.

Burtchaell, George Dames. *Genealogical Memoirs of the Members of Parliament for the County and City of Kilkenny*. Dublin, 1888.

—— and Thomas Ulick Sadleir. *Alumni Dublinenses*. Dublin, 1935.

Carter, Elizabeth. *Letters from Mrs. Elizabeth Carter, to Mrs. Montagu, Between the Years 1755 and 1800*, ed. Montagu Pennington. 3 vols. London, 1817.

—— *A Series of Letters Between Mrs. Elizabeth Carter and Miss Catherine Talbot from the Years 1741 to 1770*, ed. Montagu Pennington. 4 vols. London, 1809.

Cartwright, James J., editor. *The Wentworth Papers, 1705–1739*. London, 1883.

Caulfield, Richard, editor. *The Council Book of the Corporation of the City of Cork, From 1609 to 1643, and From 1690 to 1800*. Guildford, Surrey, 1876.

Chesterfield, Philip Dormer Stanhope, 4th Earl of. *The Letters of Philip Dormer Stanhope, 4th Earl of Chesterfield*, ed. Bonamy Dobrée, vol. VI. [London], 1932.

[Chetwood, W. R.]. *A Tour Through Ireland*. Dublin, 1748.

The Chronological Remembrancer. Dublin, 1750.

Cibber, Colley. *An Apology for the Life of Mr. Colley Cibber*, ed. Robert W. Lowe. 2 vols. London, 1889.

Cibber, [Theophilus, and others]. *The Lives of the Poets of Great Britain and Ireland*. "Congreve," IV, 83–98. London, 1753.

BIBLIOGRAPHY

Clarendon, Henry Hyde, [2nd] Earl of. *The Correspondence of Henry Hyde, Earl of Clarendon, and of His Brother, Lawrence Hyde, Earl of Rochester,* ed. S. W. Singer. 2 vols. London, 1828.

Cobham and Congreve. An Epistle to Lord Viscount Cobham, In Memory of his Friend, The late Mr. Congreve. London, 1730.

C[okayne], G[eorge] E[dward]. *The Complete Peerage . . . by G. E. C.,* ed. the Hon. Vicary Gibbs and others, vols. I–X. London, 1910–1945.

Colville, Mrs. Arthur. *Duchess Sarah.* London, 1914.

Congreve, William. *The Double-Dealer, A Comedy.* London, 1694.

—— "Letters of Congreve to Tonson the Bookseller," *The Gentleman's Magazine,* n.s. III (June 1835), pp. 609–610.

—— *The Mourning Bride, Poems, & Miscellanies, by William Congreve,* ed. Bonamy Dobrée, World's Classics. London [1928].

Cork and Orrery, [Emily Charlotte (De Burgh-Canning) Boyle], Countess of, editor. *The Orrery Papers.* 2 vols. London, 1903.

Cosby, Pole. "The Autobiography of Pole Cosby," *Journal of the Co. Kildare Archaeological Society and Surrounding Districts,* V, 1906–08, 87.

The Court Parrot. A New Miscellany in Prose and Verse. "The Secret History of Henrada Maria Teresa," pp. 13–22. London, 1733.

Curtis, Edmund. *A History of Ireland.* London, 1936.

The Daily Post (London): November 25, 1723; May 6, 1728; July 15, 1732.

Davies, Rowland. *Journal of the Very Rev. Rowland Davies, L.L.D.,* ed. Richard Caulfield. Camden Society Publications, no. LXVIII, 1857.

Davies, Thomas. *Dramatic Miscellanies.* "Congreve," III, 331–487. London, 1783–84.

Dean, C. G. T. *The Royal Hospital, Chelsea.* London, 1950.

Delany, Mrs. Mary. *The Autobiography and Correspondence of Mary Granville, Mrs. Delany,* ed. [Augusta (Waddington)], Lady Llanover. 3 vols. London, 1861.

Dennis, [John] editor. *Letters Upon Several Occasions.* London, 1696.

A Description of the Gardens of Lord Viscount Cobham at Stow in Buckinghamshire. Northampton, 1748.

Dobrée, Bonamy. *Restoration Comedy, 1660–1720.* "Congreve," pp. 121–150. Oxford, 1924.

[Dryden, John, and others]. *Examen Poeticum.* London, 1693.

Dryden, John. *The Letters of John Dryden,* ed. Charles E. Ward. Durham, North Carolina, 1942.

—— *The Works of John Dryden,* ed. Sir Walter Scott, vol. II. London and Edinburgh, 1808.

An Elegy On the much Lamented Death of Mr. Prime Serjeant Fitz-Gerald. Dublin, n.d.

The Female Faction: or, The Gay Subscribers. A Poem. London [1729].

FitzGerald-Uniacke, R. G. "The FitzGeralds of Castle Dodd," *Journal of*

BIBLIOGRAPHY

the Cork Historical and Archaeological Society, vol. III, no. 33 (1894), p. 199.

Fleming, James. "Historic Irish Mansions. No. 179: Castle Harrison, Co. Cork," *The Weekly Irish Times*, October 7, 1939.

Gay, John. *The Poetical Works of John Gay*, ed. G. C. Faber. London, 1926.

Gilbert, Sir John T., editor. *A Contemporary History of Affairs in Ireland, From 1641 to 1652*. 3 vols. in 6. Dublin, 1879–80.

Gildon, [Charles]. *A Comparison Between the Two Stages*. London, 1702.

[Gildon, Charles, editor]. *A New Miscellany of Original Poems*. London, 1701.

Gosse, Edmund. *Life of William Congreve*. London, 1888.

Graves, J[ames], editor. "Unpublished Geraldine Documents," *The Journal of the Royal Historical and Archaeological Association of Ireland*, IV, Part I, 1876, 157–166.

Harris, Walter. *The History of the Life and Reign of William-Henry*. Dublin, 1749.

Hazlitt, William. *Lectures on the English Comic Dramatists*. "Of Wycherley, Congreve, Vanbrugh and Farquhar," pp. 133–176. London, 1819.

Henley, W. E. *The Works of W. E. Henley*. "Congreve," V, 241–248.

HMC, *Fifth Report,* Part I. London, 1876.

—— *Seventh Report,* Part I. London, 1879.

—— *Fifteenth Report,* Appendix, Part VI. London, 1897.

—— *Egmont,* vol. I, Part I, pp. v–lxxii, London, 1905; II, v–xvii, London, 1909.

—— *Ormonde,* n. s., vol. II, London, 1903; n. s., vol. VII, London, 1912; n. s., vol. VIII, London, 1920.

Hodges, John C. "Congreve's Library," *The Times Literary Supplement*, August 12, 1949, p. 521.

—— *William Congreve The Man*. New York and London, 1941.

Hopkins, Charles. *Boadicea*. London, 1697.

Hunt, Leigh, editor. *Dramatic Works of Wycherley, Congreve, Vanbrugh, and Farquhar. With biographical and critical notices.* "Congreve," pp. xix–xxxviii. London and New York, 1866.

Ilchester, [Giles Stephen Holland Fox-Strangways, 6th] Earl of, editor. *Lord Hervey and His Friends, 1726–38*. London, 1950.

[Jacob, Giles]. *The Poetical Register: Or, The Lives and Characters of the English Dramatick Poets*. London, 1719.

Jeaffreson, J. Cordy. *A Book About Doctors*. "Messenger Monsey," II, 69–88. London, 1860.

Johnson, Samuel. *Lives of the English Poets,* ed. George Birkbeck Hill. "Congreve," II, 212–234. Oxford, 1905.

BIBLIOGRAPHY

The Journals of the House of Commons of the Kingdom of Ireland, I and II. Dublin, 1796–1800.

Ketton-Cremer, R[obert] W[yndham]. *Norfolk Portraits.* "Dr. Messenger Monsey," pp. 85–95. London [1944].

[King, William]. *The State of the Protestants of Ireland Under the Late King James's Government.* London, 1691.

Kippis, Andrew, and others, editors. *Biographia Britannica,* "Congreve," IV, 68–72. London, 1778–1793.

Lamb, Charles. *Essays of Elia,* ed. Alfred Ainger. "On the Artificial Comedy of the Last Century," pp. 161–168. London and New York, 1903.

—— *The Letters of Charles Lamb,* ed. E. V. Lucas. 3 vols. [London, 1935].

[Lambe, Thomas]. *Lycidas, A Masque. To Which is added Delia, A Pastoral Elegy; and Verses on the Death of the Marquis of Carmarthen.* London, 1762.

Lascelles, Rowley. *Liber Munerum Publicorum Hiberniae.* 2 vols. [London, 1824–1830].

A Letter of the Earl of Corke, To the State at Dublin. London, 1642.

Lewis, Samuel. *A Topographical Dictionary of Ireland.* 2 vols. London, 1842.

A List of the Claims as they are Entred with the Trustees At Chichester-House on College Green Dublin, On or before the Tenth of August, 1700. Dublin, 1701.

Lodge, John. *The Peerage of Ireland.* 7 vols. Dublin, 1789.

Ludlow, Edmund. *The Memoirs of Edmund Ludlow, 1625–1672,* ed. C. H. Firth. 2 vols. Oxford, 1894.

Luttrell, Narcissus. *A Brief Historical Relation of State Affairs from September, 1678 to April, 1714.* 6 vols. Oxford, 1857.

Lynch, Kathleen M. "Congreve's Irish Friend, Joseph Keally," PMLA, LIII (1938), 1076–1087.

—— "Henrietta, Duchess of Marlborough," PMLA, LII (1937), 1072–1093.

Macaulay, [Thomas Babington, 1st Baron]. *Critical and Historical Essays,* ed. F. C. Montague. "Leigh Hunt," III, 3–48. London, 1903.

MacLysaght, Edward, editor. *Calendar of The Orrery Papers.* Dublin, 1941.

Markham, Sir Clements Robert, *A Memoir of Archbishop Markham, 1719–1807.* Oxford, 1906.

Marsh, F[rank] G[raham]. *The Godolphins.* [New Milton, Eng.], 1930.

Memoirs of the Celebrated Persons Composing the Kit-Cat Club. London, 1821.

Montagu, Mrs. Elizabeth. *Elizabeth Montagu, The Queen of the Blue Stockings; Her Correspondence, 1720–61,* ed. E[mily] J. Climenson. 2 vols. London, 1906.

BIBLIOGRAPHY

———— *The Letters of Mrs. Elizabeth Montagu,* ed. Matthew Montagu. 4 vols. London, 1809–1813.

———— *Mrs. Montagu, Queen of the Blues,* ed. Reginald Blunt. 2 vols. London [1923].

Montagu, Lady Mary Wortley. *The Letters and Works of Lady Mary Wortley Montagu,* ed. [John Stuart Wortley], Lord Wharncliffe. 2 vols. London, 1898.

Morrice, Thomas. *A Collection of the State Letters of the Right Honourable Roger Boyle, The First Earl of Orrery.* 2 vols. Dublin, 1743.

[Newman, Jeremiah Whittaker]. *Memoirs of the Life of Robert Adair, Esq.* London, 1790.

Playfair, William. *British Family Antiquity.* 9 vols. London, 1809–1811.

Poems on Affairs of State, From 1620, to this present Year 1707, vol. IV. London, 1703–1710.

Pope, Alexander. *The Iliad of Homer Translated by Alexander Pope, Esq.,* vol. VI. London, 1750.

———— *The Works of Alexander Pope,* ed. Whitwell Elwin and W. J. Courthope. 10 vols. London, 1871–1889.

Prendergast, John. *Ireland from the Restoration to the Revolution, 1660 to 1690.* London, 1887.

Pue's Occurrences, June 2, 1705 [under title *Impartial Occurrences, Foreign and Domestick*]; and vol. XLVI, from Tuesday May 9 to Saturday May 13, 1749.

Reid, Stuart J. *John and Sarah, Duke and Duchess of Marlborough.* London, 1915.

Rowe, Nicholas. *The Works of Nicholas Rowe, Esq.* 2 vols. London, 1747.

Sadleir, T[homas] U[lick]. "The Register of Kilkenny School (1685–1800)," *The Journal of the Royal Society of Antiquaries of Ireland,* LIV (1924), 55–67, 152–169.

Saunders's News-Letter, January 8, 1783.

Scott, Sir Walter, Bart. *The Private Letter-Books of Sir Walter Scott,* ed. Wilfred Partington. London, 1930.

Shaw, W. A., editor. *Calendar of Treasury Books & Papers, 1735–1738.* London, 1900.

The Sixth Report of the Deputy Keeper of the Public Records in Ireland. Dublin, 1874.

A Sketch of the Life and Character of the Late Dr. Monsey. London, 1789.

Smith, Charles. *The Ancient and Present State of the County and City of Cork,* ed. Robert Day and W. A. Copinger. 2 vols. Cork, 1893.

Somerset, Frances [Seymour], Duchess of. *Correspondence Between Frances, Countess of Hartford (Afterwards Duchess of Somerset,) and Henrietta Louisa, Countess of Pomfret, Between the Years 1738 and 1741.* 2 vols. London, 1806.

Spence, Joseph. *Anecdotes, Observations, and Characters of Books and Men,* ed. S. W. Singer. London, 1820.

BIBLIOGRAPHY

Steele, Sir Richard. *The Epistolary Correspondence of Sir Richard Steele.* London, 1787.

[Steele, Sir Richard, Joseph Addison, and others]. *The Spectator,* vols. I and III. London, 1744.

Suffolk, Henrietta [Howard], Countess of. *Letters To and From Henrietta [Howard], Countess of Suffolk and Her Second Husband, The Hon. George Berkeley; From 1712 to 1767.* 2 vols. London, 1824.

Swift, Jonathan. *The Correspondence of Jonathan Swift, D.D.,* ed. F. Elrington Ball. 6 vols. London, 1910–1914.

—— *Journal to Stella,* ed. Harold Williams. 2 vols. Oxford, 1948.

—— *The Poems of Jonathan Swift,* ed. Harold Williams. 3 vols. Oxford, 1937.

Taylor, D. Crane. *William Congreve.* London, 1931.

Taylor, John. *Records of My Life.* 2 vols. London, 1832.

Tenison, C. M. "Cork M.P.'s, 1559–1800," *Journal of the Cork Historical and Archaeological Society,* second series, I (1895), 524–525.

Thackeray, William Makepeace. *The English Humourists of the Eighteenth Century.* "Congreve and Addison," pp. 55–104. London, 1853.

Thomson, Gladys Scott, editor. *Letters of a Grandmother, 1732–1735.* London, 1943.

[Thomson, James]. *A Poem to the Memory of Mr. Congreve, Inscribed to her Grace, Henrietta, Dutchess of Marlborough.* London, 1729.

Tuckey, Francis H. *The County and City of Cork Remembrancer.* Cork, 1837.

Turner, F[rancis] C[harles]. *James II.* New York, 1948.

Vanbrugh, Sir John. *The Complete Works of Sir John Vanbrugh,* ed. Bonamy Dobrée and Geoffrey Webb, vol. IV. London, 1928.

Vigors, Urban. "Rebellion 1641–2 Described in a Letter of Rev. Urban Vigors to Rev. Henry Jones," *Journal of the Cork Historical and Archaeological Society,* second series, vol. II, no. 19 (1896), pp. 289–306.

V[oltaire], [François Marie Arouet] d[e]. *Lettres Ecrites Sur Les Anglois et Autres Sujets.* Basle, 1734.

Walpole, Horace. *Horace Walpole's Correspondence with Thomas Gray, Richard West and Thomas Ashton,* ed. W. S. Lewis, G. L. Lam, and C. H. Bennett, Yale Edition of Horace Walpole's Correspondence, vols. XIII–XIV. New Haven, 1948.

—— *The Letters of Horace Walpole,* ed. Peter Cunningham, vols. I, III, IV. Edinburgh, 1906.

—— *Reminiscences,* ed. Paget Toynbee. Oxford, 1924.

White, James Grove. *Historical and Topographical Notes, &c. on Buttevant, Castletownroche, Doneraile, Mallow, and Places in Their Vicinity.* 2 vols. Cork, 1905.

BIBLIOGRAPHY

Williamson, J. Bruce. *The History of the Temple*. London, 1925.

Wilson, Charles. *Memoirs of the Life, Writings, and Amours of William Congreve Esq.* London, 1730.

Wilson, Henry. *Wonderful Characters.* "Messenger Monsey," III, 131–148. London, 1821.

Windham, William. *The Diary of the Right Hon. William Windham,* ed. Mrs. Henry Baring. London, 1866.

[Young, Edward]. *Love of Fame*. London, 1728.

Index

Members of the peerage appear under their titles in chronological sequence. All names of wives follow those of their husbands. Works listed separately by title are confined to periodicals and anonymous publications.

INDEX

INDEX

Collyer, Catherine (Alexander), 137, 173

Colville, Mrs. Arthur, 160, 178

Condé, Louis II de Bourbon, Prince de, 56

Congreve, Colonel William, father of the dramatist, 37, 156

Congreve, William, the dramatist
Character and personality, 1, 2, 4, 6–7, 9, 11, 12, 13, 14, 16, 32
Critics of: Henley, 1, 141; Dryden, 2–3; Addison, 11; Johnson, 12; Macaulay, 12; Leigh Hunt, 13; Lamb, 13; Thackeray, 13; Voltaire, 13; Dobrée, 13–14, 21–22; Gosse, 14–15, 21, 23; Thorn-Drury, 15; Taylor, 15–16, 23; Hodges, 16; Lynch, 16; Hazlitt, 21
Ill-health, 4, 5, 7, 11, 12
In Ireland: childhood in Youghal, 37; matriculates at Trinity College, Dublin, 25, 37, 150; a visitor, 54
In London: at Arundel Street, 18, 19, 35; at Surrey Street, 18–19
Letters from: to Pope, 4, 5; to Lady Mary Wortley Montagu, 5; to Dennis, 7–8; to Keally, 9, 16–17, 18, 23, 24, 27–36, 54, 55, 56; to Luther, 17; to Edward Porter, 19, 20; to Mrs. Porter, 19–20
Letters to: from Pope, 4; from Lady Mary Wortley Montagu, 5, 6; from Dennis, 8–9; from Addison, 9; from Keally, 29
Politics, 4, 7, 12, 31, 36, 150
Relations of: with Dryden, 1–3; with Tonson, 2, 15, 16; with Swift, 3–4; with Pope, 4–5; with Gay, 4, 7; with Lady Mary Wortley Montagu, 5–7; with Henrietta, Duchess of Marlborough, 5, 7, 10–11, 14, 21, 59–67, 77, 90; with Dennis, 7–9, 12; with Addison, 9; with Steele, 9; with Keally, 9, 16, 17, 23, 27–36, 54, 55, 56; with Anne Bracegirdle, 9–10, 14, 20–21; with Delaval, 11; with Cob-

ham, 11; with Mein, 15, 17–18, 20, 33, 34, 36, 55; with Luther, 15, 17; with Fitzgerald, 15, 16, 17, 34, 35, 36, 37, 54–56, 57; with Amory, 15, 17, 55; with Lord Shannon, 16, 57; with the Porters, 18–20; with Lord Godolphin, 21, 64, 81
Reputation: as a man, 1, 2–3, 5, 11–15; as a dramatist, 11, 12, 22
Scholarship, 1–2
Visits to: Ashley, 6; Tunbridge Wells, 7–8; Stowe, 11, 19; the Continent, 15, 18, 20; Ilam, 19
Will, 10, 19, 21, 60, 64, 145, 159, 176
Writings: *The Old Bachelor*, 2, 54; *The Double-Dealer*, 2, 3, 54, 144; *Love for Love*, 11, 54; *The Way of the World*, 3, 22; "Humour in Comedy," 7; *The Judgment of Paris*, 32; "Of Pleasing; An Epistle to Sir Richard Temple," 143; "Letter to Viscount Cobham," 143; "Jack French-Man's Defeat," 150; *The Tears of Amaryllis for Amyntas*, 159; "To the Right Honourable the Earl of Godolphin," 159

Conron, Richard, 52

Conron, Margery, 52

Corelli, Arcangelo, 93

Cork, Richard (Boyle), 1st Earl of, 40, 42, 151, 152, 157

Cork, Richard (Boyle), 2nd Earl of, see Burlington, Richard (Boyle), 2nd Earl of Cork and 1st of

Cork and Orrery, Emily Charlotte (De Burgh-Canning), Countess of, 178

Court Parrot, The, 159, 178

Cranworth, Robert Monsey (Rolfe), 1st Baron, 173

Cromwell, Henry, 47, 153

Cromwell, Oliver, 25, 47, 152, 154

Cross, Hawes, 53, 155

Cross, Mary (Fitzgerald), 49, 53, 155

Cruikshank, Dr. W. C., 136

Cuffe, Agmondisham, 25, 26, 27

Cuffe, Hugh, 39

INDEX

Cuffe, John, 57, 158
Cuffe, Captain Joseph, 25
Cuffe, Martha (Muschamp), 26
Cuffe, Joseph, son of Captain Joseph
Cuffe, 25

Daily Journal, The, 159
Daily Post, The, 159, 160, 164, 178
Davies, Rowland, Dean of Ross, afterwards of Cork, 53, 178
Davies, Thomas, 66, 160, 178
Davis, Sir Paul, 45
Dean, Captain C. G. T., 172, 178
Delany, Mary (Granville), 96, 164, 166, 178
Delaval, Captain George, 11
Dennis, John, 7, 8, 12, 142, 178
Dering, Sir Edward, 50, 155, 156
Dering, Helena (Percivall), wife of Captain Daniel Dering, 50
Description of the Gardens of Lord Viscount Cobham at Stow in Buckinghamshire, 143, 178
Desmond, Maurice FitzThomas, 1st Earl of, 37
Desmond, Gerald FitzJames (Fitzgerald), 14th Earl of, 37, 39
Dewes, Anne (Granville), 96
Dixon, Mary (Fitzgerald), 39
Dobbins, William, 48
Dobrée, Bonamy, 13, 21, 27, 146, 147, 178
Docwra, Anne (Vaughan), Baroness, 151
Donegal, Arthur (Chichester), 3rd Earl of, 18
Dorset, Charles (Sackville), 6th Earl of, 54
Downes, Hon. Mrs., 57
Drummond, Robert Hay, Archbishop of York, 95, 166
Dryden, John, 1, 2, 3, 9, 11, 141, 143, 178
Dungarvan, Lord, *see* Burlington, Richard (Boyle), 2nd Earl of Cork and 1st of
Dupplin, Lord, *see* Kinnoull, Thomas (Hay), 9th Earl of

Eccles, John, 32
Elegy on the much Lamented Death of Mr. Prime Serjeant Fitz-Gerald, 157, 178
Elizabeth, Queen of England, 25, 30, 38, 150
Ellis, John, 24, 28
Etherege, Sir George, 11–12
Evelyn, Sir John, 68, 85, 161
Evelyn, Lady Anne (Boscawen), 68, 160

Female Faction, The, 65, 160, 178
Ferland, Mary, 88
Fitzgerald, Anne, *see* Legge, Anne (Fitzgerald)
Fitzgerald, Catherine, 49, 157
Fitzgerald, Charity, daughter of William Fitzgerald, 49
Fitzgerald, Elinor, *see* Blesington, Elinor (Fitzgerald), Countess of
Fitzgerald, Elizabeth, *see* Gibbings, Elizabeth (Fitzgerald)
Fitzgerald, Elizabeth, *see* Lloyd, Elizabeth (Fitzgerald)
Fitzgerald, John, 41, 153
Fitzgerald, Mary, *see* Cross, Mary (Fitzgerald)
Fitzgerald, Richard
Ancestry, 37–38, 150
Career: M.P. for Strabane, 38–39; deputy Clerk of the Crown in Court of Chief Pleas, etc., 39; sent to England as member of committee of Irish House of Commons, 40; in England as special agent of Lords Justices, 41–43; collector in Wales of assessments for Ireland, 44–46
Character and personality, 44, 45, 46
Domestic life: marriage, 38; at Castle Dod, 39; kindness to relatives, 39; children, 41, 45–46; death in Wales, 46, 154
Relations of: with Sir Philip Percivall, 38, 39, 41, 44–46; with the Lords Justices, 42–43; with Davis, 45; with Inchiquin, 46

INDEX

Godolphin, Lady Mary, *see* Leeds, Mary (Godolphin), Duchess of
Gooch, Benjamin, 124–125, 130, 131–132, 171
Gosse, Sir Edmund, 2, 14–15, 21, 23, 141, 144, 146, 175, 179
Graves, James, 179
Grenville, Hon. James, 103
Grey, Lady Sophia, 94

Halifax, Charles (Montagu), Earl of, 9, 11
Hare, Francis, 80, 163
Harris, Walter, 147, 179
Harrison, Henry, 57
Hartstonge, John, Bishop of Ossory, afterwards of Derry, 148
Hartstonge, Sir Standish, 29, 148
Hazlitt, William, 21, 145, 179
Henley, W. E., 141, 179
Hertford, Countess of, *see* Somerset, Frances (Seymour), Duchess of
Hervey, John (Hervey), Lord, 88, 89, 164, 179
Hinton, Edward, 26, 147
Hodder, John, 39, 41, 43, 47, 48
Hodges, John C., 16, 144, 150, 157, 159, 165, 179
Hogarth, William, 127
Holdernesse, Robert (D'Arcy), 4th Earl of, 108, 166
Homer, 1, 2, 5, 142
Hopkins, Charles, 143, 179
Horace, 104, 112, 122, 143
Howard, Mrs., *see* Suffolk, Henrietta (Hobart), Countess of
Howard, Hugh, 29, 31
Hume, John, Bishop of Oxford, 107, 168
Hunt, Leigh, 13, 59, 67, 142, 180

Inchiquin, Murrough (O'Brien), 1st Earl of, 43, 46, 153, 156
Irvine, Anne (Howard), Viscountess, 65

Jacob, Giles, 144, 179
James II, King of England, 25, 26, 52, 53, 147

Jeaffreson, J. Cordy, 172, 179
Jellet, Anne, 145
Jennings, Richard, 59
Jennings, Sarah, *see* Marlborough, Sarah (Jennings), Dowager Duchess of
Jephson, Colonel William, 43, 44
Jersey, Judith (Herne), Countess of, 61, 159
Johnson, Samuel, 12, 13, 110, 144, 179
Journal of the Cork Historical and Archaeological Society, 145, 151, 154, 178–179, 182
Journal of the Royal Historical and Archaeological Association of Ireland, 179
Journal of the Royal Society of Antiquaries of Ireland, 147, 181
Journals of the House of Commons of the Kingdom of Ireland, 148, 150, 151, 152, 155, 180
Juvenal, 1, 112

Keally, Elizabeth, *see* Barry, Elizabeth (Keally), sister of Joseph Keally
Keally, Elizabeth, daughter of Joseph Keally, 24, 25, 30
Keally, Elizabeth, granddaughter of Joseph Keally, 24
Keally, Ellen, *see* Fitzgerald, Ellen (Keally)
Keally, "Jeane," niece of Joseph Keally, 57
Keally, John, father of Joseph Keally, 25, 175
Keally, Elizabeth (Cuffe), 25, 26
Keally, John, brother of Joseph Keally, 24, 25, 28, 29, 32, 57, 158
Keally, Hannah (Stepney), 24
Keally, John Baptist, nephew of Joseph Keally, 24, 58, 158
Keally, Joseph
  Ancestry, 24–25
  Career: called to Irish Bar, 28; M.P. for Doneraile, 29; Recorder of Kilkenny, 29; Attorney-General of Palatinate of Tipperary, 29; Commissioner of Appeals, 30
  Character and personality, 32, 33, 34

INDEX

Legge, Anne (Fitzgerald), 41, 45, 47, 153
Leicester, Robert (Sidney), 2nd Earl of, 41, 44, 154
Leicester, Philip (Sidney), 3rd Earl of, 46
Leicester, Sir Thomas Coke, Baron Lovel, afterwards Earl of, 96
Lewis, Samuel, 180
Lincoln, Catherine (Pelham), Countess of, 101, 102, 167
Lisle, Lord, see Leicester, Philip (Sidney), 3rd Earl of
Lloyd, Captain Owen, 153
Lloyd, Elizabeth (Fitzgerald), 41, 53, 153
Lovel, Lord, see Leicester, Sir Thomas Coke, Baron Lovel, afterwards Earl of
Luther, Henry, 15, 17, 31, 52
Luther, John, 17
Luttrell, Narcissus, 146, 147, 148, 180
Lynch, Kathleen M., 16, 21, 144, 145, 180
Lyttelton, George (Lyttelton), 1st Baron, 111, 120, 127, 132, 169, 171

Macaulay, Thomas Babington, 1st Baron, 5, 12, 13, 142, 144, 180
Markham, Sir Clements Robert, 167, 180
Markham, William, 101, 167
Marlborough, John (Churchill), 1st Duke of, 54, 59, 62, 65, 72, 73, 78–79, 80, 89, 156, 163, 181
Marlborough, Sarah (Jennings), Dowager Duchess of, 59, 62, 65–89, 95, 97, 161, 162, 163, 176, 181
Marlborough, Henrietta (Churchill), Duchess of
Character and personality, 59, 78–80, 89, 90
Domestic life: marriage, 59; children, 60, 83–89, 162; patronage of artists, 61, 66, 85, 160, 164, 182; visits to Bath, 64, 159; last illness and death, 89
Letters from: to Lady Mary Wortley Montagu, 61; to her mother, 67, 68–74; to Berkeley, 67; to Tonson, 67; to Mrs. Howard, 67–68; to Mrs. Clayton, 68; to Lady Evelyn, 68; to Mrs. Matthews, 73–74
Letters to: from her mother, 69–70, 73; from Dean Jones, 79, 163; from Lord Blandford, 85
Relations of: with Congreve, 59, 60–67, 75, 77, 90; with Swift, 60; with Pope, 60–61; with Lady Mary Wortley Montagu, 61; with her mother, 68–89, 160, 162; with her husband, 64, 81–85, 159; with her children, 84–89, 162, 164; with the Prince of Wales, 88, 164; with Hervey, 88–89; with her father-in-law, 162; with her father, 163; with Thomson, 143, 182
Reputation, 14, 59, 61, 62–67, 75–76, 77, 86, 160, 163, 165
Will, 88, 163
Marlborough, Charles (Spencer), 5th Earl of Sunderland and 3rd Duke of, 82
Marsh, Frank Graham, 180
Mary, Queen of England, 54, 112
Mason, John Monck, 24
Matthews, Mrs. (Henrietta, wife of Admiral Thomas Matthews?), 73–74
Mein, Charles, 15, 17–18, 20, 24, 29, 31, 33, 34, 36, 55, 145, 148, 176
Memoirs of the Celebrated Persons Composing the Kit-Cat Club, 180
Messenger, Augustine, 112
Monck, Charles, grandfather of Elizabeth (Monck) Keally, 30
Monck, Charles, son of Henry Monck, 25
Monck, George, son of Henry Monck, 24, 25
Monck, Henry, father of Elizabeth (Monck) Keally, 30
Monck, Thomas, son of Henry Monck, 25
Monsey, Clopton, 112, 170
Monsey, Dr. Messenger
Ancestry, 111–112

192

Career: a country doctor, 113, 114; cures Lord Godolphin, 114–115; Lord Godolphin's resident physician, 116, 124; the doctor of Whig statesmen, 119–120; prescribes for Mrs. Montagu, 128, 129, 130; Physician of Chelsea Royal Hospital, 116, 132–134

Character and personality, 111, 113, 116, 122, 125, 126, 128–129, 131–138

Domestic life: birth, 112; marriage, 113, 170; birth of daughter, 113; in Bury, 114, 115; at Lord Godolphin's London house, 116, 117; at North Mimms, 98, 99, 118; visits to Norfolk, 116, 117, 123, 131–132; at Claremont, 118; at Wotton, 118, 130; at Chelsea Royal Hospital, 132–134, 136; active old age, 130, 131–132, 134; death, 136

Education: at Woodbridge Grammar School, 112; at Pembroke College, Cambridge, 112; studies medicine in Norwich under Wrench, 113; admitted extra licentiate of College of Physicians, 113, 170

Letters from: to the Duchess of Newcastle, 99, 114–116, 118–119; to Mrs. Montagu, 112, 129–130, 133; to Lord Lyttelton, 120; to Bulwer, 123, 135; to Joseph Windham, 123; to William Windham, 124; to the Duke of Newcastle, 124; to his daughter, 129; to his grandson, 133; to William Windham's son, 135; to Lord Carmarthen, 136; to Dr. Cruikshank, 136

Letters to: from the Duke of Leeds, 107–108, 119; from Lord Carmarthen, 108; from Lord Chesterfield, 119–120; from Lord Bath, 120; from Garrick, 122; from Dr. Gooch, 124–126, 130, 131–132; from Mrs. Montagu, 126–129, 130–131; from Lord Lyttelton, 132

Relations of: with the Duchess of Leeds, 98, 99, 119; with the Duke of Leeds, 99, 102, 107, 108, 119; with the Duchess of Newcastle, 99, 114–116, 118–119; with Lord Carmarthen, 108, 136; with Miss Talbot, 110, 127; with Miss Carter, 110; with Mrs. Montagu, 110, 111, 112, 126–131, 133; with his father, 112; with Wrench, 113; with Lord Godolphin, 114–118, 132; with Sir Robert Walpole, 119; with Lord Chesterfield, 119–120; with Lord Lyttelton, 120, 132; with Lord Bath, 120, 121, 122, 126; with Garrick, 120–123; with Bulwer, 123, 135; with Dr. John Taylor, 124; with Dr. Gooch, 124–126, 131–132; with his daughter, 124, 129, 130–131, 137, 173; with Dr. Ranby, 125, 133; with his grandchildren, 126, 130, 133, 137; with Dr. Adair, 133–134; with William Windham's son, 135; with Dr. John Taylor's son, 135, 137; with John Wolcot, 136

Verses, 123, 136–137

Views on religion, 134–135

Will, 137, 173, 176

Monsey, Anne (Dawney), 113, 170

Monsey, Robert, 112, 170

Monsey, Mary (Clopton), 112

Monsey, Thomas, grandfather of Dr. Monsey, 112

Monsey, Elizabeth (Barber), 112

Monsey, Thomas, brother of Dr. Monsey, 112

Montagu, Charles, see Halifax, Charles (Montagu), Earl of

Montagu, Elizabeth (Robinson), 95, 103, 110, 111, 112, 119, 120, 126–130, 132, 133, 168, 169, 171, 172, 177, 180, 181

Montagu, John (Montagu), 2nd Duke of, 96

Montagu, Mary (Churchill), Duchess of, 68, 75, 78–80, 87, 96

INDEX

INDEX